MW01235169

Dr. Beare's Daughter

Growing Up Adopted, Adored, and Afraid

A TRUE STORY

JANICE JONES

Dr. Beare's Daughter
Growing Up Adopted, Adored, and Afraid
A True Story

Copyright 2024 Janice L. Jones
All rights reserved

No part of this book may be reproduced or transmitted in any form or by any means, electronic or mechanical, including photocopying, recording, or by any information storage and retrieval system, without permission of the author.

This is a work of creative nonfiction. The events portrayed are presented to the best of the author's memory, and verified with research. All persons in the book are real. The names and identifying characteristics of some individuals have been changed to protect their privacy. Dialogue has been created consistent with the author's memory of persons and events.

Summary: In this true story set in the 1950s and '60s, an adopted only child finds herself an outlier in her small town of Celina, Ohio, while struggling to be the golden child she imagines her charismatic doctor-daddy and easily hurt socialite mother really wanted, while also coping with the strict rules of the Catholic Church.

Daddy's Little Girl
Words and Music by Bobby Burke and Horace Gerlach
© 1949 Ocheri Publishing Corp.
All Rights Reserved
Reprinted by Permission of Hal Leonard LLC

The Great Pretender
Words and Music by Buck Ram
Copyright © 1955 by Panther Music Corp.
Copyright Renewed
All Rights for the World excluding Brazil and Mexico Administered by Peermusic (UK) Ltd.
International Copyright Secured All Rights Reserved
Reprinted by Permission of Hal Leonard LLC

ISBN 979-8-9890978-0-7

For my children

Ralph Jones and

Rachel Smith

And my grandchildren

Luka Jones

Niko Jones

Andrew Jones

Charlie Jones

and

Those who come after

At that, Silver-hair woke in a fright,

and jumped out of the window and ran away

as fast as her legs could carry her, and never went near

the Three Bears' snug little house again.

—Robert Southey, *The Three Bears*

From the Author

Dear Reader,

I am seventy-seven years old, and time moves so quickly now, I could sneeze and find myself to be eighty. I feel compelled to share my story with the world, because stories must be told, or they die with the person who lived them.

As you read, I hope you find connections between my story and your own, and that you find in those connections that somehow, we are all family.

Contents

May 3, 1981

Daddy was dying in the hospital's hospice wing. He was drifting in and out of a coma, each breath a strangled gurgle. Mother and I were sitting with him. It was late afternoon, and we'd been there since early morning. With her heart condition and diabetes, Mother looked so old and used up that I was afraid she might faint.

I took Daddy's hand and told him I was going to take Mother back to the apartment.

He stirred, opened his eyes, and fixed them on me. "Go take care of her . . . Kiddo." His voice was a raspy whisper. He took a labored breath, then muttered, "Make sure . . . she eats . . . takes her insulin . . . put her to bed . . . then . . ." His voice ran out.

I said, "We'll be back in the morning to sit with you."

He opened his mouth, closed it, opened it again. "I won't be . . . here . . . in the morning . . ."

I turned to Mother and said, "I'll be right back." I went to the nurse's station and asked Daddy's nurse, "Can you tell me if my father will last the night?"

She looked at me kindly, shook her head, and said, "I'll be very surprised if he does."

I felt a boa constrictor wrap itself around my heart. I walked back into Daddy's room. Mother saw me, got up, and walked wearily into the hall, expecting me to follow.

I went to Daddy. I kissed him gently on the forehead. His eyes fluttered open. He said, "I'm going to die, and not . . . one . . . of my family will be here . . . with me." The boa constrictor tightened its coils and squeezed.

Searching my face, Daddy whispered, "Take your Mother home. Then come back, Kiddo. I'll wait . . . for . . . you." His eyes closed and forced a tear down one sallow cheek.

That vicious snake clamped down on my heart and tried to force the life out of it. I grabbed the IV pole to keep myself from falling. . . .

My folks think I'm so cute and sweet.
That's all they talk about.
But then, they may be prejudiced --
You see -- they picked me out!

MY NAME IS *Janice Lucinda*

MY FOLKS *Arthur Mattie Beare*

MY BIRTHDAY IS *June 6th /47*

Mrs. J. Beare
Celina Ohio.

Mommy and me
Photo by Paul Beirsdorfer

1
The Three Beares

My birthday is June 8, 1947, but I wasn't born. I was adopted. When I was four-and-a-half months old. My parents named me Janice Lucinda. *Janice* because "it couldn't be shortened into something gawd-awful" and *Lucinda* after my new mother.

The first thing I remember is sitting on my mother's lap in the big chair while she read me The Book.[1] I can't forget it because she read it to me every day my first few years.

~~~~

Every day, I have to sit still while Mommy reads me The Book. In The Book, a happily married couple were sad because they had no babies. So they went to a Home to choose one. The Book showed three babies at the Home, floating in high chairs on an all-white page. They were wearing bibs and waving spoons like they were hungry, but no one was feeding them. There were no mommies in the Home. The only grown-up was a lady on another page talking on the phone. *Why doesn't The Book show her face?*

The happily married couple looked at the first baby and didn't want him. *What was wrong with him?* The wife held the second baby on her lap. Then the married couple just knew he was their chosen baby. *How did they know that? They didn't even look at the third baby. What happened to him? And that first one who had something wrong with him?* The couple took their chosen baby home. The Book showed the baby with his new parents, grandparents, aunts, and uncles, all with happy faces. *Thank goodness he has a real home with real people to love him. The Home is an empty place where no one pays attention to the babies.*

Every time Mommy shut the book, she said, "That's how we got you. I was so excited the day we went to Dayton to pick you up. Other mommies and daddies have to take what they get, but we *chose* you. And that makes you special."

The Home must be in Dayton! If Mommy and Daddy hadn't picked me, I'd still be floating around in the Home, hungry. Why did they choose me? They have dark hair and nice skin. I have red hair and ugly freckles. Didn't the home have any babies that look like them? If they decide they don't like me, can they take me back?

Then Mommy said, "Like the couple in the book, I love you as if you were my own." *Since I'm not her own, I'm glad she loves me anyway.*

Daddy never read me The Book. He sat with me in the big chair and played me his favorite record on the Scott—his giant radio that had a record player. Daddy sang along with the record about how I'm the pot of gold at the end of his rainbow and I'm sugar and spice— everything nice. He lifted me up in his strong hands and held me above him, so my face was right on top of his. He smiled, his brown eyes got shiny, and he sang, "And you're Daddy's Little Girl."[2]

Daddy doesn't love me AS IF I were his own. He thinks I AM his own.

Daddy was Doctor Ralph Beare. Our last name is said "bear"— like the big, hairy animal that lives in the woods. One of Daddy's ancestors added that fancy E. It's quiet. Don't say it.

Daddy had an artist draw my picture, and he hung it above the Scott. Mommy's sisters made a plaque that sat on the Scott. Three bears (without the e)—a papa bear, a mama bear, and a baby bear. Under the picture, it said:

Ralph, Lou, and Janice

"The Three Beares"

Portrait by Paul Beirsdorfer

Sometimes I wish it was the FOUR Beares. If I had a brother or sister . . . I only have Dainty and Doss, my special friends. I'm the only one who can see them.

We lived in Celina. It's a little city in Ohio. From the time I could walk, Daddy took me with him to the grocery, the gas station, the bank, the hardware store, the newsstand, the drugstore, the hospital, the tire and supply store—everywhere. People always stopped to talk to him. They thanked him for saving their mother's, grandma's, or baby's life. Then they bent down to tell me about it. "Your daddy was out to my farm to help my wife who was in a bad way while having our baby.

Daddy and me going all those places

While Doc was delivering our baby in the bedroom, Grandpa had a heart attack in the living room. Your daddy ran back and forth and saved Grandpa, my wife, *and* the baby." *Everybody likes Daddy. He's a hero.*

Daddy took me with him on house calls to the farms. Even when I was just four, he had me hold the pan of syringes. The syringes had on cotton jackets, and the pan had alcohol in it. I had to be careful not to spill it. *Daddy trusts me with an important job.* On Sundays, after Mass and a restaurant dinner, Mommy took her nap. While she napped,

Daddy took me for fast drives in the country to road races and drag races. We went into the pits so Daddy could look at engines and talk to men about how to make the cars go faster. I got tired of standing in the sun, hearing about horsepower and superchargers. *Shouldn't I be the one staying home and taking a nap? I need my nap.*

Even though my name is *Janice*, most grown-ups thought it was *Doctor Beare's Daughter.* I was maybe five years old and waiting for Daddy outside a store when a big boy teased me. "Where'd you get all those freckles?" I looked at my shoes and wished he'd go away. He said, "Your name should be Spot."

They don't wash off. I've tried.

A man walked up and grabbed the boy's ear. "Don't you know who that is?" He pointed at me and said, "That's Doctor Beare's Daughter."

All the grown-ups in town know me.

The boy hung his head and said, "I . . . I didn't know. . . . Sorry, Miss Beare." Then he ran off. *Being Doctor Beare's Daughter is better than being just Janice.*

My House Had a Waiting Room

In the summers, we lived in our lake cottage, but the rest of the year, The Three Beares lived in our house-in-town—that big white house with a doctor's office on the corner of Main and Wayne Streets. Our front door was on Main. The office door was on Wayne. It was the old Hierholzer house that Daddy bought after the big war and divided into a house and office. The house was sorta surrounded by our church, Immaculate Conception (everyone calls it IC), the grade school, high school, and convent. Daddy liked living at his office. It was easy for him to get what he needed when he had to go on house calls. But Mommy wanted a new house away from the doctor's office. Right after the war there was a ban on building new, so Daddy promised

The house-in-town seen from Main Street

The office seen from Wayne Street

The house-in-town was sorta surrounded by Immaculate Conception Parish.
Map by Janice

her that one day he would build her dream house. I liked having the office right there because I could go in when it was closed and get tongue depressors, swabs, adhesive tape, and tiny paper cups to make things. I liked sitting in the waiting room and looking at the pictures in the *Highlights for Children* magazine. I even liked the smell, which was made of alcohol, rubber gloves, and floor wax.

2
I'm Trouble & Ignorant, Too

There were things about me that surprised Mommy, and she had a lot to say about them. Every day, she said, "Janice. You must have been born with a phonograph needle stuck in your throat."

There was always lots in my head that wanted to come out my mouth, and I tried hard not to speak until spoken to—even when I thought I might bust. But sometimes I couldn't hold it in. If I said the wrong thing while we were getting groceries in the P & B, Mommy pinched my arm and hissed through her teeth, "Everyone can hear you. Where do you get such crazy ideas?" *I don't know. I didn't know they were crazy.* "Don't say them out loud. What will people think?" *They'll think Mommy adopted a crazy child.*

Mommy liked to say, "Janice. Shut the door. Were you born in a barn?" *I wasn't born. I was adopted.*

When I was very naughty, Mommy said, "Now I have to cut a switch from the grapevine." We had three grape arbors in our big yard. She cut a vine from one and switched my bare legs. It stung some, but she didn't switch hard. *I wish I could stop making her do that.*

I Cut Her Quick
Cutting Mommy's quick was the worst thing I ever did. I was still just four, and all of a sudden, she wouldn't look at me. "Mommy, are you mad at me?"

Her face was tight. "You cut me to the quick."

My tummy tied itself in a knot. "What did I do?"

"You know what you did."

Did my phonograph-needle mouth say the wrong thing again? No—I've been playing quietly all morning. Did I leave the door standing open again? That's not it—that only irks her. I irk her a lot.

"I don't know what I did, Mommy."

"Well, if you don't know, I'm not going to tell you."

The knot in my tummy pulled itself tight. "I'm sorry, Mommy."

She mocked me. "I'm sorry. I'm sorry. You're the SORRIEST girl I know. You cut me to the quick. Sometimes I wish I could GIVE YOU BACK."

My tummy flip-flopped. *She doesn't WANT ME anymore. How can I make her see that I DIDN'T MEAN to cut her quick?* I followed her around the house, begging her. "Please, please, forgive me."

Her ears couldn't hear me. So I yelled, "I'M SORRY, MOMMY. I'M SORRY. I'M SORRY."

She still couldn't hear me. I sat down in a corner, hid my face, and cried. My tummy knot tried to spit up, but nothing came out. I got the hurty kind of hiccups. My heart started screaming like it was being killed. *Mommy might take me back to the Home. And nobody else will pick me.*

When my eyes ran out of tears, my heart went on screaming. It took a whole week for Mommy to love me again. *I must NEVER cut her quick again.*

Sometimes other people cut Mommy's quick. When Mommy took me shopping in Dayton, the shop ladies said, "What a beautiful granddaughter you have."

Mommy's face always went stiff. Sometimes she snapped, "I'm her MOTHER." Other times she stuck her nose in the air, grabbed my hand, and fast-walked us away. I could see by the shop-ladies' faces that they didn't mean to cut her quick.

I guess I'm a lot of trouble to take care of. That must be why we have Louella. She lived with us some of the time. She did the housework and watched me so Mommy could go to her parties and meetings. Mommy belonged to important clubs like the Mercer County Medical Auxiliary and the Doctors and Lawyers' Wives Club.

GODDAMN IGNORANT

I always asked Daddy lots of questions, about lots of things, because he knew everything. He usually smiled and told me the answers, but this one time, while I was still real little, he said, "Why are you asking me that?"

"I want to know, is all."

"Aren't you smart enough to figure it out? No child of mine could be so GODDAMN IGNORANT. I can't stand IGNORANCE."

He spat his words at me like watermelon seeds. His voice was so nasty that his words could have dripped snot. *Daddy is smart. His own child would be smart. Instead, he got me. I feel sorry for him. I feel sorry for me.* I tried to keep my sorry inside, but it came out my eyes in tears.

"Why are you crying?" Daddy demanded. "You're too GODDAMN SENSITIVE."

Now my sorry jumped out my throat in sobs. Cold fingers pinched me up and down. Lightning hit me in the chest. *I'm going to split down the middle.* I sat on the floor and wrapped my arms around me. *I've got to hold myself together. Daddy doesn't hit, but his words tear me apart.*

Mommy said, "Ralph. She's hasn't even started school yet. How's she supposed to know anything unless she asks?"

Yes. How? And how am I supposed to know which questions are the goddamn ignorant ones?

Now Daddy was looking at Mommy. "You think it's my fault she doesn't know anything? Why would you think it's MY fault?"

It's MY fault. I'm the ignorant one who asked the ignorant question.

"You shouldn't talk to me this way. I deserve better from you. It's a crying shame—that's what it is. A GODDAMN, SONOFABITCH, CRYING SHAME."

Now Mommy was crying, too. *Look what I've done.*

Mommy said, "Ralph. You're not making sense. You're getting irrational."

"Sonofabitch. There you go again. Thinking terrible things about me. You don't respect me. You don't love me; you don't give a tinker's damn about me; my patients care more about me than you do. SHIT. What did I just tell Janice about crying? You're as ignorant as she is. I'm surrounded with goddamn ignorance. I can't stand it."

Mommy pinched her lips shut. Daddy threw up his hands, and said, "MY." Then he tramped out of the room. And out of the house. He drove away.

Will he come back? What's to happen to Mommy and me if he doesn't?

"Ralph gets so irrational at times," Mommy said to no one. "His mother was the same way."

Mommy thinks this whole thing is Daddy's fault. I'm pretty sure it's mine. I hugged my sides together and ran to my room. I threw myself on my bed and stayed there, holding myself together until my body fell asleep.

Later Mommy woke me up and called me for supper. Daddy was there at the table. *He came back.*

Daddy cut the tenderloin from the T-bone steak in front of him and put it on my plate. He cut another piece of steak and gave it to Mommy. *Daddy got his rational back. I don't ever want to make him lose it again.*

Mommy sighed and said, "Just once, I'd like the tenderloin."

Why does he always give me the best part? I better not ask why. It might be a goddamn ignorant question.

3
Relatives and "Relatives"

I had a grandpa—Daddy's father, Wellard Beare, who was retired
and living in Versailles, Ohio, about fifty miles from Celina. Sometimes he phoned Mommy. "Mrs. Beare," he would say. "I'm hungry."

His wife had died a long time ago,
and sometimes he missed us and
wanted some home cooking. Then
he came and stayed at our house a
few days until he had his fill. Any
meat that Mommy was cooking got
this from Grandpa: "Mrs. Beare, can
you get a little gravy out of that?"

I wasn't used to having anybody
to play with, except Dainty and
Doss, and they weren't real. Daddy
was always busy in the office or
taking me somewhere. Mommy had
other things to do. Cooking. Or
sitting in a chair. Or taking her afternoon nap. Louella was usually busy,
too. But Grandpa played with me.

With Grandpa at the house-in-town

When I was maybe four or five, Daddy bought a new refrigerator. Grandpa tied a loop of rope to the empty box. He put the rope around his middle, snorted like a horse, and pulled me in that box all over the big yard of the house-in-town. Mommy finally put a stop to that game, saying, "Janice. You're wearing Grandpa out."

I liked horses so much that Grandpa bought me a metal horse with wheels and springs that I could ride on the sidewalk. *When I grow up, I'm going to ride the real thing.*

My very own horse

When I did something wrong, Daddy lost his rational, Mommy cut a switch, but Grandpa just said, "Tut, tut, tut, Kiddo. That's not the way."

When Grandpa was in our house, Daddy never lost his rational. Sometimes I could tell that he was just holding it in. After Grandpa went home, it always came out. When I missed Grandpa, I went into his room, opened the bureau drawer, and looked at his pajamas and razor. *I wonder what he's doing right now in Versailles?*

There were a few other Beares in Celina because Daddy's younger brother was his partner in the office. They called each other "Doctor Ralph" and "Doctor Paul." Uncle Doc was married to Aunt Ginny. Daddy told me that they came to Celina when I was just three, bringing along my cousin John, who was two years older than me. Then they had a daughter, right after they came. I wished I could play with my cousins, but we only saw them on birthdays and Christmas because Daddy said he and Uncle Doc wanted to keep the families separate. Daddy said he saw Uncle Doc all day in the office and that was enough for him. *It's not fair that I can't see my cousins much just because Daddy and Uncle Doc get tired of each other.*

Mommy had eight brothers and sisters. Her big family lived in Indiana and Illinois, so we saw them less than Uncle Doc's family. There were tons of cousins. The ones in my generation were grown-ups, so at the reunions, I played with their children who were more my age. I liked being part of the big, happy jumble, but I didn't really belong to them. It was Mommy and Daddy who adopted me; the rest of them hadn't had any say about it.

"Aunts" and "Uncles"

I may not have had much family around, but I had "aunts" and "uncles." These were Mommy and Daddy's good friends. "Uncle" Charlie and "Aunt" Mildred Cron were the closest friends. Aunt Mildred walked into our house anytime—the back door was unlocked all day. She was the only person I knew with red hair, like me. She had long red nails that gave the best back scratches. Uncle Charlie and his brother owned Cron Tire & Supply Company. Daddy took me there a lot, looking for some car part. I liked riding the freight elevator to the second floor. The shelves were full up to the ceiling with all kinds of parts. It smelled like metal, dirty fingernails, gasoline, and oily rags. I always took a big breath to take it all in.

Aunt Mildred and Uncle Charlie lived in a big white house on Johnson Avenue, and I liked to hide in its many rooms. I played by myself a lot in the big yard. Aunt Mildred and Uncle Charlie's children were grown and gone.

Daddy bought the two big, empty lots next to Uncle Charlie's house. Someday Daddy would build Mommy her dream house there. Mommy and Aunt Mildred talked a lot about what the house would look like.

"Aunt" LaVaun Nickel was always working in her huge garden. She wore overalls and a straw hat, like someone in Mommy's *Better Homes and Gardens* magazine. "Uncle" Paul owned Nickel Hardware on Main Street. When Daddy took me downtown, I liked to run into Uncle Paul's store to say "hi" and dig my hands down in the big tubs of nuts and bolts. They felt smooth and cool on my fingers. Aunt LaVaun and Uncle Paul had no children. *I guess they don't need any, or else they would have gone to the Home to get one.*

"Uncle" Rock Riley was president of Citizen's Commercial Bank.

"Aunt" Helen and "Uncle" Rock Riley

He and "Aunt" Helen lived across town. They had a boy my age named David.

David and I played together while our folks visited. He was much more fun than Dainty and Doss. David and I played War with three decks of cards. We built things with Lincoln Logs. We played "ranch" with plastic horses. I loved being with David because he was so much fun. Our mommies and daddies called us using one word: "Janicendavid!" *Yup, that's us, all right.*

Janicendavid

I loved my "aunts" and "uncles" because they made our big, lonely house feel warm. Mommy always reminded me that they weren't my REAL aunts and uncles because I wasn't related to them like I was to Mommy's brothers and sisters and Uncle Doc and Aunt Ginny. *That makes no never-mind to me. I'm not related to the REAL ones either.*

Mommy and Daddy had many more good friends, like Owen and Mary Pogue, who owned Pogue's Men's Store. I had to call them "Mr." and "Mrs.," but I liked to think of them as "Owen" and "Mary." One time we met them down in Florida at an orange grove, and Owen held me up, so I could pick oranges off a tree. After that, I adored him. Every night before I got into bed, Mommy listened to my prayers. I had people I was supposed to God-bless. "God bless Mommy and Daddy. God bless Grandpa, and Uncle Doc, and Aunt Ginny." One night I surprised Mommy and added: "And God bless Owen Pogue."

Then there were the Shorts, the Longs, the Sharps, and the Dulls. Earl Dull was Daddy's lawyer. Earl Dull and Don Short were partners in the Short and Dull Law Firm.

I spent as much time as I could with the "aunts" and "uncles." I liked to use their grown-up words, even if I didn't always get them right.

4
City Life, Country Life

The House-in-Town

In fall, winter, and early spring, we lived in our house-in-town. It *bustled* (one of Uncle Rock's favorite words) with all kinds of good noise. Through the dining-room wall, I could hear the sounds of the office—the cries of babies when they got their shots; the muffled blare *(muffled blare—what a pair)* of the waiting-room TV; Daddy's booming voice, talking to a patient.

"I SEE YOU HAVE SOME PILES HERE."

(Piles of what?)

"THIS IS THE CAUSE OF YOUR RECTAL ITCHING AND BLEEDING."

Oh, oh. I know where the "rectal" is.

Main Street made its own flavor of noise. At the red light out front, motors revved. Then tires squealed. Horns honked. Cars backfired. Holey mufflers growled like a pack of mad dogs. *Where are all those people going?* Main Street was also US 127. Big trucks roared through town and sometimes, at night, pulled across the parking spaces under my window so the drivers could sleep. Then their idling engines hummed me to sleep, too. *Where do the men who drive the trucks live? Do they have families back home who miss them?*

Half a block away, the IC church bells rang the Angelus twice a day. *Who's in the church, ringing those bells? The nuns in the convent across Wayne Street must be stopping their chores to pray.* On down Wayne Street a long ways, the furniture-factory whistle signaled time to go home with a long fweet! I always ran to the front-room window to watch all the people leaving work drive up Wayne and turn onto Main at the light. *They're a big human family—way bigger than The Three Beares, and I want to be part of it somehow, even if they're out there and I'm in here.* Sometimes Mommy let me put on my coat and watch them from the front porch. *Are they going straight home, or do they have to stop at the P & B first?*

Early every morning, Daddy got up and went to the hospital to do surgery. Mommy woke me after he left. While I had breakfast, I looked at the pad of paper on the table by the phone to see what Daddy had written there. Sometimes it was numbers. He liked to figure his money. Other times it was drawings of people's insides with arrows and lines and circles. *What part of a person's innards is that? Is he going to take it out or just do something to it?*

At 11:30, Daddy came home from the hospital for lunch. Then he napped in the back room for an hour. Mommy's job was to keep me quiet, answer the phone, and wake Daddy up at one, when it was time for afternoon office hours.

Watching the world go by from the front porch

After Daddy went into the office, Mommy went upstairs to take off her girdle and have *her* nap. Then it was *my* job to keep me quiet. I sat on the living-room sofa and watched the traffic go by or tried to build a house out of Mommy's bridge cards. Sometimes I played

Candyland, pretending I was the green playing piece and Grandpa was the red one. I had given up on Dainty and Doss. *I wish I had a dog to play with. David has a dog, and it's his good friend. Every time I ask Daddy for a dog, he says we don't need any "damn dog."*

After Mommy's nap, she started dinner. Daddy liked his supper hot and on the table when he walked in the door from the office. But Mommy never knew when that might be because there were no appointments to see the doctors. Patients came when they needed to and sat in the waiting room until the nurse opened the door and said, "One for Doctor Ralph" or "One for Doctor Paul." The office closed after the last patient had been seen. When it got past five o'clock, Mommy always said, "Janice, go count the cars."

I ran outside and counted the cars on Main, then around the corner on Wayne. If there were lots of cars, dinner was going to be very late, and I was going to get very hungry. When only a couple of cars were left, I went to the kitchen door that led into the office drug room. I slowly cracked it open because there were always patients standing against the other side of the door, waiting to pay their bill to the nurse or to get a prescription filled from the big bottles of pills, liquids, and powders on the shelves above the cash drawer.

I would hiss, "Psssssssst" through the door crack to get the nurse's attention. This amused the patients, and one of them once said, "Some-one better tell Doc there's a snake in his office." The nurse showed me on her fingers how many of the last few patients were Daddy's.

～～～

Daddy kept records on his patients, but he never kept one on me. So when a new dose of vaccine came in, he couldn't remember the last time I'd been boosted. When I saw him come in the house with a syringe in his hand, I ran and hid behind the big chair in the living room. Daddy brought the shot to me. He didn't even fish me out of my hidey-hole but just got hold of an arm. OUCH. *Sigh.*

One day, while I was maybe five, Daddy came in the house from the office with a little girl my age. He said, "I thought you might play with Jenny here a little while."

Yippee. I never get to play with other little girls. We dressed up my dolls. It was a big time. I caught the measles from her. I was pretty sick, and Daddy took care of me. I caught the mumps the same way, from a different little girl. I asked Daddy why he made me sick on purpose. He said there were no vaccines for measles and mumps, and he wanted me to be immune before I started school. He also wanted me to have them while I was little and he could take care of me, because they were way worse if you got them when you were older. *Daddy made me sick for my own good.*

There were lots of parties in our house-in-town—Aunt LaVaun called them "big bashes." I knew a party was coming when Daddy took me to the liquor store for cases of the stuff. At the party, all the "aunts" and "uncles" and other important people in Celina would be there. Sometimes Uncle Doc and Aunt Ginny came, but mostly not. They had their own friends.

There was always a bartender in one corner of the dining room. Hired girls in frilly aprons passed silver trays of stuff you could eat with your fingers. And there was always a buffet *(help-yourself)* supper.

After the big crowd left, Daddy got out the poker table, and the "aunts" and "uncles" played until late. Daddy let me sit on his lap, and he taught me to play five-card stud. When he had to go to the bathroom, I played his hand for him. I lost most of his chips before he came back. Everyone thought this was funny. Even Daddy.

I loved the grown-up parties because there were lots of people in our house that made it feel alive and hopping. If I didn't want to be sent to my room early, I had to keep my mouth shut. If I *had* to open my mouth, I stuffed it with the nearest *delicacy.* I got that word from Aunt Helen. I chomped on stuffed mushrooms and heard all the gossip. I chewed sauerkraut balls and learned secrets about people in Celina. I was like one of the pitchers in Mommy's old saying: "Little pitchers have big ears."

Mommy played bridge at our house-in-town every Friday afternoon with Aunt Mildred, Aunt LaVaun, and Mary Pogue. On every-other-Tuesday, she played with three tables full of lady friends. They wore gloves and fancy hats. When offered a petit-four *(Why not petit-six, or -eight?)*, the ladies fussed. "Oh, I shouldn't. I couldn't. Well, maybe just one." Then they nibbled ever so daintily. (I learned *nibbled* and *daintily* from Mary Pogue.) They worried about their figures. Mommy didn't worry about hers. She was way bigger than all her friends. This made her unhappy—sometimes.

Mommy also had tea parties. I wasn't supposed to be at those, so I hid under the dining room table behind the long tablecloth. One time I heard Mommy say, "Ralph and I went shopping in Dayton last Thursday and stopped on our way home at a diner in the country. I saw Ellie Weissman with John Greggs, sitting together on the same side of a booth. *Mr.* Weissman and *Mrs.* Greggs weren't there."

There were gasps from the ladies, then Mommy said, "Ralph and I left before they saw us." *Why didn't Mommy want them to see her? Sounds like they were being naughty. Is she gonna tell on them to Mr. Weissman and Mrs. Greggs? She should, now that everyone else knows.*

Aunt LaVaun said, "Lou, my neighbor Mrs. Schultz is very sick. Do you know what's wrong with her?"

"I had no idea she was sick," Mommy said. *Mommy probably knows what's wrong with Mrs. Schultz, and lots of other people, too, but she has to pretend she doesn't. Mommy can only gossip about things that happen OUTSIDE the office. And that goes for me, too.*

Living at the house-in-town meant we had to look just right when we went out because somebody, or lots-of-somebodies, might see us. I thought of all those somebodies as the Eyes of Celina. Dinner, shopping, church, or visiting—Mommy chose my clothes. But sometimes she said, "Janice, go put on a dress."

I always asked, "Which one?"

She always answered, "Any one—just go put on a dress."

I picked one that felt good and put it on. But when I went downstairs, Mommy said, "Not *that* one! Now go change."

I never get it right the first time! "Which one do you want, Mommy?"

"Any one but that one! And comb your hair."

I'll put on the newest, scratchiest one. She always likes the scratchy ones. I combed my hair and showed myself to her.

"That's brand-new! We're saving that one for Mass on Sunday."

I always had to try on three or four before she finally threw her hands up. "It will have to do, or we'll be late. I hope somebody doesn't see us."

I hope so, too. I must look gawd-awful.

Being Real at the Cottage

Hurrah. It's time to move to the cottage. In late spring, Mommy, Louella, and I threw our clothes and lots of other stuff into Mommy's Cadillac, and we hauled it to the cottage. We had to make several trips. *Whew. I can't wait to put all this stuff away and find my shorts.* At the cottage, nobody cared if I wasn't dressed just right. *The Eyes of Celina must not see very far from town because sometimes I get to wear my swimsuit all day.*

Our cottage was on Harbor Point, a peninsula that sticks out into Grand Lake St. Marys, a huge lake with Celina on the west end and St. Marys on the east. Harbor Point is really an island because there's

Playing in the ivy in front of the cottage

a channel that cuts it off from the mainland, and the only way onto Harbor Point is over the rattly wooden bridge by the boathouse or a little footbridge over the channel in the state park.

Our cottage was right on the lake with a big screened porch. Outside the porch was some grass, then our seawall, and then the lake spread out everywhere. I loved listening to it's music: The waves slapped the seawall—lap-lap-lap. Fish jumped—splash, splash . . . splash. Voices of boaters carried across the water—"THAT THERE IS DOC BEARE'S COTTAGE."

Sometimes we heard a sonic boom. Daddy said that the jets from the Air Force base in Dayton used the wide-open space over the lake

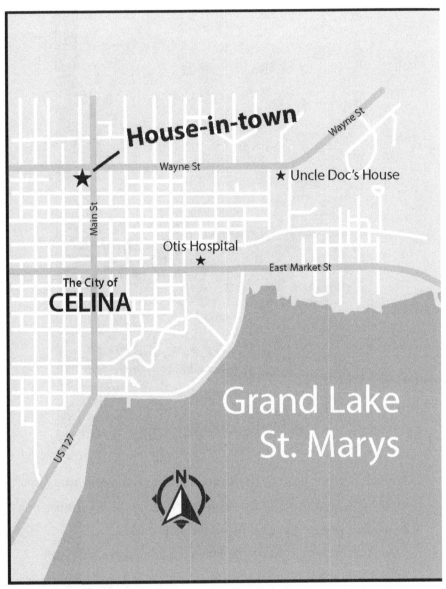

to break the sound barrier. Every spring, the first couple of booms made me jump. Then I got used to them, and I waved in case the pilot might see me.

At night, instead of big trucks humming me to sleep, the lake's splish-splashings were my lullaby. Every morning, the birds' chitters woke me up. *They're saying, "Get up, Janice. Come out and play."*

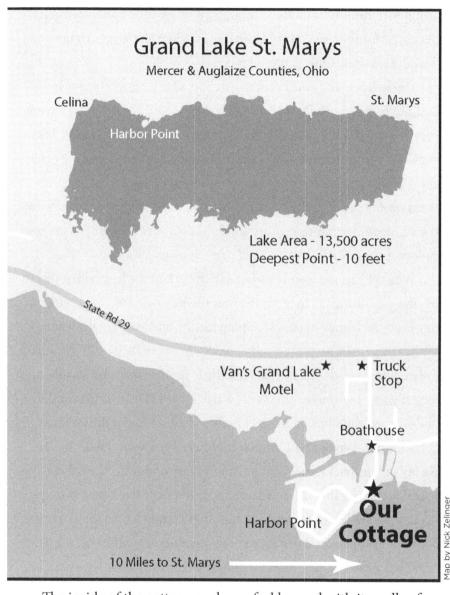

Map by Nick Zelinger

The inside of the cottage made me feel hugged with its walls of knotty *(not naughty)* pine, furniture made of canes, and jute rugs that felt tickly on my bare feet. The big stone fireplace kept us warm, and picture windows brought the lake right inside the house.

The Pogues had a cottage on Harbor Point, too. Mary Pogue walked to our cottage in her bathing suit, and she and Mommy floated around in inner tubes. I liked to grab an inner tube and join them because Mommy was relaxed and happy when she was with her friend, and she let me in on the talk.

Uncle Rock and Aunt Helen also had a cottage on Harbor Point. So I got to play with David every day. David and I liked to turn over rocks in the shallow water by the fishing pier to find crawdads. He showed me how to pick them up, so I wouldn't get pinched. They were slimy and wiggly, their legs and pinchers going like crazy. We put them on the grass, and they raced back to the water. Then we wiped the slime off our hands on David's shorts. *I'm not supposed to get my clothes dirty, but it's okay if David does because he's a boy.*

We explored the woods and marsh in back of the boathouse, meeting the wild things as they went about their day—opossums, skunks, muskrats, raccoons, snakes, snapping turtles, and long-legged wading birds. Sometimes we picked cattail reeds and wove them into placemats. Other times we played with David's little metal cars in his sandbox, which was a big tractor tire. Afterward, Louella cleaned my sandals and washed the sand off my feet before she'd let me in the cottage.

At night, David and I hunted night crawlers with a flashlight, or we lay on our backs on a blanket, looking for shooting stars above the lake. David said that the stars were heaven's fiery freckles. I snugged up against David, so I could feel him there while we watched the sky. We were just Janicendavid, being real together. *David is real all the time, but I can only be real with David when we're alone. I have to be Doctor Beare's Daughter the rest of the time. David is the only one who knows me when I'm being real, and he likes me anyway.*

"Hang on, Larry"

Daddy's little wooden Penn Yan fishing boat hung in a hoist on our seawall. "The Chris" was our eighteen-foot mahogany Chris Craft inboard that "belonged" to Mommy. To ride in the Chris, we had to go to the boathouse, which was run by our neighbor Carl Morley. Carl's crew rolled the Chris out of the Quonset to the big hoist and dropped her in the water. Then Daddy drove her down the long channel to the open lake, where he could throttle down. I loved a family ride in the Chris, with the air whipping my hair and bits of spray tickling my face. *It's something The Three Beares do together, and nobody gets mad when we're out on the lake. I wish we could go out in the Chris more often.*

In 1951, when I was still four, Daddy bought two hydroplanes that he named after Mommy and me. *Lou-Jan I and Lou-Jan II.* Daddy

Me in Lou-Jan I with Daddy at the boathouse

Larry driving Lou-Jan II

got a crew together to race the boats. He was the mechanic, and our driver was Larry Kruger from Neptune, Ohio. When he started driving for us, he was just sixteen. The rest of the crew were Bob Kruger (Larry's dad), Uncle Charlie, and sometimes Carl from the boathouse, . . . and ME. My job was to *always* stay in Daddy's sight and *never* get in the way. Daddy gave me my own crew shirt with *Lou-Jan* in red letters inside a red circle on the back. *See my crew shirt, everybody. I'm "Jan."* "Lou" didn't wear a

My crew shirt

crew shirt. She wore a dress and watched the races from a lawn chair with Aunt Mildred and the other onlookers.

Right before the start of a race, I jammed my fingers in my ears. BOOOOOOMMM . . . a cannon on a barge fired, and the tight pack of boats roared past. The crowd yelled, "IT'S A START!"

There's Larry fighting for the lead with one hand on the steering wheel and the other on the throttle. He was kneeling in *Lou-Jan II's* shallow box, going more than sixty mph over the water. The water was moving, too, and it made Lou-Jan II bounce, skip, tilt, and slide wild. *Hang on, Larry.* The hydroplane races were exciting and scary—they made my heart crawl up into my throat. Larry won a lot of races in the Lou-Jans. When he won, my heart busted open with a big gush of joy.

A Crying Shame

At the cottage, Daddy liked a big plate of crappies or a couple of catfish for dinner. I didn't mind fishing, but I wanted to throw them back in. I didn't want to eat them. Every time I was faced with a fish on my plate, I could see it. Alive. Gasping for air. Wildly flapping its tail. Its googly eyes on me, saying, "Oh, please. Throw me in the water."

One Friday night at dinner, while I was still very small, Daddy put some fish on my plate. "Well, dig in." Daddy fork-pointed at my fish.

I looked at Mommy. "Please, may I have something else?"

"What else? This is Friday. We're Catholic."

Why do Catholics have to eat fish on Fridays? Whoever made that one up? Someone who likes fish as much as Daddy; that's who. "May I have some watermelon?"

Daddy dropped his fork and looked at me. "Don't be silly. You like fish. They are delicious and good for you." He took a bite and said, "Mmmm."

I don't like fish. YOU like fish. I put a bite of fish in my mouth. My mouth tried to spit it out. I looked at Mommy. Her face made me swallow. My stomach bucked at getting fish. It wanted to get rid of it. I ran into the kitchen, hopped on my step stool, leaned over the sink, and gagged and gagged and gagged.

Daddy said, "What's the matter with Janice?"

Mommy said, "She doesn't like fish."

"She's MY daughter. Of course she likes fish."

Doctor Beare's Daughter . . . GAG . . . LOVES fish. I wish . . . GAG . . . I was her.

"It's because of that raw oyster you fed her," Mommy said.

"What are you talking about?"

"When Janice was still in her high chair, you fed her that raw oyster and made her swallow it. When she spit it back up, you never should have put it down her the second time. Or the third. Or the fourth. Or the fifth. It put her off fish."

"You think it's MY fault? If you knew that oyster would put her off fish, then why did you let me give it to her?"

"You think it's MY fault?"

"Well, you're her MOTHER. It's not possible for a CHILD OF MINE to not like fish."

He's forgotten . . . GAG . . . that I'm adopted again. He does that . . . GAG . . . all the time. Mommy NEVER . . . GAG . . . forgets it.

"Ralph. You're getting irrational."

Oh, oh. I'd better do . . . GAG . . . something fast.

"SONOFABITCH." Daddy slammed his hand on the table, making the dishes jump. "I've got a wife who thinks everything's my fault and has no respect for me. And now you tell me I've got a daughter who doesn't like fish. . . . It's A GODDAMN CRYING . . ."

I had swallowed my gag and was back in my seat at the table. "I needed a drink of water. Now I'm going to eat my fish."

Daddy shut up, but his mouth was still hanging open. He was watching me carefully. Mommy rolled her eyes.

I stuffed some crappie in my mouth, chewed, and (gulp) swallowed. I said, "Mmmm." My tummy turned itself inside out. I fed it (gulp) another bite.

"Mmmm," Daddy said and set to eating his dinner like nothing had happened.

Right after dinner, I threw that crappie back in the water—of the toilet. I wiped my face and told my poor tummy, "You'd better learn to keep it down. We're going to have to do this every goddamn Friday. It's a crying shame. That's what it is."

The next Friday, Mommy made spaghetti for dinner. The sauce had mushrooms instead of meat. "Thought we were having fish," Daddy said.

"I forgot what day it is," Mommy said.

"If you forgot what day it is, then how come there's no meat in the sauce?"

"I remembered after I cooked the spaghetti."

"MY."

It was just one word, but it meant, "How could anyone be so GODDAMN dumb."

Mommy nodded at me, and I dug in.

"I'm going fishing tomorrow," Daddy said.

Sometimes Mommy served tuna on Fridays. I managed to eat a little bit of it because it came out of a can and did not look like it had once been part of a fish. I held my nose and pretended it was chicken. Most Fridays, I wished I'd been adopted by Protestants.

5
I Couldn't Have... Could I?

I have a gray-and-white secret from Mommy and Daddy. It was November 1952. I was five, and we were back at the house-in-town. My secret was almost found out when The Three Beares were walking up the slate sidewalk from the garage to the back door.

Daddy said, "What's a cat doing sitting on our step?" When it saw us, the gray-and-white cat darted into the shrubs. "Janice, have you been feeding a stray?"

"Uh, no." *It's not much of a lie. I never fed it. I only gave it a drink of milk.*

"Stay away from it."

Daddy doesn't like dogs, and I guess he doesn't like cats, either.

In late March, we thought winter was over, but it turned bitter cold and

My gray-and-white secret

started to snow. I looked out the window. The gray-and-white cat was lying in the middle of the yard, snow swirling around her. I put on my coat and went out to see what was wrong. There was a bit of black fur against the white fur on her chest. It moved. *It's a kitten.* I ran into the office. Daddy was in the drug room with a patient, filling a pill envelope.

"Daddy. The stray cat is having kittens."

"I told you to leave that cat alone," he said.

"Daddy. She's having kittens in the middle of the yard. IN THE SNOW."

He excused himself from his patient, got his coat, and went with me to the cat. He took a look, then tramped through the snow to the garage. I followed him. He grabbed a box of new glass medicine bottles. "Take all the bottles out of the box, Kiddo. The wood shavings they come packed in is good insulation." He cut off the top flaps of the box and cut a flap on the side for a door. He gave me the box of wood shavings and said, "Take this. I need some things from the house."

I took the box and ran back to the cat, just in time to watch the next kitten, covered in a clear sack, slide right out of her. *So that's how babies are born.*

Daddy came back with a hammer, some tent stakes, and a tarp. First, he cleared the snow away from the cat and her kittens—she was heaving, trying to have another one. Then he surrounded mother and babies with the wood shavings to make a snug nest. Next, he turned the box upside down over the family. Finally he put the tarp over the box and staked it to the ground. Then he said, "I have to get back to my patient, and you have to come in the house. This is the beginning of a big storm."

Through the kitchen window, I watched the snow pile up on the cat's new roof. *I hope they're doing okay in there.*

The next morning, I left a pan of warm milk in the melting snow by her door. She waited until I left, then stuck her head out to drink. A few days later, she carried a kitten by its scruff across the alley to the abandoned livery stable with its saggy roof. She made six trips in all. Thanks to Daddy, she and all her kittens made it through the storm. *Daddy's a hero, all right.*

~~~~

Before I was old enough to start school, Daddy always took me with him to the hospital when he was called in for emergencies. I was supposed to sit in the waiting room, but it was too boring, so I sneaked up and down the halls, peeking into patient rooms. When I recognized one of Daddy's patients, I visited them until one of the nurses found me and took me back to the waiting room. *I don't know why she always makes me leave. The patients seem to like having a visitor.*

One time, when I was at the hospital, a nurse took me upstairs to a hall outside two big double doors. "Your daddy wants you to stand right here," she said.

The doors opened, and Daddy came out wearing his scrubs and cap. He had a teeny-tiny baby in a blanket. He said, "I just helped this little girl come into the world." He used his finger to open one tiny fist, "Just look at those tiny fingers." He was smiling wide. "Look there, at her tiny toes. Her nails are so thin you can see right through them. It's a miracle, I tell you. It's a miracle every time." He chuckled.

Daddy thinks new babies are wonderful. Was I ever that little?

Daddy told the nurse, "Take Janice back to the waiting room, and tell the father he has a girl. Now I'm going to show this brand-new one to her mother."

That baby was born from her mommy, like the kittens who came from the gray-and-white cat. Was there a mommy who born me? In The Book there weren't any mommies at the Home, so I couldn't have been born like that. . . . Could I?

6
The Pot

She Never Sings Back There

People didn't travel very far in the 1950s. It cost a lot, and the insides of cars got hot in the summer. Rest stops were way far apart and had smelly outhouses. Daddy didn't care. He loved to drive. He loved far-away wild places. Every summer, he drove us thousands of miles in search of wild scenery in whatever Cadillac Mommy had at the time. Grandpa always came along. We took lots of these long trips before I was old enough to start school.

Mommy sang our way down the road, and I learned the words to her songs. Her favorites were "Meet Me in St. Louis, Louis,"[3] and the one about taking a walk in the park in May and being surprised by roguish eyes that stole her heart.[4] I liked Grandpa's company in the back seat, but road trips made me sick. My adults smoked cigarettes with all the windows up because Mommy didn't want the wind to muss her hair. The mixed-up stink of Old Golds (Grandpa's), Lucky Strikes (Daddy's), and Chesterfields (Mommy's) made me cough and my eyes run. And the twisty highways, gravel roads, and dirt ruts through woods, across deserts, prairies, and swamps, and up and down hills and mountains made my spit run and my stomach roll over. And I couldn't see where we were going over the high back of the Cadillac's

front seat. When I had to spit up, I grabbed
The Pot. Then Daddy had to stop so I could
empty it in the ditch.

The Pot

If I had to throw up too often, Daddy
made Mommy trade seats with me because
I wouldn't be as sick if I sat up front and
could see where we were going. This didn't
sit good with Mommy. She fumed about it
for a hundred miles. *She never sings back there.*

Daddy liked to stop for the night around four-thirty. Then we got
into a motel, and he brought out the brown leather case—the traveling
bar. While my adults drank cocktails, Daddy fixed me one, too. It was
a jigger of Virginia Dare wine in a big cup with lots of 7UP and ice.
Delicious.

Days on the road started early. While I was still asleep, Mommy
hauled me out of bed and stuffed me into my clothes. Daddy carried
me out to the car and plopped me in the back seat with Grandpa.
When I woke up, we stopped for breakfast. But by then I was usually
too carsick to eat. Mommy always said it would be easier if they left
me at home. *Yes, Daddy. Leave me with Louella.*

He said, "I want Janice to see things and not just read about them
in books."

*But I like books. Mommy still reads me the one about how I was
chosen. I wish she would get a new one.*

Poisonberries

I had my fifth birthday in June 1952 at the cottage. In July, Daddy
said we were going to a cooler place in the wild, someplace with
no polio—a terrible disease that could paralyze people, especially
children, so they couldn't breathe. "The world needs a vaccine for
polio," Daddy said.

We were going to Lake Nipigon in Canada, a thousand miles from
Celina. In the back seat, Grandpa told me made-up funny stories
that made me happy. When we got into Canada, the road went up
and down hills, and I had to use The Pot. A lot. Daddy stopped to
give me a break, and we got out of the car to walk around. Mommy
saw some berries on a bush. "Boysenberries," she said, and she ate a
bunch of them.

Daddy said, "It's strange that all the other bushes have been
picked clean. Why do you suppose the birds and the natives left only
those berries?"

Yes, why?

Grandpa said, "Maybe those weren't *boysen*berries, but
*poison*berries."

My stomach felt like there were worms in there, wiggling. My heart
jumped like a toad trapped in a jar. *This is what scared always feels like.
Mommy maybe ate poison. She might die any minute. What will Daddy
and I do without her? I don't want my Mommy to die. Who will take
care of me while Daddy works? Will I have to go back to the Home?*

We got back in the car and started driving again. I stood on my
toes on the floor of the back seat, rested my chin on the back of the
front seat, and stared at Mommy, waiting to see if she was going to die.

"Sit down, Janice. You're breathing on me," Mommy said. "They
were *boysen*berries."

Neither Daddy or Grandpa seemed worried, so I sat down. *I guess if
she keels over, Daddy will save her.* It took lots of miles for the worms
to settle and the toad to quit jumping.

A Big, Baked Potato

We stayed in the little village of Nipigon where there were husky
dogs in the streets. Some pulled carts of fish and vegetables. Some

ran loose. Some sat in the doorways of stores. I wanted to meet every one of them. But Daddy thought it was not a good idea. Grandpa said the dogs pulled sleds in the winter for transportation. I imagined myself in my little sled on a snowy day being pulled by a big husky dog all around Celina. People would say, "There goes Doctor Beare's Daughter and her dog." *My own dog.*

At the Hudson Bay Company Store, I begged Mommy for a figurine dog that looked like the huskies in the streets. When Daddy saw it, he said, "Why would anyone want a statue of a damn dog?" *I want my own dog more than anything. But I guess Doctor Beare's Daughter is supposed to hate dogs.*

Some days, we took long drives to see all the wild scenery around Lake Nipigon. Other days, Daddy and Grandpa went out fishing on Lake Nipigon. Daddy always took one of his catch to a restaurant, and they cooked it for our dinner. "Eat your fish," Daddy said. "You won't find any fresher fish than the big one I caught today." He ate a big forkful, then said, "Mmmm."

Mommy knows I hate eating fish. Grandpa knows I hate eating fish. But Daddy doesn't know, so we all have to pretend that I like eating fish because Doctor Beare's Daughter loves her fish. I took a bite. My mouth grew watery. *No,* I told it. I swallowed the fish. My stomach tried to heave. Mommy's face said I'd best keep it down. *Stop,* I told my poor stomach. I cut the rest of my fish into tiny bites. I slid some into my napkin and hid the rest under the skin of my baked potato. *I'm always going to ask for a big baked potato when I have to eat fish. The skin can hide a lot of fish. Daddy will think that Doctor Beare's Daughter loves baked potatoes as much as she loves fish.*

After dinner, Grandpa said, "I'm going to take Janice for a walk around town." When Mommy and Daddy were out of sight, he bought me a hot dog from a street cart and let me pet a lot of dogs. I imagined every one of them was mine.

Diamonds in the Shoebox?

On our trip home, we were stopped at the border. The guards said that someone had been smuggling diamonds into the U.S. in Cadillacs. They had Daddy drive the Caddy over a mirror that showed the underside of the car. We had to get out while the guards searched the inside. Then they opened the trunk. *Daddy wouldn't smuggle diamonds. Would he? He wouldn't. But what if the smugglers hid their diamonds in our car because it's a Cadillac?* Now the guards had our suitcases open and were pawing through our stuff. I took both of Mommy's hands. She thought I wanted to hold them. I was really hiding her rings with the big diamonds.

When they were done with the suitcases, the guards found the shoebox with the rubber band around it, next to the spare tire. It was Daddy's supply of just-in-case drugs. The guards looked inside the box, then two of them took Daddy into the office. Mommy, Grandpa, and I were told to stay put, and a guard was seeing to it. My heart was jumping wild like a crazy kangaroo. I whispered to Mommy, "Do you think the smugglers planted diamonds in the shoebox?"

"What? . . . Of course not. You have an overactive imagination."

"Then, why did they take Daddy away?"

"People smuggle drugs, too."

My heart jumped into my head, leaving a hole in my chest. Now the kangaroo was banging around inside my head, trying to get out. *What will we do if they arrest Daddy? They can't do that. He's too important.* I knew about drugs. The office drug room was full of them. Extras were in boxes in the basement. There was always a jumbled-up mess of them in shoeboxes in the cupboard above the stove in the kitchen. Drugs could kill you or save you. I knew not to touch them. They were just part of our house-in-town.

Daddy finally came out of the building with his shoebox. He put it in the trunk and slammed it shut. He looked at the guards, then pointed to the physician license plate on the Caddy and said, "For crap's sake."

We got in the car and drove off. My heart slid back into my chest where it belonged. *Those guards are goddamn ignorant. They don't know how important Daddy is.*

"We're Away"

On the last day of January in 1953, Grandpa showed up at the house-in-town and said, "Are you ready to sneak out of town, Kiddo?"

Way back when Daddy took Uncle Doc into the practice, it was agreed that Daddy would always have February off to go to Florida. Uncle Doc could have all the vacation he wanted, too, but February was for Daddy.

"More like *streak* out of town," I said. *Leaving for Florida is like making a getaway from a bank job, only it's the patients Daddy is getting away from.*

After the car was packed and aimed at Main Street, Mommy, Grandpa, and I sat in the kitchen until Daddy popped his head in to say, "Last patient." Then we used the bathroom and sat in the car with the motor running. When Daddy finished with his patient, he walked out of the office, through the house, locked the back door behind him, got into the car, and drove us straight out of town. If he didn't, there might be an emergency, and then who knew when we could leave? When we passed the Celina city limits, he said, "We're away."

Daddy escaped once again. Oh, how I love travel and The Pot.

In Kentucky, we stopped at a gas station. The attendant had black skin. I grabbed Mommy's hand and whispered, "That poor man has been burned bad by the sun."

She shushed me and pulled me away, saying, "That's his normal skin color. He's a Negro."

Back on the road, I asked, "Why aren't there any Negroes in Celina?"

Daddy answered by telling this story: "We had a Negro family move into town once. One day they went out of town to visit relatives. When they came home, they found their house had burned down. In the yard stood a brand-new truck piled with all their belongings. The neighbors said that they managed to save the family's things, but couldn't save the house. They felt so badly, they all pitched in and bought the family a new truck. They gave the man the keys and wished him luck starting over elsewhere. The family got in their new truck and left town."

If the neighbors had time to get all the family's stuff out of the house, why couldn't they save the house? Why didn't the neighbors help them find another house in Celina? Why did the family leave town to start over somewhere else? I was about to ask Daddy, but thought, *better not. Those might be ignorant questions.*

Pffttt, Pffttt, Pffttt!

I looked out the window at the hills of Kentucky, at the red soil and the shacks on the sides of the hills. Every one had a wringer washing machine on the rickety front porch. We drove through little towns where Route 25 became the main street. We passed homemade quilts for sale strung along the roadside on clotheslines. We passed tobacco barns, their sides wide open, tobacco hanging from the racks to dry.

Every few miles, I saw signs about Dog Patch: Bar-B-Que Restaurant. Bargain Barn. Free Zoo. I said I wanted to see the zoo, but Daddy said Dog Patch was a tourist trap and a smelly one at that. I imagined a bunch of people with cameras around their necks sitting on perches in a cage. *I don't think that's what he meant.*

"I wouldn't mind a barbecue-pork sandwich," said Grandpa. *Not me. My tummy is watery. I hope we get there before I have to grab The Pot.*

Each sign we passed made me want to stop there even more. "See the man feed the alligators at Dog Patch." "Free zoo at Dog Patch." "Live black bear at Dog Patch." "Only 50 (40, 30, 20, 10, 5, 3, 2, 1) more miles to Dog Patch."

"Ralph, I have to pee," Mommy said. *Does she really? I think she's doing that for me.*

Daddy sighed and pulled into the parking lot.

I dragged Grandpa to the zoo. We walked through rows of cages with birds, monkeys, and other animals. *Those poor animals. They're stuck in cages with their own poop and dirty water bowls.* Daddy had been right about the smell. It went right up my nose and punched me in the eyes from behind. It was worse than the tear-jerking cigarette fumes in the Caddy and the mean rotten stink that gassed me in the rest-stop outhouses.

We went to the restaurant, and Grandpa got his barbecue-pork sandwich. My tummy was feeling much better. The barbecue smelled so good that I asked Grandpa for a sandwich. I was about to take the first bite when Daddy came and told me, "I don't think barbecue is a good idea."

It was delicious. I ate the whole thing. In the Bargain Barn, I fell in love with a stuffed, white cat with long, luxurious fur, and Grandpa bought it for me. Back on the road, he hissed and wildly waved the cat around, making it chase me. Grandpa said the cat's name was Pffttt, Pffttt, Pffttt! because that's the noise it made. Its hair fell out, all over the back seat. Poor Pffttt, Pffttt, Pffttt! He was bald before we got to Tennessee. That's where the hills became mountains. The two-lane highway climbed up and down and around. I had to grab The Pot and up came the barbecue, leaving my throat raw and my stomach fuzzy with nausea. *When Daddy says something's not a good idea, he knows what he's talking about.* I got to sit up front—in misery for the rest of the afternoon until we stopped for the night.

Mommy wasn't happy either. When she got out of the car at the motel, her navy-blue dress was covered in white cat hair. It was the funniest thing. I put my hands over my mouth to keep from laughing. I was pretty sure that laughing out loud was not a good idea. It took three cocktails from the traveling bar to unruffle Mommy's feathers.

When I got into bed, I noticed that my bed had a box with a slot to insert a dime for a "relaxing massage." I asked Daddy for a dime. He said, "I don't think that is such a good idea."

"Please, please, please! I want a massage." It took a lot more "pleases" before he gave in.

I lay on the bed and put the dime in the slot. The bed began to shake. The vibrations crawled through me and made my teeth clatter. I gripped the sheets beneath my hands so I didn't vibrate onto the floor. *I don't dare escape after begging Daddy for that dime!* He was sitting up in his and Mommy's bed, watching me. When the "relaxing massage" was finally over, I got up, went into the bathroom, and threw up. When I came back to my bed and crawled in, Daddy said, "Good-night, Kiddo" and switched off the light. *I really am stupid, sometimes. Sometimes? All the time.*

They're Not Like Us

In Georgia, the mountains settled down into hills. Cotton fields spread out everywhere. Once in a while, we passed men, in black-and-white striped jumpsuits, joined together in groups by heavy chains attached to iron cuffs on their ankles. They were working on the roads or digging ditches along the highway in the hot sun. They were watched by guards who had pistols, rifles, and whips. "Why are those men in chains?" I asked.

Daddy said, "They're criminals. They live in camps and are put to work on the roads. They're chained together so they can't run away."

Do they have to put them in chains?

Grandpa said, "Bad boys build good roads."

"Couldn't the bad boys build better roads if they weren't chained to each other?"

"It's part of their punishment," Grandpa said. "And we sure don't want them running around loose." *I think the guns and whips are enough.*

Throughout the afternoon, we passed a few more chain gangs, and I realized that the men in chains were always Negroes, and the guards were white. "Why aren't there any white criminals on the chain gangs?"

Daddy said, "They send them to prison."

"Why do they put Negro criminals on the chain gangs but send the white ones to prison?"

"This is the South," was Daddy's answer.

"What does that have to do with any . . ."

Mommy cut me off. "You'll understand some day, Janice, when you're older."

I can't imagine what they might tell me later that would make it okay to put Negroes in chains. They're people, too. Aren't they? Daddy says, "They're not like us." Well, their skin IS a different color, but that's the only difference I see—that and those chains. And . . . I wear invisible chains every day.

Flamingos and Parrots and Dolphins and Whales

After four days on the road, we finally got to Hollywood, Florida. Our motel was right on the beach. Daddy bought me a kite and helped me fly it on the beach. Mommy and I waded in the Atlantic

Ocean and hunted seashells together. The four of us played shuffle-board. *I love doing fun things as a family.* We were staying in Hollywood so Daddy could go to the GM Motorama in Miami and look at all the new cars.

We saw a bunch of other stuff in Florida, too, like flamingos and parrots and dolphins and whales. When February was over, I didn't want to go home. *There's a lot of mountains and a whole lot of vomit between here and Celina. Why do we have to drive so far just to look at new cars and have some family fun? Can't we just visit a car dealer in Celina and play a game together in our living room?*

Mommy and me dressed for dinner in Hollywood, Florida

7
So Much to Learn

Her Mommy is Divorced

It was spring, the air smelled like lilacs, and I was roller skating on the sidewalk down Wayne Street. The grade school was ahead, just across the street. *I'll be going there in the fall. I can't wait to meet other kids my age and make friends.* I crossed over and skated on down Wayne, and another little girl was skating toward me. *Yay.* We met in the middle of the block. Jill took me to her house farther down Wayne, and her mommy made lemonade for us. When I told Mommy about my new friend, she said I could skate with Jill, but I was not to go inside her house again.

"Why? Her mommy was very nice."

"Her mommy is divorced. She might have men in the house."

I didn't see any men when I was there. "Then can Jill come here to play sometimes?"

"You're not to get too friendly with her."

"Why?"

"I told you. Her mommy is divorced." *I wonder why she's divorced? Maybe Jill's daddy got mad at her. I hope Daddy doesn't get mad enough to divorce Mommy.*

Who's a Pretty Bird?

On my sixth birthday in June 1953, Mommy's best friend, Aunt Mildred, walked into the cottage with a cake under her arm.

"Where's Charlie?" Mommy asked.

"He's just getting Janice's birthday present out of the car."

I ran to the back door and saw Uncle Charlie coming up the walk carrying a blue parakeet in a cage. My heart was banging. My head was spinning. My chest was straining.

"Happy Birthday." Uncle Charlie handed me the cage.

I thought I might fall over. *I can't fall over. I can't drop the bird. It's mine. I have a pet. What if Daddy won't let me keep it? I'll just die.* I held my breath and watched Daddy.

"Uncle" Charlie and "Aunt" Mildred

He had never let me have a pet before. *He hates dogs and cats. Does he hate birds, too? Daddy didn't say anything about the parakeet. It must be because Uncle Charlie gave it to me. Daddy thinks a lot of Uncle Charlie.*

I named my beautiful bird *Bunny*. He learned to sit on my finger, and I held him close to my lips and said, "Bunny is a pretty bird. Bunny is a pretty bird. . . ." It took a couple of weeks, but one day, when I took him out of his cage, he greeted me with, "Bunny is a pretty bird. Bunny is a pretty bird. . . ." He liked to fly around the cottage, perch on top of the curtains, or take a bath in the kitchen sink. His favorite treat was the leafy top of a celery stick. Once he learned to talk, he wouldn't stop—just like me. *Aunt Mildred and Uncle Charlie understand that a girl with no brothers or sisters needs a pet. Mommy and Daddy just don't get it.*

Shortly after my birthday, Louella left us to get married. Mommy didn't get another live-in helper because I would be in school during the day come fall. Instead, she hired a lady to come in twice a week and clean. *I'm going to miss Louella because she was nice and read to me sometimes. Now it will be just Mommy and me all day.*

Fishy Fries

I had Bunny about two weeks when I had to leave him with Uncle Charlie and Aunt Mildred because we went on vacation to Canada, to Daddy's favorite fishing place on Lake Superior. We stayed at Herron's Camp on Batchawana Bay. Mommy liked our cabin because it had an indoor flusher. Daddy and Grandpa went out on a boat every day. They caught lots of whitefish, and Mrs. Herron cooked it for us for dinner. No baked potatoes. Mrs. Herron served French fries. *How's this going to work?* I ate a French fry, then cut a strip of fish the same size, mixed it up with the other fries, doused them with catsup, and ate up the real fries.

When I was done eating, Daddy said, "Don't you want your French fries, Kiddo?"

Oh, oh. Daddy loves fries with catsup.

Grandpa grabbed my plate, scraped my *fishy* fries onto his, and said, "If you aren't going to eat your French fries, I'll have them."

Daddy looked disappointed. *I love Grandpa so much.*

It's Clear, for Christ's Sake

I was standing with Daddy on the wooden dock where they tied up the fishing boats. Looking down at the water, I could see pretty, colored rocks on the bottom just below the surface. I wanted to collect some, so I kicked off my shoes and stepped off the dock. When I hit the water, I felt like my heart jumped out of my body. It was shocking cold. I went straight down, down, down. *I'm going to die. Just like people drown in the lake sometimes back home.* Somehow, I came back up, thrashing. Daddy grabbed me and hauled me onto the dock. "What the Sam hell?" he bellowed. "What were you thinking? That water is eight feet deep."

Daddy's a hero again. I hung my dripping head in shame. My teeth were knocking together, and the air made my skin hurt.

"Look." Daddy pointed to the water. "It's CLEAR for CHRIST'S SAKE. You can see all the way to the bottom. It only looks shallow. It's not like the green water in Grand Lake." *It sure isn't.*

Daddy marched me back to the cabin and told Mommy, "Dry her out, and warm her up." *Yes, please. I'm so GODDAMN COLD.*

Afterward, Grandpa took me for a walk in the woods and used his pocket knife to make me a whistle from a twig. *I'm so glad Grandpa comes with us on vacations.*

Born in a Barn

The Cadillac hopped and shook as it crept along the ruts of a cart track through the woods. *Shouldn't there be a real road that goes to a village where people live?* Daddy and I were going to the Ojibway village, not far from the fishing camp, taking boxes of blankets, clothes, and other useful things we'd brought from home to Daddy's friend and favorite fishing guide, Joe Tom Sayers—chief of the Ojibway people.

When we came out of the woods, racks of whitefish were drying in the

Chief Joe Tom Sayers

sun. Log cabins were strung out in a line along the rocky shore. Children were running around, laughing and playing a game. *This looks like a poor place where the people don't have much.*

Joe Tom thanked Daddy for his gifts, then gave him a present—a hooked rug that his wife, Mary Jane, had made. While we were driving back to camp, I said, "A chief is an important man, so how can he be poor?"

Daddy said, "The Ojibway people don't think of themselves as poor. They are proud and independent. They fish for a living, live off the land, and trade for any other things they need." *They may have what they need, but they don't have anything else. We have a lot of everything else, but I don't think all our stuff makes us any happier than them. I wish I was part of a village instead of our lonely family of three.*

I looked at the rug in my lap. It was beautiful, with a native paddling a canoe on a lake. When we got back to camp, I jumped out of the car and ran to show it to Mommy.

Later, Grandpa noticed that the Caddy's front passenger door was standing open. When he went to close it, he surprised a skunk that had gotten in the car. It sprayed the inside, then shot out of the car, stopped, gave Grandpa a dirty look, and walked off.

"How in the living goddamn hell did that happen?" Daddy asked Grandpa.

"Don't know," Grandpa said. *It's because I was born in a barn.*

Daddy let out a long string of cuss words, and then he and Grandpa cleaned the inside of the car the best they could with a bar of soap and a hose. That left it wet, and the smell was still awful. When we started for home, we sat on our raincoats. Mommy tied a scarf over her head, and we rolled down the windows. We held our noses—for six hundred miles. *Mommy's gonna get a new Caddy just as soon as we get home. All because I'm so goddamn forgetful.*

I'll Do It

I was glad to be back on Harbor Point with David. One day, he had a box of drinking straws, took one, lit one end, and smoked it. He tried to get me to smoke straws with him. I couldn't make myself do it—it was too much like cigarettes. Another time, under a cottonwood tree, he said he'd give me a dime if I would pull my pants down in front of him. *A dime will get me two frozen Milky Way bars from the boathouse. I'll do it. It makes no never mind to me if David sees me. Mommy told me that she and Aunt Helen gave us baths together when we were littler.*

8
This Is Shocking

After we got back from vacation in July, Aunt Ginny had a baby, and Mommy took me to Uncle Doc's to see my new cousin, Anne Elizabeth. When I looked at her sleeping in her crib, I remembered the new baby Daddy had shown me at the hospital. She had been born from her mommy, like Anne had been born from Aunt Ginny. On the way home in the car, I asked Mommy, "Are all babies born to mommies?"

"Yes, of course."

"Then I was born to a mommy before you got me?"

"Well . . . er . . . er . . . yes."

My heart was galloping. I needed big breaths. *I had a real mommy who gave me away. She didn't want me.* A humongous wave crashed into my heart. I wanted to scream and cry at the same time. Instead my voice got small, and I squeaked out, "Why did she give me away?" My heart galloped faster. My shoulders and neck hurt. My fingers made fists. *I'm about to hear the terrible truth about me. I'm not sure I want to know.*

Mommy sighed like she didn't want to say. "There are many reasons for giving a baby up for adoption. It's usually so the baby can have a better life than the mother can provide."

"Do you know what happened to my real mommy?"

The Caddy jerked toward the ditch. Mommy hit the brakes and stopped so fast on the shoulder that gravel flew everywhere. She glared at me and said, "I'm your REAL mommy. I became your REAL mommy when we adopted you."

I'm getting REAL close to her quick. I better quit. I owe Mommy and Daddy everything. They could have left me in that empty Home. After I knew that I was born to a mommy, sometimes when I got mad at my parents, I hoped someone was looking for me. At the same time I hoped no one would come to take me away.

9
"Beare"

Making Mommy Proud

I'd be starting first grade in September (1953), so in August, Mommy took me shopping for new clothes. We did this twice a year. The Goldstein family, owned shops on Main Street that made up a department store, and Lil Goldstein ran the children's shop. She went to New York to order clothes for her store. While she was there, she ordered just one of some things for me that would go good with my red hair. That way, Mommy could be sure that whatever I wore wouldn't be seen on another little girl in town. *Another thing I don't understand.* The new clothes were always scratchy and made me fidget.

When we got home from shopping, Mommy sat down and opened her arms to me for a hug. I jumped into her lap. She put her arms around me and said, "You're my big first-grade girl." *It feels so good when Mommy is proud of me.*

Harold's Little Girlfriend

I had to ride the bus to school from Harbor Point because we didn't move back to town until late September. When the school bus screeched to a stop in front of our cottage, it had already picked up all the kids out on the farms. I got on and looked for a seat, but the bus seemed full. *Am I supposed to just stand here?* The driver closed the door, and the bus pulled out with a lurch, throwing me against the nearest seat.

I grabbed the back of it and saved myself from landing on the laps of the two kids sitting there.

"Watch it," they said.

"Sit down," the driver commanded.

Panic rushed into my chest. *There's nowhere to sit. What am I supposed to do now?*

"Here!" called a voice at the back of the bus. An older boy was waving at me. I made my way back to him. He shoved the boy next to him up against the window, smushing him into the glass. Then he scooted himself up against the squashed boy to make a space for me. I sat down next to him. He said his name was Harold Putoff, and he was in fourth grade at IC.

Every day after that, when I got on the bus at Harbor Point, Harold was at the back with an empty seat next to him. The other boys teased him. "Here comes your little girlfriend."

Harold always smiled and said, "You're just jealous." He didn't seem to mind, and I sure didn't either.

An Alien from Space

In my classroom at IC, I found my name on a card on the second desk between George Adams and Fred Cooper. I sat and looked around. I didn't know anybody. Our teacher, Sister Mary Alma, introduced herself and took attendance. When it was time for Mass, she called out, "Adams. Beare. Cooper." And motioned for us to stand.

"Beare" is me. What'd I do?

We jumped up, and everyone else lined up behind us. We marched out of our classroom, down the hall, out the front door, across the playground, and into church. The rest of the IC students were there. In our pew section, the girls sat together with the boys behind us.

The inside of Immaculate Conception Church was big and fancy —three long aisles, rows of pews everywhere, and three altars at the front. Above the main altar was a wall of statues; the largest was the Blessed Virgin Mary, whom we Catholic kids called the BVM. Two confessionals stood, one next to each side altar. The ceiling was so high

you couldn't hit it even if you threw a ball really, really hard. In the center was a dome of stained glass, and right in the middle of the dome was a brown eye inside a triangle. When I saw it staring down at me, I wanted to crawl under a pew. *That must be the Eye of God. Watching me. Waiting for me to do something wrong. I better watch myself.*

After Mass, we went back to our classroom and had religion class, then writing class. One of the girls talked back to Sister in writing class, and Sister

Immaculate Conception Church

Inside Immaculate Conception Church

spanked her in front of everyone. She stood still and didn't cry. I felt bad for her. *Nuns can be mean. I'm never going to talk back to one.* After writing class, there was recess on the playground. All us girls grouped together.

One girl with a jump rope said to me, "Oh, you're *her.* My daddy told me Doctor Beare's Daughter would be in my class. I'm supposed to be nice to you and ask you to jump rope."

Before I could say, "I'd like that," another girl said, "Your daddy brought me and my sisters."

"Daddy has delivered many babies in Mercer County."

"You talk like a grown-up."

Then somebody else said, "I see you in church on Sundays. How did your mommy get so fat?"

"I don't know." *That's so mean. Mommy can't help it.*

Suddenly, everyone was throwing questions at me. I felt like I was one of those aliens I saw on TV, and I had just landed on the playground.

"Do you know you're adopted?"

"Yes."

"Aren't you curious about where you came from?"

"No." *Curious is ungrateful to Mommy and Daddy.*

"What's it like to be an only child?"

"It's okay." *Sometimes I want brothers and sisters, like my cousins.*

"What's it like to be rich?"

"It's okay." *I'm rich? I guess. Maybe.*

"Where'd you get that red hair and all those freckles?"

"I don't know." *I came that way from the Home.*

"My mommy said the dress you wore to church last Sunday was paid for by her gallbladder operation. Whose gallbladder paid for this one?"

I was desperately trying to think of an answer when she said, "Mommy always looks for your old clothes in the rummage sale. I hope she gets this one when you're done with it."

Then the girl who had to be nice to me said to the others, "Let's jump rope." She gave one end of her rope to another girl, and they walked a ways from us and began twirling it. The rest of the girls got in line. I was about to go stand at the end of the line when the girl whose mommy had her gallbladder removed said, "You better not jump rope with us. It will wrinkle up that good dress."

She doesn't want me to get in line. I stood there, alone, waiting. *Surely the girl who has to be nice to me and ask me to jump rope will notice and call me over.* She didn't. I got a nasty, sinking feeling in my chest—an alone-and-left-out feeling. *They don't like me because I'm different. I have red hair and ugly freckles, I'm adopted, I'm rich, and my dress is nicer than theirs. I talk too adult.* I didn't know what to do, so I sat down under a nearby tree—just me and my nasty, sinking alone-and-left-out feeling.

Then I heard one girl say, "What's wrong with her?"

Another one said, "She thinks she's too good for us because her daddy is a doctor—she's a snob." *That's not true. I don't think I'm too good for them. I just want to be friends. So what if Daddy is a doctor? That makes me a snob?*

The next morning, I was hoping that everyone had forgotten I was a snob, but the girls ignored me. The boys didn't ignore me. They teased me. One boy pointed at me and said, "Beare has cooties." *Now my name is just, "Beare." I'd rather be "Doctor Beare's Daughter." People like her.*

Then the boy scooped up some imaginary cooties from my desk and threw them at another boy, who tossed them on to yet another boy, as if they were lit firecrackers. The nasty, sinking, alone-and-left-out feeling came crawling back into my chest.

Another boy said, "I know where you got those freckles. The old cow pooped dung in your face." Then several boys were pointing at me, saying, "Cow dung." That got a big laugh. *Why are they so mean? Somebody, please tell them I'm not a snob. Somebody tell them I'm just another little kid—like them.*

That afternoon, in one of the bathroom stalls, I found out I was more than just a snob. I overheard one of the girls say, "Beare is teacher's pet."

Another voice said, "Sister asks Beare to pass out the papers and calls on her, even when she doesn't raise her hand."

Does Sister really do that? . . . She does! Why does she do that? I imagined my face on the body of a pug dog, curled up in Sister Alma's lap, while she petted me with one hand and used her other hand to smack all the other kids with her ruler—no, a yardstick. Hard. *Wait. Sometimes she really does pet me on the head. Yipes! I really am her pet.* Then she would always say, "Janice, you're a lucky girl to have been adopted by such wonderful parents." *You don't know what it's like to live with them.*

Sister Alma wasn't the only nun who did this. Every once in a while, a stray nun would spot me outside church or in a store downtown, pat me on the head, and remind me of my good luck. One of them caught me in Uncle Paul's hardware store once, and another time a nun I didn't even know got her holy mitt on my head ("You lucky girl") in the P & B. I never did see it coming. If I had, I would have ducked.

Not only was I ignored or teased in school, but during morning Mass, my classmates stared at me. All their eyes on me and God's big, brown one up above was too much. *Why are they doing that? How can I get them to stop?*

It went on until one day after Mass, Sister Alma asked me, "Why can't you sit still in church?"

The next day when everyone was watching me, I watched me, too. I scuffed my feet on the kneeler, I wiggled in my seat, I bit my nails, I scratched my leg. I flipped through the pages of the hymnals. I twirled my hair. Then I watched the other children. *They're as still as robins, listening for worms.* So I made me sit still, too. After a few seconds, my body wanted to move, and I fidgeted. I had to get quiet all over again. *Sitting still in church is almost impossible.* To keep from looking like I was moving, I swallowed. I wiggled my toes inside my shoes. I recited my spelling words in my head. *It's still hard. But look. They've stopped watching me.* I worked hard at sitting still in church. And whenever I slipped up, I was reminded by all those eyes jumping right back on me. I slipped up a lot.

Give Me a Kiss

When we moved back into town, I missed riding the bus with Harold. At least I had Bunny to wish me a *good morning* and greet me when I came home. I taught him to play "dead bird" when I pointed my finger at him and said, "Bang." If I said, "Give me a kiss," he pecked me ever so gently on my lips. *Bunny is my best friend, and he makes the house a happier place by amusing Daddy and Mommy. Even I can't do that.* Bunny often perched on the rim of Daddy's glasses and crooked his neck to see himself in the lenses. Then he bobbed his head and yakked to himself. When Daddy took his glasses off, Bunny hopped on Daddy's head and slid around on the bald spot, flapping his wings to stay on. That made Daddy laugh out loud.

Bunny liked to sit on Mommy's shoulders. He would walk behind her neck from one shoulder to the other to see what she was making for dinner. She might slip him a single pea or nub of corn. Bunny spent more time out of his cage than in it. At night, I put him back in his cage and covered it. "Good night, Bunny."

"Good night, Bunny," he said.

He has a good sense of humor. I think I do, too.

Every morning, I cleaned his cage and moved it to the back room so he would be there to greet me when I came home from school.

She Pointed Her Cigarette at Me

One day in school, I surprised myself and took a chance . . . so big and scary it felt dangerous. Sister Alma had us work in pairs to practice our spelling words. Debby and I were quizzing each other. "Spell *crown*," Debby said.

"C r o . . . would you like to come to my house after school? I have lots of games we could play . . . w n." *Why did I do that? She's going to laugh at me. She's going to tell the other girls that "Beare" asked her over to play.*

"Okay. But I'll have to call my mother from your house to let her know."

She said yes! How 'bout that.

After school, I told Mommy, "I brought a friend home to play."

"I see that."

After Debby called her mother, we went upstairs to my room and played Monopoly. Before we finished, Mommy came in my room and said, "It's time for Debby to go home."

Not yet. "Please, Mommy, can Debby stay for dinner? We want to finish our game."

Mommy's face went stiff.

"I could call my mother and ask her," Debby said.

Mommy's stiff face managed to smile at Debby. "We might eat late, and I'm sure your mother wants you home before dark."

Daddy can drive her home later. I was about to say so, but Mommy's blue eyes suddenly looked black. "Janice, put the game away, and say goodbye to your friend. Then I need you to count cars." *Aw, heck.*

I walked with Debby to the end of our block, ran back to count the cars, and went to the kitchen where Mommy was waiting for me. Her face was pinched, her eyes poking into me. "Don't you ever again" —she pointed her cigarette at me—"ask me in front of another child if they can stay for dinner."

"Why not?"

Mommy never smacked me, but she looked like she wanted to. "You embarrassed me. I have dinner planned for the three of us. I don't have enough for a guest at the last minute."

"So . . . next time I should ask you when my friend can't hear us?"

Mommy shook her head. "You need to ask a day ahead of time if you can bring a friend over. I don't really know Debby's mother."

"Do you think she might be divorced and have men over?"

"You say the most ridiculous things. Debby's mother is a widow who has to work for a living."

"I thought you didn't know her."

"I don't *really* know her—I know *of* her."

"Well, what if I get invited to go to someone else's house after school?"

"You mean you would rather be with somebody else than come straight home to see your Mommy?" Her face was changing—from mad to hurt.

Uh oh. "I'd rather be with you than anybody, Mommy." *If her quick gets cut—that is NOT good.*

"Hmmm." She turned her back on me and opened the cupboard to take out a pot. I took Bunny out of his cage and taught him a new trick.

The next day in school, I heard the other girls ask Debby, "What's Beare like at home?"

"She was nice," Debby said. "You should see her house inside. She has her own room. With two closets. And her own bathroom. The doorbell is real chimes with long golden tubes, and the whole down-stairs has wall-to-wall carpet."

"Nobody has that," another girl said.

Really?

"No wonder she's a snob," said another.

The next week, Debby asked me to go to her house after school. I told her I couldn't. I didn't invite anyone else to my house again either.

10
Charred Rubble

Old People Are Smarter

Since I didn't have friends at school, I found some new ones . . . all by myself. Clyde was about Grandpa's age, and he ran the furniture store in the old house right across the alley from our house-in-town. The furniture store was one of two houses between my house and the grade school. On Saturdays, I sneaked away to visit Clyde. If there were no customers in the store, he would be alone, dusting the furniture. Dusting made him bored, so we played hide-and-seek. There were so many good places to hide with all that furniture. When Mommy realized I was gone, she would come to get me and apologize to Clyde for my bothering him.

He always said, "Leave her here, Mrs. Beare. She's not bothering me."

Mommy always said, "Are you *sure* she's not bothering you?"

Like she can't imagine me being somewhere without bothering people.

Clyde always said, "I'm sure," and Mommy would let me stay a little longer.

I found two more friends on my own. In the house on the other side of the furniture store lived old Nora Fortman and her really old father, Joe. In the afternoons, they sat on their front porch. I took the long way home from school—past their house, instead of up the alley —and popped up onto their porch to say, "Hi."

Nora and I sat on the porch swing, and her cat crawled into my lap. Joe sat in a wicker chair. He was always wearing a brown sweater and a flat hat. We talked about the weather, the goings-on in the parish, and Joe's health, which was never good. I couldn't stay long, in case Mommy came looking for me. *I love old people. They aren't mean like the kids at school, and they're always glad to see me. I think they're smarter than younger people, too.*

Makes a Person Hum

One night, sirens jerked me awake. I heard the pumper truck pull out of the fire station—two blocks south of us—and head north on Main. I hopped out of bed and ran to the window that faced Main to see it roar past our house and turn west, onto Wayne Street, and pass out of sight. Then I heard it stop. I ran to my other window that faced the alley. Across the alley, red flames were shooting up in the air, and black smoke billowed everywhere.

The furniture store burned down. When the remains were cleared away, all that was left was a sad, empty lot of charred rubble. I sometimes wandered around the empty lot or sat on the blackened-stone threshold and threw little rocks from the rubble at imaginary targets. I missed Clyde something terrible. His family had another store downtown, and he went to work there. *Mommy doesn't seem to notice he's gone, and she won't let me go all the way downtown by myself. I can't tell her I miss Clyde because she'll know he was important to me. She'd be cut to the quick. I'm glad she lets me love Daddy and Grandpa.*

When the winter weather set in, Nora and Joe disappeared from their porch. Even Nora's cat was nowhere to be seen. *I'm so lonesome, I could cry.*[5] I'd heard those words in a song on the radio. I hummed it a lot.

Why'd You Come Back?

February. No cootie-throwing boys. No whispering-about-me girls. Florida, here I come. Three days of hugging The Pot in the hazy back seat was gonna be worth it to get away from school. Sister Alma gave Mommy a big packet of workbook pages for me so I wouldn't fall behind.

That year we stayed on the Gulf of Mexico at Sarasota and went to the Ringling Bros. and Barnum & Bailey Circus, where I had my picture taken with a famous clown.

We went to Cypress Gardens, where we saw world champion water-skier, Dick Pope Jr., ski barefoot. *Someday I'm going to waterski behind the Chris.*

We went to Silver Springs where I watched a Hollywood film crew shoot an episode of the TV

Me, at the Ringling Bros. Barnum and Bailey circus in Sarasota with clown Charlie Bell and his little dog

show *Sea Hunt. It's amazing—the things you can see when you travel. It's too bad it takes all that driving to get there.*

When I went back to school in March, one of the boys said, "Beare. I thought you'd moved. Why'd you come back?" *I wish I hadn't.*

11
She's Growing Old

One of a Kind

That spring (1954) Mommy took me to Goldstein's for my Easter outfit—a frilly, scratchy dress and coat and a straw hat decorated with flowers, berries, ribbons, and netting that hung over my eyes, like Mommy and her friends wore. Then Lil proudly showed us a purse that was a small hexagon box, decoupaged with flowers, lined with velvet, and sporting a handle of clear glass—the most beautiful thing I'd ever seen. *Please. Please. Please. I crossed my fingers.*

"It's one of a kind," Lil said. "The designer never makes two exactly the same."

"We'll take it." Mommy sounded thrilled.

I snatched it up and carried it around the store, swinging it by the handle. When I got home, I found things to put in it: a lacy hankie, a sample vial of perfume, a rain hat from Uncle Rock's bank, and a quarter. When Easter Sunday came, I put on my new itchy clothes. Mommy had a new outfit, too, special-ordered from Goldstein's Women's Shop. Daddy bought us corsages. Mommy's had big, purple orchids, and mine had pink rosebuds. Daddy pinned them on our coats. *He's so proud of us.*

As we walked down the alley to church, I swung my purse by its crystal handle and felt very grown-up. As we climbed the front steps of the church, lots of grown-ups smiled and said, "Happy Easter, Doctor and Mrs. Beare. And Janice."

When we walked up the main aisle of the church, I held my head high. Then I saw a few of the girls in my class, sitting here and there with their parents. I could tell they were watching me. One of them was staring at my purse. Her forehead was frowning, and her mouth was tight. When I got into the pew, I took off my coat and laid it over my purse. *Having something so beautiful is no fun when other people hate you for having it. Why do they do that? I'll never carry this purse again. And I'm going to hide it so Mommy can't put it in the rummage sale.*

Why Didn't I Know?

I loved spring at the house-in-town because summer and the cottage couldn't be far behind. By the grape arbors, some straggly tulips hung on in memory of those long-ago Heirholzers who'd built our house. In school, we planned a special program for Mother's Day, making big cardboard letters that spelled M-O-T-H-E-R. My job was to hold the O. When our big day came, our mothers sat in the small auditorium. Those of us carrying letters lined up off-stage, the M being first. While the rest of our class sang, each letter walked out onto the stage in order. The song went like this:

> M is for the million things she gave me,
>
> O means only that she's growing old,
>
> T is for the tears she shed to save me
>
> H . . . E . . . R. . . . Put them all together, they spell MOTHER.
>
> A word that means the world to me.[6]

When it was my turn, I walked out onto the stage, smiling and holding the O. *Mommy will be proud of me.* I saw her in the audience with the other mothers. Next to them, Mommy looked old and bulky. She was smiling, until she saw me. Then her eyebrows jumped. Her lips flattened out. She looked like she was about to cut a switch from the grapevine. *Am I wearing the wrong dress? No—she picked it herself.*

Am I holding the O upside down? It's an O. It can't be upside down. What am I doing wrong?

After the program, the mothers came to our classroom for tea and cake. Mommy found me and got me by the arm, her long, red nails digging in. "Why were *you* holding the O?"

"That's the letter Sister gave me."

"Why didn't you pick some other letter?"

"Because Sister gave me *that* one."

"Sometimes you just cut me to the quick."

"It wasn't me. It was Sis . . ." She had me out the door and halfway up the alley to home. "But Mommy . . . school isn't out yet."

Mommy pulled me along. "Mother's Day is the most important day of the year to me. Now it's spoiled." *Why did Sister have to give me the O? Why didn't I know better than to carry it? Doctor Beare's Daughter would have known better.*

At Least for a While

After school let out on the last day of first grade, I came home with my report card in an envelope and gave it to Mommy. She opened it, read it, and said, "You have been promoted to grade two."

I want to feel her being proud of me again. "Mommy, can I sit on your lap?"

She opened her arms for me. I curled up on her lap and said, "I'm your big second-grade girl."

She smiled and gave me a squeeze, then said, "Oh. My big second-grade girl." *Things are all right again—at least for a while.*

12
Where Are You Going with that Crowbar?

*B*ack at the cottage for the summer of 1954, I was feeling proud of the Lou-Jans. Lou-Jan II had broken the Grand Lake record by more than 6 mph. Larry was a daredevil driver, and Daddy was always in his shop at the cottage, making sure the little Mercury engine could beat the competition. He made his own fuel with nitromethane.

L to R: Larry, Daddy, and Bob Kruger with some of the Lou-Jan trophies

The Daily Standard Reprinted with permission

Dr. Beare Gives Kruger Credit For Setting Grand Lake Record

Dr. Ralph Beare, owner of the outboard hydroplane that set a record Sunday on Grand Lake, today gave credit for the record to his driver, Larry Kruger.

"I just happen to own the boat" Dr. Beare, who functions as his own mechanic, said.

Larry really ran a great race. Everybody was talking about the last two laps, when he was clocked at over 70 MPH."

The new record of 65.3 MPH betterd the old one by more than six MPH. The old record, set by Mike Lemon last year was 59.2 MPH.

Dr. Beare explained that the record is only for the course on Grand Lake and will not be recognized officially by the American Power Boat Assn. While the St. Marys Boat Club is a member of the APBA, the race wasn't ran under official rules. The official world record for boats of that class is just a fraction over the record set by Kruger.

Kruger, who lives in Neptune, said afterward that he was driving to win, but had no idea that he was setting a record. Infact he didn't know that he had until he "read about it in the paper."

The record-setting boat was powered by a Mercury-25 engine.

He liked to fire the engine up dry, for a few seconds, just to hear it scream. The stand shook, and the shop filled with blue smoke that choked me.

Carl from the boathouse, who lived catty-corner across the road from us, always said that nitro wasn't to be messed with. Whenever he heard the engine start up, he came out of his house to see if the shop

Kruger Wins Two More Trophies

Larry Kruger of Neptune, who set a new Grand Lake record last Sunday picked up two more trophies yesterday at Indian Lake. The boat races there were held in connection with the current sesquicentennial celebration at Russell's Point.

Kruger, competing with drivers from several parts of the country, won both heats in the A-hydro and D-hydro events.

The latter of these two events was won while piloting Lou Jan II, the boat owned by Dr. Ralph Beare of Celina which set the new Grand Lake record.

The Daily Standard Reprinted with permission

was going to explode. I always ran across the road just in case he was right.

Larry was young and fun. When the drivers hung out, he let me tag after him. We all sat on a couple of boats with our feet hanging in the water, kicking our gray tennis shoes that used to be white. Sometimes we stood around in the water near the boats; the drivers' pants were always wet to the knees. They bragged, teased, joked, and sometimes splashed water at each other or at me. I splashed water back at them, which made them laugh. *I'm part of the gang.*

That summer, we raced on the Detroit River, the Great Lakes, and Lake DePue in Illinois. We took the Lou-Jans to New York to race on Lake Champlain. Lou-Jan II had a big reputation. She couldn't be beat. But there was that one time. . . .

We were late to the races, making it just in time to get Lou-Jan II in the water. I was watching the race with Daddy, Uncle Charlie, Carl Morley, and Bob Kruger. Larry was running in a pack of boats when the pack disappeared into a turn. We could never see the boats in the turns because of the spray from all the rooster tails. Larry was almost always first out of a turn. But not this time. A couple of boats came out, but no Larry. *Where is he?* The whole pack was out now, but still no Larry. I was holding my breath. *Where is he? Did he flip? Was there a crash?* Larry shot out of the turn. "There he is," Uncle Charlie cried. Larry was chasing down the pack. Lou-Jan II skipped and streaked over the water. She was flying. Butterflies danced in my stomach. I held my breath some more. Larry was gaining on the pack.

Daddy yelled, "Just look at that sonofabitch go."

I'm looking. Everyone's looking. The crowd was yelling and pointing. The announcer's voice was climbing higher and higher. I was jumping up and down, screaming, "Go! Go! Go!"

Larry picked off the boats in the pack like they were putt-putting along, trolling for bass. The crowd's roar grew so loud, it drowned out the thunder of the engines when Larry blew past the leader and shot across the finish line. Carl threw his hat on the ground and jumped on it. Daddy and Bob pounded each other on the back. Uncle Charlie picked me up and swung me in a circle. Joy surged through me—I threw my arms out to the sides and swooped through the air like a bird.

"Something's wrong!" yelled Carl.

Uncle Charlie let me down so fast, he almost dropped me. Larry was coming full throttle at us. It looked like he was going to drive Lou-Jan II right onto the rocks. A few feet from shore, he cut the engine, jumped out of the boat, and grabbed the bow. Daddy and the men ran over the rocks and into the water. Then they were all holding up the bow. Daddy was yelling for the crane to pick up the boat. *What's happening?* When the boat was lifted in the air, I saw a big hole in the bow. *How did that happen?* If Larry had slowed down, Lou-Jan II would have sunk.

Later, Larry told us that in the turn, another driver had rammed him. On purpose. *Why would anyone do that?* I saw that driver walk off into the woods. *Is he going off to hide? Maybe he has to pee.* Carl saw him, too. He grabbed a crowbar out of the toolbox and went after the man. Uncle Charlie called out, "Carl! Where are you going with that crowbar?"

"I'm going to kill that son of a bitch."

There's going to be a fight.

Uncle Charlie and Daddy ran after Carl, grabbed him, and walked him back to our pit. Bob and Larry had stayed with me. Bob said, "If I'd gone with Carl, I'd have helped him."

I'd have helped him, too.

After Uncle Charlie and Daddy walked Carl back to our pit, Daddy and Larry went to file a complaint against the driver. When they returned, Daddy told us, "Because we were late getting here, everyone thought Lou-Jan II was a scratch. So one of the other owners bet a lot of money on his boat. When we showed up, he got worried and paid one of the other drivers a hundred dollars to take Lou-Jan II out of the race." *A hundred dollars is a lot of money. I wonder how much money the big bettor lost? I hope it was millions.*

"I Want to Ride the Barrels."

Later that summer, we went on vacation to Yellowstone National Park and Jackson Hole, Wyoming. The drive across Nebraska, the Black Hills, and the Badlands was so hot that Daddy couldn't stand it, and we rolled the windows down. Hot air blasted through the car, but not a single hair on Mommy's head moved. Daddy said, "Summer travel can be damn hot sometimes."

It got cooler when we drove through the Rockies. We saw blue hissing holes and mud pots at Yellowstone and the snow-covered peaks of the Teton range, but the best thing was the Jackson Hole rodeo. Girls competed in a barrel-racing competition, racing their horses around three barrels in a pattern called a cloverleaf. Then they galloped flat-out across the finish line. *I want to be a cowgirl. Someday I'm going to ride the barrels.*

Feeling like a cowgirl somewhere in South Dakota

13
The War with the Devil

The Snob Wants to Sob

"Daddy, can I go to public school with David and the other Harbor Point kids?"

"Don't be silly."

The summer of 1954 was over, and I dreaded going back to IC for second grade. I told David I was worried about the boys being bullies. He said, "Look 'em in the eye and say, 'Sticks and stones may break my bones, but words will never hurt me.'"

When I got on the bus, there was Harold Putoff, in the back, saving my spot. I threw myself onto the seat beside him. He gave me a big smile, and I leaned my head on him. He didn't mind it. *Maybe school won't be so bad this year. Maybe everyone forgot about my reputation as a snob.*

Before I spent five minutes in my new classroom, I had my head patted by Sister Protasia, who thought I needed to be reminded how lucky I was to have fallen into the lap of rich and wonderful Doctor and Mrs. Beare. *Grrrr.* As soon as I got away from her, one of the boys said, "Beare, you smell bad." Sister, who wasn't any taller than us kids, looked him straight in the eye, which made him whimper and scramble to his seat.

She must have learned to do that in nun school. I tried it on the next boy who teased me, and he said, "Look at Beare's face. Her freckles are turning red."

I thought about saying "Sticks and stones . . . ," but it was a sad lie. *Their words make the SNOB want to SOB. Oh wait, that's funny. How can I feel like crying and think something is funny at the same time?*

~~~~~

I was sorry to move back to the house-in-town and miss the bus rides with Harold. When I walked down the alley to school, I wanted to keep going on down Wayne Street, past the furniture factory and right on out of town. Instead, I turned my back on my classmates and told myself, *the snob wants to sob.*

After school, when I came in the back door of the house-in-town, I let it slam behind me. When Bunny heard it, he called out, "Mommy. I'm home." He learned that all by himself. Whenever the phone rang, he said, "Doctor Beare's residence." Sometimes when I was talking to him, he interrupted me. "Janice, you talk too much." That one always made me laugh out loud. *My funny Bunny—hah. Sounds like he's a rabbit, but rabbits can't fly.*

Souped Up

Daddy bought a 1955 Thunderbird that fall and decided to soup it up. And he thought I should be right there with him, helping. "Hand me a torque wrench . . . that's a socket wrench. Go get a torque wrench from the shop . . . hurry up. . . . That's an adjustable wrench. Go get a torque wrench . . . goddamnittohell. That's a pipe wrench. What made you think it's a torque wrench? SOME PEOPLE don't know their own ass from a hole in the ground. Why don't you know the difference?"

I probably come from a long line of people who don't know their own asses from holes in the ground.

When Daddy's hands were too big to work in a small space, he told me to do it—whatever it was that he was struggling with. When

I didn't understand his instructions, it made him mad. "Why are you turning it THAT WAY? I said COUNTER-clockwise, not CLOCK-wise. Can't you read a clock? Don't you know how to tell time?"

I knew it was past time to hide when he told me to help him. I hate working on cars. Thank goodness he took the T-bird to the dealer to get the safety harnesses put in.

When Mommy saw the harnesses, she rolled her eyes and said, "What are you going to do with that car that you need seat belts?"

"See how fast it can go," he said. "Want to take a ride?"

Mommy shook her head and went into the house. I imagined her getting in the little, low-down car, and buckling up. It was a very funny picture in my head.

God Bless America

Now that we second-graders were seven years old, Sister said we had reached the "age of reason." That meant we were old enough to sin. The priest came to religion class and told us about sin. Venial sins were little sins like feeling prideful or being rude. If you died with a venial sin on your soul, you went to purgatory, where you burned in fire until God was satisfied that you'd had enough. Then He took you to heaven. Mortal sins were sins against the Ten Commandments, and they made God so mad that if you died with one on your soul, you went straight to hell, where He left you to burn in fire—FOREVER. This terrified me because the priest was surely talking about me. I was a liar and a cusser, and I sometimes thought bad thoughts about my parents and the kids at school.

The only way to get clean of a mortal sin was to go to confession, where you told your sins to a priest, and he gave you God's forgiveness. I couldn't wait to make my first confession and get all those mortal sins off my soul.

The confessional was three booths wide with purple-velvet curtains. The priest sat in the center booth. The penitents knelt in the side booths, facing a screen with a panel. When the priest pulled back the panel, I made the Sign of the Cross and began, "Bless me, Father, for I have sinned. This is my first confession. I talked back to my daddy four times and disobeyed my mommy once. I took the Lord's name in vain twice. Maybe more. Maybe three times. Maybe seven. I lied once, no, twice, no only once. I'm sorry for all my sins."

Father said, "Remember to always honor your father and mother. Lying is the work of the devil, and blasphemy is a violation of the Third Commandment, 'Thou shalt not take the Lord's name in vain.' Now, make your Act of Contrition."

"Oh my God, I am heartily sorry for having offended you. I detest all my sins because I dread the loss of heaven and the pains of hell. . . . I resolve to sin no more and to avoid the near occasion of sin." *How can I avoid the occasion when I live with Mommy and Daddy?*

Father absolved me and was about to slide shut the panel when I said, "Father . . ."

"Yes?"

"I need something I can say when I feel like cussing that isn't blasphemous."

"How about *God bless America.* That isn't blasphemy."

"Thank you, Father."

Transubstantiation

Sister said we were now "in a state of grace and ready to receive First Communion." Father told us that the priest performs a miracle during Mass that changes the host and wine into the body and blood of Jesus. This is called the miracle of transubstantiation—that was one of our spelling words. Father says we can't go to heaven without Holy

Communion. *I always knew Protestants can't go to heaven. Now I know why.*

First Communion was a big deal. All us girls had white dresses and veils to show that we were pure. *For once, my dress is like the other girls'.* The boys wore white suits. *Sister says they have a harder time staying pure because they have the devil in them.*

Mommy and Daddy gave a big party at the house, and I had to wear my white dress, act very devout, and get my picture taken. Parts of the day were fun, but I kept thinking about Daddy's soul. He took Holy Communion on Sundays, but he only went to confession once a year to do his "Easter duty." He cussed most every day. *He mixes mortal sin with Communion all the time. Daddy is playing with fire—*

Looking devout for the camera with Daddy and Mommy

hellfire. I cried myself to sleep that night for my poor father who was certainly going straight to hell when he died. I worried about Aunt Mildred, too. She used to go to Confession most every day until the priest told her, "If this is all you have to tell me, you're wasting my time." She never went back.

After making my First Communion, I carried my breakfast to school every day because we had to fast overnight before receiving Jesus at morning Mass. If someone didn't take Communion, we all knew he or she had committed a mortal sin. There was always a priest in the confessional during Mass. We could get confessed and be back out in time to go to Communion. This saved a lot of kids from being embarrassed. *I'm one of them.*

The Blessed Virgin's Promise

A week after First Communion, we got our scapulars—two little rectangle-scraps of wool, connected by long strings. *What do I do with this?* Sister showed us how to put the strange thing over our heads and tuck it under our clothes, so one scrap of wool rested on our chests and the other on our backs.

That itchy thing

One rectangle had a picture of the BVM and the words, "Behold the garment of salvation." The other rectangle said, "Whosoever dies wearing this scapular shall not suffer eternal fire." A wonderful feeling whispered through me like a spring breeze that smelled of lilacs and chased out the always-there worry that death might catch me by the throat with a mortal sin on my soul. *This is what it feels like to feel safe.* I floated through the rest of religion class. But soon I had a problem. I asked Sister, "Is my scapular supposed to itch?"

She said, "It's the devil, trying to get you to take it off. You must resist."

I resisted and itched and wriggled and itched. It felt like patches of fire on my skin, burning and blistering. I prayed to the BVM for help. *The devil isn't going to win.*

That night when I undressed, Mommy saw the bright-red mess the scapular had made on my chest and back. She went straight to Daddy. She shoved my scapular at him like it was a skunk she'd caught spraying her shoes.

He said, "She's allergic to wool."

"She wears wool skirts all the time," Mommy said.

"But they're lined. How can she have allergies? Nobody in my family is allergic to anything." *He's forgot again.*

He tossed my scapular in the trash can. Then he went into the office and came back with lotion, which Mommy smeared all over my chest and back.

That night I tried to sleep, but all my worries about dying in sin came back. *I don't care how much it itches. I need the BVM's protection.* I sneaked downstairs and rescued my scapular.

For two days, I slathered myself with lotion and wore the scapular. I sat at my desk and did my work while a goddamn war with the devil went on under my dress. *Whoops! I just committed the sin of blasphemy.* I went to confession. After getting absolution, I asked, "Father, if you die with a mortal sin on your soul, you go straight to hell. Right?"

"That's correct."

"If you die wearing a scapular, you won't go to hell. Right?"

"That's our Lady's promise."

"What happens if you commit a mortal sin while wearing a scapular, and then you die?"

"The scapular is worn to remind you of your devotion to Mary, so you won't be tempted to sin while wearing it."

But . . . I just confessed to the mortal sin of blasphemy that I committed WHILE WEARING my scapular.

"Father, does your scapular itch you?"

"MY scapular? Well, er . . . no."

"Do you wear it ALL the time?"

Whoosh. The panel slid shut. Father had moved onto the kid on the other side. I left the confessional and went to kneel before the statue of the BVM and said my penance. Then I took off my scapular and laid it at her feet. My wonderful feeling of safety lay there with it. I left them both behind. The crummy worry crept back into my chest, where it hunkered down to stay. *There's always something to worry about. Especially for Catholics.*

Mondays and Thursdays

Shortly after First Communion, Mommy fired our "help" and got a new one. Roberta had a lot of energy and was always happy. She liked me to talk to her while she worked. I looked forward to Mondays when she cleaned house all day and Thursdays when she did laundry. When I came home from school, I might find her standing in her socks on a blanket, atop the dining room table, cleaning the crystals of the chandelier, or at the kitchen sink, polishing Mommy's tea service. Roberta always wanted to know how my day had gone. And she wanted me to know about life when she was a girl, growing up on a farm. I wished every day was Monday or Thursday.

The last day of second grade, I ran home to give Mommy my report card. She opened it, read it, and held out her arms. I crawled onto her lap. She hugged me and said, "Oh. My big third-grade girl." *I never want to get too big to do this.*

14
Drive, Ralph!

Right after school was out for the summer, I had my eighth birthday. The next day we left the cottage for another road trip. My stomach vomited its way through lots of mountains: the White Mountains, the Green Mountains, the Adirondack Mountains, and the Allegheny ones, too. We stayed on Cape Cod so Daddy could go deep-sea fishing for bluefin tuna. I went with him and Grandpa out on a charter boat. We managed to land a big one, but nothing like the one we saw hanging on the doc. *I'll never be able to eat tuna and pretend it's chicken again.*

That's enough tuna for several grocery stores.

In early August, the Lou-Jans were going to race on Lake Michigan, so Bob and Larry took the boats to Petoskey early on Saturday. Daddy had to work in the office all day, and we were going to drive up early Sunday for the finals. I couldn't wait to go to the races. I couldn't wait to wear my crew shirt. I couldn't wait to hang out with the drivers and watch Larry win. During dinner on Saturday, the phone rang. Daddy accepted a long-distance call from Petosky. I put down my fork to listen. *Something must be wrong with the boats.*

"Uh, huh . . . Uh huh . . . The hell you say. . . . What hospital? . . . I'm on my way." He slammed down the receiver. The phone jumped off the table and dangled by its cord. The receiver clattered onto the floor and blasted a dial tone. Bony fingers wrapped themselves around my heart.

"Larry—" Daddy's voice got quiet and deep—"went swimming with some of the other drivers. He dove off a pier, but the water was shallow, and he hit his head on the bottom." Those bony fingers were squeezing, now. Daddy swallowed big, then went on. "The impact broke Larry's neck. He's paralyzed."

"NO," Mommy said.

The bony fingers squeezed so hard, my heart made big bangs, and chills raced up and down my back. "What's 'paralyzed?'" I asked.

Daddy put a gentle hand on my shoulder and said in a kind voice, "It means that Larry can't move his arms or legs, Kiddo." Then he said to Mommy, "I've got to get up there," and he headed for the door.

"Wait," Mommy cried. "I'm coming with you."

Daddy said, "I'm driving the T-Bird to make better time."

"I'm coming with you." Mommy grabbed up the hanging phone and called Roberta to come stay with me. Then she grabbed her purse and ran out to the cars. I ran after her. Daddy was already in the T-Bird. Mommy yanked open the passenger door. The car was so low that she had to hang onto the open door with both hands, squat into a sit, and stuff herself backward into the seat. *I didn't think she could do that.*

She was having a time fighting with the safety harness. "Janice. Buckle your mother in," Daddy yelled.

I ran to the car and started sorting out the straps. Mommy pushed my hands away and said, "Step back, Janice." Then she said, "Drive, Ralph!" She yanked the door shut on her dress, leaving part of it hanging out the bottom. Daddy took off, raising a cloud of gravel dust. The bottom of Mommy's dress flapped as the T-bird drove out of sight. I sat down in the white swirling haze and cried gravel-dust tears until Roberta pulled in. She hopped out of her car, sat in the dust with me, and held me.

Later, Roberta let me stay up and watch TV with her until the station played the national anthem and signed off. We stared at the test pattern a few minutes, then went to bed. Roberta slept in my room in the other twin bed. It felt good to have her there. I fell asleep thinking of Larry. *Does he know what happened? Can he see? Can he talk?* I woke up over and over. Each time, I saw Roberta sleeping in the other bed I remembered that my nightmare was real.

Larry died on Monday morning. He was only twenty years old and already one of the top drivers in the country. But most of all, he was my friend.

Two days later, I saw him lying in a casket at the funeral home. *It's Larry, but he's not really in there. How can a person leave their body behind like that? He wasn't Catholic, so he had to take all his sins along with him. Is he in heaven? He liked to cuss. Does that mean he's in hell?* The thought of Larry in hell was more than I could stand.

After the funeral, we went to Larry's house. At one point, I felt so sad that I ran out of the house and sat on the front step. His sister came out and sat beside me. A boxer dog came up to us, wagging its tail, and Larry's sister hugged the dog and cried into its fur. "This was Larry's dog," she said.

I wanted to cry with her, but she deserved to cry more than me because he was her brother—not mine. *I always did wish he was mine.*

Daddy sold the Lou-Jans. He said his heart wasn't in hydroplane racing any more. I hid my crew shirt under the layers of old clothes in the guest-room chest, where no one ever looked. *Just in case Mommy decides to throw it away, and then it will be gone, just like the Lou-Jans.*

Injuries Are Fatal

CELINA—Larry Kruger, 20, widely-known boat racer from Celina, died at 4 p.m. today in Little Traverse hospital, Petoskey, Mich., of a broken neck suffered in a dive into shallow water Saturday night.

Relatives here were informed that Kruger dived from a lake pier at Oden, Mich., after qualifying Saturday for outboard motorboat races at Petoskey last weekend.

Kruger was pulled from the water by Dan Preston, 20, also of Celina, who left here with him early Saturday to compete in the races. Kruger has been driving the Lou-Jan entry of Dr. Ralph J. Beare, Celina surgeon, for some time.

The victim's parents, Mr. and Mrs. Robert Kruger, and Dr. and Mrs. Beare were in Petoskey for the races. The parents and Dr. Beare remained at young Kruger's bedside.

Why Won't You Dive?

Three weeks after Larry died, I was at my last day of Miss Mary's swim class at the Celina Municipal Pool. Mommy was sitting with the other mommies, watching the lesson. Our final test was to dive off the pool deck into the deep end. I walked to the side of the pool and hooked my toes over the edge. *This will be easy. I'm a strong swimmer. Mommy will be proud.* I put my palms together, raised them over my head, and tried to push off, but my toes were stuck to the edge of the pool. I looked down at the water, breathed in some air, and tried again to launch. Nothing happened. My body had made up its mind. *Why can't I dive?* Miss Mary said, "Janice, go to the end of the line. You can try again."

The line moved forward as each of my classmates found their courage and dove in. Then it was my turn again. It was no good. My toes wouldn't unstick. Miss Mary said, "Don't worry. You'll be able to do it next year."

After the lesson, Mommy got me by the arm, her nails digging in. "Why didn't you dive? All the other children dove in but no, not my Janice."

Miss Mary was suddenly there. "Mrs. Beare! Don't you know why Janice wouldn't dive? It's because of Larry."

Mommy looked embarrassed. She said, "Oh, I didn't think of that."

I didn't think of that, either.

Miss Mary winked at me. Right in front of Mommy. *She thinks my feelings are important. I wish Miss Mary was my big sister.*

15
Sometimes it Feels Like Too Much

"The Great Pretender"

On Thursdays, Daddy's office closed at noon, just like all the businesses downtown did. When I got home from school on a Thursday, my parents whisked me out the door so fast I learned to use the bathroom at school before heading home. Dinner out of town, so Daddy could escape the phone for a while. No Nora and Joe's on a Thursday.

Daddy might drive us to Dayton for shopping at Rike's Department Store before finding a restaurant, or to the Wooden Shoe Inn in Minster for their fried chicken in a basket. Other favorite places were the Milano Club—Lima's fancy Italian restaurant—and the Fairway Restaurant in Decatur, Indiana. *What's a hundred miles when you want to eat dinner?*

Every Sunday noon we ate at Koch's Cafeteria in St. Marys. Then Daddy drove around the lake following the shore for at least another hour before we got home. *Out to dinner, I hate it. I especially hate being stuck in the car with my parents. Their evil cigarettes take away my appetite, and there's always the chance of a "discussion" in the front seat. Daddy and Mommy never "argue."* On one of those long, Sunday afternoon drives around Grand Lake, in November 1955, a song jumped out of the Caddy's radio and made me hold my breath to listen.

Oh yes. I'm the great pretender
Pretending that I'm doing well
My need is such
I pretend too much
I'm lonely but no one can tell . . .
Too real is this feeling of make-believe
Too real when I feel what my heart can't conceal
Yes, I'm the great pretender
Just laughing and gay like a clown
I seem to be what I'm not, you see
I'm wearing my heart like a crown
Pretending that you're still around.[7]

That song is talking to me, and I have to hear it again. When I got home, I turned on the Scott and sat there until they played it. Then I changed channels and waited to hear it again. I memorized the words and sang it over and over, aloud and in my head. *What is it about this song? I can't hear it enough.*

The Man Who Knew No Fear

On a Thursday night in December 1955, Mommy, Daddy, and I were watching Disneyland on TV. The show was *Davy Crockett, King of the Wild Frontier.* Davy was brave—"the man who knew no fear." *I wish I knew what it felt like to be calm inside. Davy could grin down a bear. I know a couple of Beares I'd like to grin down.*

Walked His Legs Off

On Christmas Eve, Daddy gave me a coonskin hat, just like Davy's, and a 45 rpm record of "The Great Pretender." I put on my coonskin hat and played the record until time for bed. The day after Christmas, when I took "The Great Pretender" off the turntable, I accidently closed the turntable drawer on the record and broke it in half. All the air went right out of me.

Mommy said, "You have no idea what your Daddy did to get you that record. He walked his legs off all over Dayton to find it for you, and all the record stores there were sold out. Then he walked all over Lima, and all those stores were sold out, too. He finally found one in Fort Wayne, Indiana."

Daddy did all that for me? I can't ask him for another one. I sadly dropped my broken record in the trash.

A few days later, Daddy casually handed me a new copy, saying, "Be more careful with this one." *I wonder what city he walked all over to get this one? Daddy loves me an awful lot. Sometimes it feels like too much.*

16
She Could Have Killed Me

Too Far Gone

Daddy popped in from the office, gave Mommy a packet of pills, and told her to give me one to prevent carsickness. Then he went back to work. It was February 1, 1956, and time to leave for Florida. Mommy gave me a pill, but at the last-patient warning, I didn't seem relaxed, so she gave me another.

R. J. BEARE, M. D.   P. E. BEARE, M. D.
Residence Phone 2110   Residence Phone 3135
O F F I C E   P h o n e 3 7 7 7
Corner Wayne and Main Sts.   Celina, Ohio
AFTERNOONS—1:30 - 3:30 P.M. Except Thursday and Sunday
THURSDAY and SUNDAYS by APPOINTMENT

TAKE	Every _____Hours
	_____Times a Day
	_____Each Meal
_____ Tablets	_____If Needed
	_____At Bedtime

We had just passed the Celina city limits when I fell asleep. After a while, Grandpa tried to wake me up. But I was too far gone. He yelled at Daddy, "Something's wrong with Janice."

Daddy drove off the road and found me unconscious. He asked Mommy how many pills she had given me. I stayed unconscious the rest of the day. For once, Grandpa's being there didn't stop Daddy. He laid into Mommy about how ignorant she was and how she could have killed me. He kept it up until he wore his voice hoarse, Mommy ran out of tears, and they fell asleep at the motel. Mommy told me all about it the next day in the ladies' room of a gas station. She was hopping mad at me, like it was all my fault. *I love Mommy, and she doesn't mean to hurt me. But sometimes, when she wants things her way, she sacrifices me, and it's scary.*

On Fire

We went to Daytona Beach, where we stayed at the Sagamore, an apartment-motel right on the ocean. My adults were happy, so we had fun, and it was an easy time. Until Daddy took me to the Grand National stock-car races at the Daytona Beach Road Course.

Part of the course was right on the beach. The best view was from the top of a sand dune, overlooking the turn where the cars left the sand and took to the pavement. They fishtailed wildly around the turn, and anything could happen. Daddy gave me a bottle of pop, perched me on the dune, and told me to stay put. Then he went to look close-up at the cars. By the time he came back, my skin hurt and was pink.

When we got back to the Sagamore, Daddy blamed Mommy. "Why the hell wasn't she wearing long sleeves? Where was her goddamn hat? Didn't you rub her down with sun lotion?"

Mommy had already had enough of being yelled at over the car sickness pills. She came back at him. "You took her to the race. Why didn't you put her long-sleeve shirt on her and see she had her hat on?"

"Because you're her mother."

"Her hat and shirt were *in the car.* All you had to do was put them on her."

My skin is on fire. Is this what burning in hell feels like?

"Are you saying this is my fault?" Daddy said.

It's my fault because I'm so much trouble to take care of.

"She should have been wearing them when she left the motel. There you go again, thinking bad things about me. You don't give a tinker's damn about me, for crap's sake."

He went to the cupboard, found the shoebox, and pawed through it. He came up with a bottle of aspirin and a tube of hydrocortisone cream. "Well, I'll be a son-of-a-bitch. There's no Benadryl." He turned back to Mommy and said, "You didn't pack any goddamn Benadryl."

"It's your shoebox," Mommy pointed out.

"You're a nurse for Christ's sake."

Mommy's a nurse?

"I *was* a nurse," Mommy said. Her face looked dreamy, like she was faraway.

Daddy took one aspirin from the bottle and slapped it into Mommy's hand. "Give Janice this aspirin. *One* aspirin. Do you hear me?" He was about to put the aspirin bottle back in the shoebox, thought better of it, and stuffed it in his pocket. Then he threw the tube of cream at Mommy. "Put this on her sunburn. I'm going to a drugstore and get some goddamn Benadryl." He ripped open the outside door so hard the jalousies rattled. Then he looked back at Mommy and said, "Goddamn it. This is Florida. The sun is closer to the earth here. You should know that. The ignorance." He slammed the door so hard that two of the jalousie windows fell out onto the sidewalk and broke. "Shit. Now look what you made me do. Call Mr. Anderson."

The Andersons own the goddamned Sagamore.

Lou and Lee

While Daddy thought the best thing about Daytona was the big race, I thought it was Mrs. Anderson's two little Pekingese, named Lou and Lee. She let me walk them twice a day. They yipped and nipped at each other as they pranced and bounced along the sidewalk, tangling their leashes in knots. I wanted a dog so much, it hurt as bad as the sunburn.

He Changed

After we were back home at the house-in-town, Mommy was in her room one night, sitting at her vanity, getting ready to go to a party. I liked to watch her pick out her jewelry and put on her perfume. She always spritzed me with a little puff. "When did you become a nurse?" I asked her.

She picked out a little gold pin from her jewelry box and put it in my hand. "This is my nursing pin. I got it when I graduated nurse's training in Saint Louis."

"Daddy went to medical school in Saint Louis. Is that where you met him?"

"Yes. I was walking in the park, and a friend introduced me to him. It was in May, like the song."

That's why she sings the one about walking in the park—and the one about meeting Louie in St. Louie. "Why did you go to Saint Louis, Mommy?"

"I grew up in Illinois. My poppy died when I was twenty. When I was twenty-two, Mama died, and I was left to live with my oldest brother. I saw an ad in a magazine from a hospital in Saint Louis. They offered nurses training in return for work in the hospital. So I went to Saint Louis."

She was brave to do that.

Mommy went on. "Ralph and I planned to have lots of children, just like my big family. I can't remember my mama not being pregnant. The years she didn't have a new baby were the years that she miscarried. Her children were the jewels in her crown."

Poor Mommy. She only has one jewel, and it's a fake. "When did you decide to adopt a baby?"

"We had been married for fifteen years, and I'd never been pregnant. Still, I hoped—until I had to have a hysterectomy. Then I knew if we wanted a child, we would have to adopt. I was already forty-one, and Ralph was forty. He was against it. He was afraid we would get someone else's bad seed. I had to talk him into it."

It's a damn good thing I've learned how to pretend I'm Doctor Beare's Daughter.

Mommy leaned toward me like she was going to tell a secret and whispered, "Ralph was engaged to a girl back in Versailles when he met me."

He was? Then how . . .

She straightened up, looked in the mirror, tossed her head, poked at her hair, and said, "He broke his engagement to marry me." She looked proud. Then her face changed to sad, and she said, "Ralph was wonderful for a while; then he changed." She put her pin back in the jewelry box and said, "He's waiting. I have to go."

Why did he change?

17
Step on a Crack

After dinner at the house-in-town, Daddy always sat in the living room and listened to music on the Scott. I liked to listen too, so I would creep into the living room with Bunny and lie down in the corner. Daddy didn't know I was there. His eyes were closed, and he kicked his foot in time to the beat. The heel of his right wingtip had worn a slit right through the carpet, down to the horsehair pad. Music was powerful. The beat, the tune, the words of a song jumped right out of the radio, grabbed me by my ears, and busted up my thoughts. Lost in a song, I traced the swirls on the carpet while Bunny followed along. He tried to hop on my hand. One night, in early March, not long after we had come back from Florida (I was eight and in the third grade), Daddy was playing a record of piano music. It was soooo beautiful. "Daddy. Will you buy me a piano?"

"Huh?" His eyes opened. "I didn't know you were there, Kiddo."

"I want to learn to play the piano like the record."

"What happens when you get tired of practicing and quit? What will we do with a piano then?"

"I'll never get tired of music."

"But will you get tired of practicing?"

"I don't think so, but I don't really know."

I thought that was the end of it, but the very next day, I came home from school and found a brand-new Wurlitzer spinet in the dining room. I was even more surprised when Daddy sat down and played a song all the way through. *I didn't know he could do that.* I learned that his mother could play most any instrument and had taught Daddy and Uncle Doc to play piano when they were children.

Daddy arranged for me to take piano lessons after school, one day a week, with Mrs. Morrow. I got to walk all the way across town to her house by myself. On Saturday mornings, I went back again for music-theory class with her other students. And for those fifteen blocks, I made sure I didn't step on a crack just in case what Mommy once told me was true—"Step on a crack, break your mother's back."

For the first block along Main Street, the sidewalk was made of bricks. *I'd better walk on the grass. Wait. The spaces between the bricks are just spaces—not cracks.* I trotted along—for the first block. The rest of the way to Mrs. Morrow's had cement sidewalks, and every slab had a crack or two or five or seven. I leaped and tiptoed and must have looked tipsy. The first few trips to Mrs. Morrow's were dreadful. Then I learned the cracks and even which block I was on when I stepped over them. I passed a lot of houses but didn't know what they looked like. It didn't matter. I had a mission.

I Read Them All

"Adams. Beare. Cooper." Sister lined us up one afternoon to walk in formation to the public library. It was on the next block up Main Street from my house. *I must pass it every week on the way to Mrs. Morrow's but never saw it before.* We learned to use the card catalogue and saw where the children's books were shelved. Then I got my own library card. I loved books, but there weren't that many of them in our house. *Now I can read all the books I want.*

On Saturday mornings, on my way home from Mrs. Morrow's, I stopped at the library and checked out seven or eight picture books, lugged them home, and read them while Mommy and Daddy took their naps, and then I took the books back. When I returned them, the librarian said, "Janice, you're supposed to *read* these before you bring them back—not just look at the pictures."

I told her that I *had* read them and needed more. I worked my way through all the picture books, then started on the chapter books. I read all of them, too. I thought the librarian was a good friend because I saw her so often. She found me books for older children that she thought were okay for me to read. I liked learning new facts about the world from nonfiction, but it was the stories—the fiction—that had the stuff I was desperate to learn.

Safer Alone

When I was alone, I felt safer than when I was with people because I wouldn't say some gawd-awful thing and be a snob, or crazy, or goddamn ignorant. Often, when Mommy thought I was playing outside in the yard, I would go sit in church by myself. The doors were always unlocked. The inside was lit only by a rack of red votive candles burning at the back of the church and what light sneaked in the stained-glass windows and dome. I didn't mind God's eye looking at me when I was alone; He could see I was behaving myself.

I sat in the back pew and looked at the Pieta—the life-size statue of the BVM holding her dead son Jesus across her lap after He had been taken down from the Cross. He was wearing the crown of thorns that tore his skin. He had holes in his hands and feet, too, where He had been nailed to the Cross. He had a big bloody slash in his chest where He'd been run through with a sword. *God sent Jesus to Earth to die for my sins. I brought this on Him. If God can do anything, why couldn't He have found a better way to save me?*

An Angry Little Voice

In April, I was practicing to play in my first piano recital. I had a lot of trouble with a fast run of notes. No matter how many times I played it, I made the same mistakes. I was about to give up when Bunny flew into the dining room and tried to perch on my right hand while I was playing. My hand was moving too fast for him, but he flapped and squawked and fought to stay with it, until he finally slid off. I stopped playing, he hopped back on, and we were off again. I became just as determined to fix my mistakes as my brave little bird was to stay on my hand. Thanks to Bunny, I played well at the recital.

Daddy was quite proud, and this made me very happy . . . until he bragged to some of the other parents, saying, "Playing piano runs in my family. My mother was very musical."

My face felt hot. My tummy tumbled. My fingers rolled up into tight little balls. An angry little voice, buried deep inside me, distantly shouted: "I don't know where my talent for music came from, but it's not from YOUR mother." *Daddy forgets I'm adopted. He thinks I should forget, too. I have to forget, otherwise I'm ungrateful.* I pushed down my anger and shushed the little voice inside me. *I can make it be quiet, but I can't forget. Why can't I just forget?*

18
A Box of Dirt

It was May. Mother's Day was coming. Daddy had always picked out my present to give Mommy and it never made her happy. I decided that this time, I was going to show her how much I loved her by getting her present all by myself. I asked Daddy for some money and to let me go downtown by myself. "Where do you want to go?"

"I want to go to Rankin's because they have lots of pretty things."

At Rankins, they seemed to be expecting me. I didn't know what to get, and then I saw it—a large, pink brandy snifter with gold words in French written on it. It could be filled with fancy soaps or flowers, or just anything. *It's beautiful. Mommy loves fancy things.* I had it gift-wrapped and picked out a funny card. *This Mother's Day, I'm gonna make Mommy smile.*

When the day arrived, she unwrapped the box and took out the brandy snifter. She held it up and looked it over. Then she set it down on the kitchen table and said, "Why on earth would you think I'd like such a gaudy thing?" Next, she read my card and said, "This is a funny card. Mother's Day isn't a joke." Mommy's eyes filled up with tears.

I felt like there was a little bird inside me, pecking me everywhere. *I'm right here in front of you, Mommy. I'm your child. I love you. Why can't that be good enough? Her own child could give her a box of dirt, and she'd love it. I HATE Mother's Day. And right now I don't like Mommy either.*

19
Quicksand

Catching a Great Vocabulary

When we moved to Harbor Point, the summer of 1956, there was a new neighbor across the road—Mrs. Wilson, a widow and a writer. Her novel *White Witch Doctor* had been on the best-seller list for a year and was a Hollywood movie. At night, through open windows, I could hear the tap-tap-tap of her typewriter keys. I wanted to know a real writer, so one day when she was outside, I went over and asked her about her garden. She invited me in for a glass of juice, and her living room was lined with shelves and shelves of books. *It's a library.*

She'd written several books and was working on a series of young-adult novels for the United Nations Children's Fund. The books were set in various countries to help children learn about different peoples and cultures. *Books are powerful. You can learn so much about the world and people outside Celina.*

Mrs. Wilson had been a missionary in the Middle East, and her pen name was Louise Steintorf. She never spoke of her Steintorf husband, but she liked to talk about her second husband, Doctor Wilson, who she called "my Henry." She said that she moved to Harbor Point after her Henry died to live near her sister. But now her sister wanted nothing to do with Mrs. Wilson. I felt sorry for her. It must have shown on my face, because she gave me a smile and said, "I'm going to stay and make the best of it." *That's what I have to do, too. All the time.*

Because it was summer, I couldn't get to the library, but Mrs. Wilson said I could borrow any of her books. *I want to read them all.* If Mommy saw me reading "too much," she'd tell me to put the book down and go do something. So I took up fishing—in a place where Mommy wouldn't see me. Now that I'd had my ninth birthday, I was allowed the run of Harbor Point by myself. That freedom went beyond the bridge to the boathouse, where I could buy minnows or a frozen Milky Way bar. I was even allowed to ride my bike all the way to the truck stop on 29 to get air in my tires. Right behind the boathouse was a wild area along the channel that was usually deserted. Mommy would never see me there.

I packed one of Mrs. Wilson's books in my creel, along with a sandwich and some dough balls for bait. I grabbed a cane pole and a campstool and went to my spot and threw my hook in the water, but I didn't bother to bait it. I ate my sandwich and read about growing up in foreign lands. When I had read all of Mrs. Wilson's books, I started on her books by Pearl Buck. One day, while reading *A House Divided,* there was a character in the story named Doctor Henry Wilson. When I took the book back to Mrs. Wilson, I asked how her husband's name came to be in Pearl Buck's book. She said, "Oh, Pearl and I are good friends."

Mrs. Wilson had other famous friends. One day while "fishing," I read a speech of Eleanor Roosevelt's that Mrs. Wilson had written. *I'm so lucky that Mrs. Wilson moved in across the road. She's different from anybody else in Celina, yet everybody likes her—except maybe her sister. Might people still like me even though I'm different? Some maybe, but I don't think they go to IC.*

Daddy: "Did Janice go fishing today?"
Mommy: "Yes."
Daddy: "Did she catch anything?"
Mommy: "No."

Exploring

In July, Uncle Charlie sold his part of Cron Tire and Supply to his brother and bought Van's Grand Lake Motel on Route 29. He and Aunt Mildred sold their house and moved into the owners' apartment in the motel.

Just past the boathouse and behind the deserted 4-H camp lay a woods with trails, and one led to a small beach. David and I weren't allowed to go into the woods alone, but we were allowed to explore it together. We knew where all the trails led and liked to wade at the beach. Now, I wondered whether I could find a way from that beach to the back of the motel. I set off alone. After I got to the beach, I took off my shoes and waded along the edge of the woods until I thought I might be even with the back of the motel. Then I re-shoed myself and snaked my way through the trees and brush and came out on a marsh. Someone had laid boards across the boggiest ground, so I walked across them and came out of the marsh right behind the motel. *I did it. I'm an explorer.*

When I strolled into the motel office, Aunt Mildred asked, "Where did you come from?" She looked past me. "Is Lou here?"

"No. I came by myself."

"You walked along the highway?" Her face showed she was shocked, maybe even afraid.

"I came through the woods and over the marsh."

"Does Lou know?"

That sounded different—deeper, solemn. It made me shiver. I shook my head.

Aunt Mildred touched the phone, then stopped and said, "Let's go find Uncle Charlie in the garage. There's ice cream bars in the freezer."

Good ol' Aunt Mildred. She understands that sometimes a girl just has to have a secret from her Mommy.

After that, an ice cream bar was my reward every time I made the trip to the motel. I followed Aunt Mildred and Roberta (who also worked at the motel) around while they made up the guest rooms or helped Uncle Charlie with odd jobs. I never heard Uncle Charlie curse, not even when something went wrong with his fix-it projects. *Uncle Charlie, Grandpa, and Uncle Doc never curse. What is it with Daddy? I hate it when he curses at me, but when I feel like cursing, then I like it. That makes it very hard not to do.* When it was time for me to go home, I noticed that Uncle Charlie followed me at a distance until I was over the marsh.

One day, on the way home, I wandered off the trail in the woods and stepped in a mud pit. I sunk in. Past my knees. *It's quicksand! Goddamn it, sonofa . . . God bless America. It's going to pull me under. I'm going to die. I haven't been to confession since school let out. I'm going to hell. I have to make an Act of Contrition and hope for the best.* "Oh my God, I am heartily sorry for having offended you. I detest all my sins because I dread the loss of heaven . . ." *Wait. I'm not sinking. It's not quicksand.* But I still couldn't pull either leg out of the mud. *Now what? I might not be found for days. I could starve to death . . . be eaten by a bear . . . I could . . .*

"Why are you standing there in the mud?"

It was David. He had appeared out of nowhere. "Why were you praying? And why are you back here by *yourself?*"

I was so glad to see him, I felt like crying. Since I didn't want to cry in front of him, I shot back, "Why are *you* back here by *yourself?*"

With the help of a strong branch that had fallen off a tree, David pulled me out of the mud. He also pulled me out of my shoes; they were still down there somewhere. I followed him, barefoot, my legs caked with mud up to my knees. When I walked past the boathouse, Carl's wife, Sarah, gave me a long look. She must have called Mommy, because she was waiting for me at the back door of the cottage.

"Janice got stuck in some mud back in the woods," David told her. "I pulled her out."

"Well," said Mommy. "Now you know why you're not allowed to go back there alone. What if you hadn't been with David?"

"Yeah. What if?" David said.

"Where are your shoes?" Mommy asked.

David shook his head, sadly.

As Mommy was cleaning me up, I said, "Can you take me to the house-in-town on Saturday morning? I'd like to play the piano. Then I can ride home with Daddy for lunch."

"I suppose so. We'll go when the stores open. We have to buy you some new sneakers."

I'm going to Saturday morning confession at church. Then I'll play the piano really loud in the house, so Daddy will hear me in the office and know I'm where I'm supposed to be. My parents don't need to know what a big sinner I am.

Protestants Have All the Fun

After dark, the Harbor Point kids played hide-and-seek at the big light pole. While some kids hid behind shrubs and under overturned boats, I liked to hide with David because he found the best places. One night, when we were looking for a good place to hide, David got the idea to climb an antenna. Many cottages had three-sided antenna towers with rungs, right next to the house. We climbed up one and lay next to each other on the roof. It was glorious. We were out of reach of the rest of the world with only ourselves to answer to. *I could stay here with David and never go home, and no one could find me.*

"Olly, olly, oxen free," came the call from the base of the light pole.

David stood and said, "Watch this." He walked over to the far side of the roof, then ran across it to the antenna, stomping his feet as hard as he could. Then he spidered down the antenna.

I heard raised voices inside the house. *God bless America.* I fairly slid down the antenna. If David hadn't caught me, I'd have fallen into the bushes. He took my hand and pulled me along as we ran away. We made it to edge of the yard, before a man came out with a flashlight to look around. Then he climbed his antenna to see what might be on the roof.

David looked at me and said, "Fun. Huh?"

I could only nod. *David isn't afraid to do something wrong, like I am. He doesn't worry about sin or about his parents finding out. That's because he's a Protestant. I wish I was more like that, but I'm not.*

20
The Power of War Paint

In August, Grandpa threw his grip in the trunk of the Caddy, while Daddy set the tripmeter to zero. It was July, and we were headed for Chicago to find the east end of Route 66, and Daddy was going to drive it all the way to the Pacific Ocean.

As we drove off, I peered in between all the cottages as they went by for my last glimpses of Grand Lake for a while. I was awake because Mommy hadn't given me a pill. I would have to face plains, hills, mountains, deserts, and scads and scads and scads and scads of cigarettes, wide awake and woozy. *The car will be HOT, and I'll need The POT.* My stupid poem made me smile, for a few miles anyway.

Route 66 covered 2,248 miles of steep slopes, dangerous curves, and narrow lanes. It made driving to Florida seem like a hop, skip, and a jump. And our trip to Wyoming, a skate around a long block. Good thing Grandpa had lots of new stories. We took lots of side trips and saw lots of amazing stuff. My tummy turned itself inside out. Repeatedly.

Globe, Arizona, was celebrating the town's seventy-fifth jubilee, and the streets were full of people and action—like a scene in a Western movie. Many of the men were wearing guns, and they all had beards, except for the Apache on their painted ponies, suddenly charging down the street, waving their bows, whooping. People on the streets screamed, and cowboys pretend-shot at the Apache.

During lunch on the sidewalk outside a café, a horse-drawn jail wagon lumbered up the street. "Whoa." The wagon stopped. Two lawmen jumped off and arrested a man on the sidewalk. They hand-cuffed him and locked him in the jail wagon. Daddy and Grandpa suddenly left their sandwiches on their plates and went into the café.

"I'm just going to pay the bill," Daddy said, over his shoulder.

Mommy wrapped their sandwiches in napkins and stuffed them in her purse.

I said, "But we are not—" she snatched my sandwich from my hand "—done with lunch."

"They're arresting men without beards, so we'll finish our lunch in the car, then vamoose out of town," she said.

The jail wagon moved on. I could see the handcuffed man looking out between the bars in the rear of the wagon. I felt sorry for him. All he did was shave. Daddy and Grandpa came back. We had to walk several blocks to the car, and I saw a wanted poster tacked to a post. It had a picture of a clean-shaven man and these words:

> *Wanted. Alive.*
> *Any man walking the streets of Globe without a beard*
> *will be arrested and thrown in jail*
> *until he pays bail to the city*
> *$100.00*
> *Local Folk and Strangers Alike*

I was on high alert now for the jail wagon. My heart was jabbing my chest from the inside. *I'm so God-bless-America scared. So what? You're always scared. Think. What will Mommy and I do if Daddy and Grandpa get arrested? Who will help us? We don't know anybody here. I know. I'll call the Short and Dull Law Firm in Celina. Thank goodness I know how to place a long-distance phone call—collect.* My chest hurt pretty bad until we were so far vamoosed that we had crossed the border into Nogales, Mexico, which was quiet. Men were asleep on the sidewalks under their big straw hats.

Daddy said, "They're taking their siestas." He didn't have to tell me why they slept in the afternoons. It was so hot that I felt like lying down in the shade, too. When siesta was over and the stores opened, Daddy bought me a sombrero. As we left Mexico and headed for California, he said, "Cadillac is coming out with air-conditioning in the fall."

We had been away from home for twelve days when we finally came to the end of Route 66 in Santa Monica, California. We took a long look at the Pacific Ocean, drove up and down the coast some, and walked around Hollywood. *I'll take Florida. It's a lot closer to home.*

On the way home, we went to see the Grand Canyon. We took a scenic drive along the rim and parked at an overlook. I sat in the car, just staring. The canyon went on forever with its pillars of rock, and it was so deep it might take a week for a rock to fall to the bottom. *How could that tiny river, way down at the bottom, have cut through all that rock?* There was a stone wall at the rim of the canyon where people were standing, taking photographs. And a dime viewer that you could look through.

"Please, may I have a dime? I want to go look through the viewer."

"We can see just fine from here," Daddy said.

"But . . . there are other people out of their cars."

"That's all right for them, but we don't need to do that," Daddy said.

"Is that because it's not a good idea?"

"It's a fine idea. It's just not something we want to do." *He doesn't want to get out of the car, so I can't get out either. It's the Grand Canyon for crying out loud. What will he do if I just get out anyway?* The thought of disobeying Daddy sent an electric shock through me. *Do I dare?*

I had my hand on the door handle when the Caddy pulled away. *I'm coming back here someday, and I'm getting out of the car.*

When Daddy finally parked the Caddy in front of the cottage, the tripmeter read 5,260 miles. I jumped out of the car, out of my clothes, into my bathing suit, and into the lake, before Grandpa had the car unpacked.

Don't Poke the Nun

"Let's begin our new school year with sharing what you all did over the summer," said Sister Ralph on the first day of grade five in 1956. "George Adams. Stand up, face the class, and tell us about your summer."

Adams stood, stammered a bit, then started talking. I didn't hear a word he said, because Beare came after Adams, and I was desperately thinking of what I would say.

"Janice Beare."

I gulped and shivered as I got to my feet. I said, "I went swimming in the lake and rode my bike." I started to sit down.

"Just a minute," Sister said. "Didn't you go to California?"

I hung my head and looked at my shoes. "Yes, Sister."

"Can you name all the states you went through?"

"I don't remember them." *Ohio, Indiana, Illinois, Missouri, Kansas, Oklahoma, Texas, New Mexico, Arizona, California, Nevada, and Mexico, too.*

"Maybe this will help." Sister walked over to the front of the classroom and pulled down a window-shade map of the United States. She motioned me to the front of the room, handed me her pointer and said, "Show us."

I dragged the pointer across the map, naming the states. When I gave it back, I wanted to poke her with it.

Then she asked, "What was the most interesting thing you saw on the trip?"

"A war party of Apache, whooping and racing their horses through town."

One of the boys waved his hand frantically and said, "Did they have guns?"

They're interested in what I'm saying. "Bows and arrows."

Another boy called out, "Were they wearing war paint?"

They're hanging on my every word. This is wonderful. "Yes. And their horses were wearing war paint, too." *That should really get them.*

Sister shook her head as if she had been swimming and wanted to get the water out of her ears. Then she asked me, "Tell us something new you learned."

"In Mexico, everyone wears a big hat and sleeps on the sidewalks in the afternoons."

"Those big hats are *sombreros* and the afternoon nap is called a *siesta*," Sister explained. *I hope she doesn't find out that I have my own sombrero. Or it will end up at show-and-tell.*

Sister pushed on, "What else did you learn?"

"That the Pacific Ocean looks just like the Atlantic, except that the waves come to shore from the other way."

"Sit down, Janice."

Compression

In October 1956, Daddy bought Mommy the car we had all been waiting for: an *air-conditioned* Cadillac. He also traded in the T-Bird and bought himself a new, 1957 model in dusk rose with a white lift-off hardtop. I thought it was a beautiful sports car, but to Daddy, it was another engine to be worked on. *Here we go again. Daddy should have adopted a boy.*

Daddy put three carburetors and a blower on the T-Bird, while I stood there and handed him tools. When he got through with the car, it sounded like a pack of motorcycles was chasing it. The men at the gas station told him he couldn't run so much compression on an engine—that it would blow up someday. *I'm not sure what compression is, but Daddy put a lot of everything on that car. I hope it doesn't blow up when I'm in it.*

21
Hey, I'm Here

Careless Mistakes

Right before Thanksgiving, report cards came out, and I got a D in arithmetic. *This proves how stupid I am. Daddy is going to get loud and irrational. He can't stand ignorance.* I handed the card to him. "Please sign this."

He read it over and said, "Get me your last math test."

I brought it to him. About twenty problems—addition, subtraction, multiplication, long division. Several had a red check mark. I hung my head. "I don't know why I get the wrong answer sometimes."

"You never had trouble with addition and subtraction before."

"The problems were only single numbers before." Daddy and I looked at the first problem. It was: 235 plus 141 equals 396.

$$235$$
$$+141$$
$$\overline{396}$$

He said, "Goddamn. Are you really that ignorant? What is three plus four?"

"Seven."

"If you know that, why the hell did you write down nine?"

"I don't know."

"MY." Daddy scanned the rest of the test. "How can a child of mine make so many careless mistakes? Shit. If I was this goddamn careless, half of my patients would be dead."

He made me rework every problem I got wrong. I was able to correct a few. Sometimes I came up with a new wrong answer. When we were finished, Daddy was hoarse, I was fighting off tears, and my chest hurt. Finally he said, "Now all the answers are correct. Do it like this on your next test." He signed my report card. *God bless America. I don't know how to do it any better on my next test.*

While I struggled with math worksheets alone in my room, Bunny strutted around on the page, stopping, lifting one foot, picking his toes, and saying, "I'm such a pretty bird." Then he picked up a corner of the worksheet, held it with one foot, and drilled a line of neatly-punched holes along the edge of the paper with his beak. Finally, he shit—right on a long-division problem. *Good aim, Bunny.*

I figured out that I could get a C or even a B on a math test if I worked all the problems, then went back and did them a second and third time to find most of my mistakes. I sometimes ran out of time before I could rework them all. I had no idea why I made so many stupid mistakes in the first place. *It must come with being ignorant.*

I Love David

It was 1957 now. One afternoon during an end-of-March snowstorm, Mommy opened the front door to grab the paper off the porch. She heard a whir of wings and saw Bunny fly off. She had gotten so used to him being on her shoulder that she forgot he was there. She got Daddy from the office, and we all ran outside to look for Bunny. I spotted him, sitting in the snow on the ledge outside of Mommy and Daddy's bedroom window, shifting from one foot to the other, his feathers fluffed, making him look twice as big and very cold. I felt my heart sinking.

"I think I can get him," Daddy said.

Mommy and I stayed in the yard, watching Bunny, while Daddy went in the house and upstairs to the window. He tried to open the window slowly, but the sash made a noise, scaring Bunny. He flew.

High in the air, across the yard, and over the high school, he flew. As Bunny grew smaller and smaller, my heart sank deeper and deeper. When he became a tiny dot, then faded into nothing, my heart drowned. Bunny was a tropical bird. He couldn't survive the cold. I cried myself to sleep that night for my poor, beautiful Bunny. Then I dreamed that Daddy had opened the window and Bunny flew back in the house and landed on Mommy's shoulder. Then I woke up and saw him fly away. Over and over, the dream, then the reality.

The next day I couldn't pay attention in school. Sister made me stay after and write on the blackboard twenty-five times: "I will pay attention in class." When I got home, David was sitting on the back step. He was bundled up and had walked all the way across town in the snow. *Mommy must have told Aunt Helen about Bunny.* "I brought something to show you," he said.

I sat next to him. He showed me a jointed, wooden snake and posed it one way, then another. Then he gave it to me and said, "You try."

My heart wasn't in it. I gave the snake back to him.

Then he said, "What do you call a funny snake?"

I shook my head.

He made the snake rear up on its tail and say, "Hissssssterical."

I couldn't help it. I smiled.

He gave me the snake and stood. "I've got to go. My mother thinks I'm playing in the snow in our yard." I tried to give him his snake. "You keep it awhile," he said.

I love David. I was smiling when I walked into the house. When I let the door slam behind me, I heard Bunny's little voice inside my head, "Mommy. I'm home." I burst into tears.

～～～

Thursday—again. My parents were waiting for me to come home from school so we could go to dinner in Dayton—again. I was feeling sad and asked them, "Please let me stay home alone."

"You can't stay home alone," Mommy said.

Roberta came in just then. "I can take her home with me," she said. "You and Doc can pick her up at my house on your way home."

"I suppose." Mommy didn't sound sure.

At Roberta's house, I forgot to be sad for a little while. Her husband, Urb, had a cocker spaniel named Betsy for squirrel hunting. While Roberta cooked dinner, I took Betsy for a walk. *Someday, I'm going to have a dog.*

When my parents came to take me home, Roberta locked Betsy in the bedroom before answering the door so Daddy wouldn't know I'd been playing with a dog. *It makes me tired to keep so many secrets.* When I said goodbye to Urb, he gave me two squirrel tails for the hand grips on my bicycle. *Urb is awfully nice, but I feel sorry for the squirrels. I can't put these on my bike. I'll give them to David. He'll think they're wonderful.*

An Old Harmonica

On Sunday while my parents were napping, there was no Bunny to keep me company. I was sad and went looking for something to make me feel better. I found an old harmonica and a yellowed instruction book in a drawer. I took them outside to the grape arbor and tried to play a song. It was impossible to blow just one note. After that, every time I was alone, I worked on it. *I'm not giving up.* I kept the harmonica a secret. It was important that nobody knew I was learning to play it. "This is just for me."

Anonymous

During English class, Sister Ralph had the boys bring hymnals from the church so we could learn the new hymn for Sunday Mass. Sister noticed a wrong note printed on the music staff in the hymnal and told everyone to get a pencil, cross out that note, and draw in the correct one.

After singing the song several times, I got bored. I flipped through the book and was reading the lyrics to a hymn on page 283 when I had an idea. I picked up my pencil and drew a staff in the margin. I wrote a series of notes on the staff. It gave me a bit of satisfaction to see my work there on the page. Then, each time we were given a hymnal in class, I would turn to page 283 and add my bit of made-up music. As I wrote the notes, the little voice inside me said, "Hey. I'm here. But I'm not allowed to be, so I'm anonymous." At Mass I always checked all the hymnals in the pew to see if any of them had my music. Sometimes I would see it, and it made me smile. I went on marking hymnals until one day in English class, one of the girls raised her hand and said, "There's writing in my hymnal on page 283."

Another girl piped up, "There's writing in this one, too." My stomach felt like it had plunged down the hill of a roller coaster.

Sister said, "Everyone turn to page 283. Raise your hand if your hymnal has extra music written there."

Oh my. My stomach hit the bottom and started to climb the next hill. A dozen hands went up. Mine shot up, too, because I had just finished marking the book I had. *Yipes. What's going to happen now?*

Sister asked, "Who did this?"

Everyone put down their hands. Especially me.

Then Sister said, "Whoever did this has defaced church property." *I didn't think of it that way.*

I stared at my desk and tried to look innocent. My heart was approaching the top of the next hill. I was having trouble breathing—

on the inside. On the outside, I sat as still as the lake on a windless day. Sister walked up and down the aisles, stopping to stare intently at each one of the boys. "This is a serious sin."

Serious sins are mortal sins. I didn't mean to sin. Her stares made some of the boys, squirm. One looked like he was going to confess just to get her to stop staring at him. Then he lowered his eyes, and she moved on. *She thinks it's one of the boys.*

She went to the front of the class and said, "Well, if you won't own up now, I expect the student who did this to come to me in private, confess, and take their punishment." Sister Ralph was the elementary school principal.

I can't confess. Everyone would know Doctor Beare's Daughter did a crazy thing. That would be like . . . like . . . the end of the world or something. Daddy would explode. Think. What am I going to do now? I'm going to get away with it, that's what, because she has no idea who did it. I'll never tell.

Then she said, "If no one owns up to this, I'll have to punish everyone."

My heart jumped off the top of the roller coaster and nose-dived to the ground. *She's going to punish everyone for what I did.*

My stomach hurt, and my heart raced around my chest the rest of the day. When I walked home, things got worse inside me. I thought I might jump right out of my skin. I didn't want Mommy to see me because she would know something was wrong. So I went into the garage. There, stacked along one wall, was Daddy's massive stash of *The Journal of the American Medical Association (JAMA)*—a pile, nearly four-feet high, six-feet long, and four-JAMAs wide. I climbed it and sat, knees to chest, on its ledge. I was surprised how strong and steady a stack of flimsy magazines could be.

If I fess up, my parents will be embarrassed of me. I can't let that happen. That would be unBEAREable. Ha. But if I keep quiet, Sister will punish everybody. I can't let that happen, either. I don't know what to do. What would Davy Crockett do? Davy wouldn't have marked up the hymnals in the first place. Then I remembered Davy's motto: "Be sure you're right. Then go ahead." My heart and stomach sunk into my legs and made them heavy. *I know what's right. Now I have to go ahead.* I walked my heavy legs back to school.

I found Sister Ralph in her office. "Janice, what do you want?"

I looked at my shoes. My heart was back where it belonged, but my ribs were squeezing it to death. "I wrote in the hymnals."

"You?"

I nodded.

She pointed to the chair in front of her desk. I sat. It took her a minute to collect her thoughts, then she said, "Doing a thing like this can be a cry for help. Is something wrong at home?"

Her words struck me like a thunderbolt. I had somehow sent out a signal that there was something wrong. *How did I let that happen? I work so hard every day to pretend that I'm just fine.* I looked Sister right in the eyes and said, "Nothing's wrong." I told that whopper with a straight face. *I'm very good at acting. I act like I'm Doctor Beare's Daughter all the time.* "I was just doodling. I'm sorry."

Sister stared at me a few seconds, then said. "Come to school on Saturday at noon. Meet me in the small auditorium for your punishment."

I turned away before my mask slipped and left. She had been concerned for me, and it made me want to cry. *I'm going to have to keep that little voice quiet. She gets me into trouble.*

On Saturday, I told Mommy that I was going to school to work on a project with some of my classmates. Then I went to morning confession and got rid of my terrible sin. Finally, I met Sister in the small auditorium. On the stage were piled *all* the hymnals from church. They covered half the stage. There must have been five hundred of them. Sister handed me a big pink eraser. She laid four more on the stage. She said, "You're to check each hymnal and erase all of your work. I'll be back in a couple of hours to check on you."

My lungs were drinking air. My hand holding the eraser trembled at the task ahead. *Well, I deserve it. Thank the BVM that I didn't manage to write in all of them before I got caught.* It was a long afternoon. I used up all the erasers. Sister Ralph didn't tell my parents what I had done. She didn't tell the rest of the class, either. *Who knew that holy virgins can be kind sometimes?*

22
The Battle of the Water Skis

Gangly

The summer of 1957, I turned ten. Shortly after my birthday in June, I met Susie, the new girl on Harbor Point. We were instant good friends. David was feeling left out, so we told him he could join our "club," but he had to pass an initiation. We had him do silly things, like moving Mommy's wheelbarrow full of dirt and flowers back and forth ten times. He passed, and we became a tribe of three.

David and I taught Susie to climb antennas and stomp roofs. And we made up a new night game that we called spooking. We wore dark clothes and walked around Harbor Point in the dark, hiding in shadows when we saw other people, following them without their knowledge. Sometimes we dared each other to look in people's windows to see what they were doing. "I like being anonymous. Just no-name me—somebody who's there, but you don't know who it is."

I admired Susie for being athletic. She could scurry up a tree like a squirrel to the treetops, while I carefully worked my way through the low limbs. She could do cartwheels and walk on her hands. The best I could do was a somersault, my long legs getting the way of each other. Mommy sometimes compared gangly me to graceful Susie, saying, "Susie glides into a room, and then here comes Janice." To make her point, Mommy lumbered across the room like a gristly bear walking on its hind legs. *Is she trying to help? I feel like I should apologize for myself and my gangly legs.*

For my tenth birthday, Daddy gave me a pair of Cypress Gardens water skis, one of which was a slalom, with an extra boot for putting one foot behind the other. The skis were signed by Dick Pope, Jr. I remembered the time I saw him ski at Cypress Gardens in Florida. Ever since then, I had wanted to learn to water ski. Well, that day had come. Daddy outfitted the Chris with a tow rope and bought a set of steps for the boat. Susie got a set of skis, too.

Karen, one of the older girls on Harbor Point, took Susie and me out in the Chris to teach us to ski. Susie came right up out of the water on her first try. But I couldn't get the hang of it. Karen had a lot of patience with me, but I couldn't get it. *My legs are too gangly, and I'm too stupid, just too . . . everything. I'll never get the hang of skiing on two skis, let alone the slalom.*

This Is Celina

One day, Mommy finished mowing the lawn and came in to sit down. "Why can't Ralph pay someone to mow the cottage grass like he does at the house-in-town?" The cottage lawn was small. Still, Mommy didn't like to exert herself unless she had to.

"I'll do it." I liked the smell of new-cut grass.

One Sunday after church, Mommy looked at the yard. "Janice, you let the grass get too long. It needs cutting." I changed into shorts, got out the mower, and started cutting the grass. I hadn't made one pass across the side yard, when Mommy was there, waving and yelling. "What are you *doing?*"

"You told me to cut the grass."

"Not *now.* This is *Sunday.* You can't cut the grass on Sunday." She threw up her hands in disgust and went back in the house.

I put the mower away and went inside to find her. "Why can't I cut the grass on Sunday?"

"This is Celina. It isn't done. Someone might see you." *I guess the Eyes of Celina can see Harbor Point, after all.* Mommy went on, "What will people think? I can't have people thinking you don't know better."

I DON'T know better—about lots of things. Why do I always think up things to do that aren't done in Celina? Can one cut the grass on Sunday in Lima? Dayton?

Mommy finished up with, "Sometimes I think you don't have the good sense that God gave a horse." *I'm dumber than a horse. Even a horse wouldn't cut the grass in Celina on a Sunday. If I didn't have to be Doctor Beare's Daughter, I'd whinny right now.*

Mommy is Pretty Smart

One day, Daddy took me out in front of the cottage by the lake. He had covered the picnic table with newspaper and laid out a sharp knife, a scaling tool, a pair of pliers, and a shop rag. Then came a whole mess of crappies and a catfish. Daddy said, "I'm going to teach you how to clean fish because your mother doesn't know how to do it. No matter how many times I've shown her, she doesn't learn."

I eyed the pile of dead bodies. Daddy showed me how to hold the catfish in a shop rag, so I wouldn't get stung by the barbed fins. Then how to skin it with the pliers and how to filet a crappie. Having been raised in a butcher shop and being a surgeon, he made short, clean work of it. "Now you try," he said.

Crappies have sticky scales that have to be scraped off. They stuck to my hands, arms, and shirt. I used my arm to brush my hair off my forehead, and the gluey scales got in my hair. *I have this nasty mess sticking all over me just to please Daddy. I hate that I can't ever be myself because that's not who my parents want.* I minced my way through

Daddy's entire catch and made sure to get lots of scales and guts on him until he finally gave up and said, "You're just as bad as your mother at cleaning fish."

That's one useful thing I learned from Mommy. I was so disgusted by the fish mess all over me that I grabbed the bar of Ivory soap that always sat in a dish on the picnic table, (for extra dirty occasions)

Harbor Point Picnic L to R: Uncle Doc, Uncle Paul, Uncle Rock, Mother, Aunt Mildred, Susie, Susie's Mom

At the cottage L to R: Daddy, John, Uncle Doc, Uncle Rock

and jumped in the lake. I gave my clothes and me a good scrubbing. Ivory *floats.*

All summer I waged my battle of the water skis, and when Daddy finally put the Chris up for the winter, Karen said, "Next year." *That's what Mommy calls wishful thinking.*

23
The Stir in the Air

Right after we moved into the house-in-town in the fall of 1957, the Cadillac dealer came to the house to show Mommy the 1958 color chart. Daddy had an agreement with the dealer for a new Caddy every other year, and it was time to say goodbye to the '56. This year, Mommy asked me to help her pick out the color. She said, "What do you think, Janice?"

I looked at the chart. *She's had about every color Caddy there is, except . . . that one.* I pointed out the chip called "Tahitian Coral Iridescent."

The dealer said, "That's a brand-new color this year. It's striking and elegant. I can't wait to see it on a car."

Mommy said, "But it's pink."

I darted off to find Roberta.

Mommy ordered a pink Cadillac. It was the only one in town. She'd had it for less than two weeks when she realized that it was causing "talk." Overheard remarks were getting back to her through the bridge club grapevine. "Did you see Mrs. Beare's new Cadillac? La de da." Or "Mrs. Beare must be planning a big party—the pink Cadillac was parked in front of the liquor store yesterday."

Mommy liked being famous for her good taste, but she hated being infamous for driving a pink Cadillac. She slouched in embarrassment when she drove it. "Why I ever let you pick the color of my car, I'll never know," Mommy said.

She asked me for my opinion, and I gave it to her, but it wasn't the opinion she wanted. I have to guess all the time what they want to hear and give it to them. I usually guess wrong.

I Like Characters

One day when I was counting cars for Mommy, I saw a girl about my age sitting on the office-porch step. Joyce Becker was waiting for her mother. She asked me if I liked to skate. I said *yes*. When Mrs. Becker came out of the office, Joyce said, "This is Janice."

Her mother said, "I know who she is." *Of course she does.*

Joyce asked, "Can we pick Janice up on Saturday when you drive me to the rink? She likes to skate, too."

Mrs. Becker said, "Janice, would you like to come along?"

Would I ever. "I'll have to ask Mommy if it's all right." *She'll never allow it. I'm sure she knows OF these people, but she probably doesn't KNOW them.*

Mrs. Becker said, "I'll just pop back in the office and ask Doc about it."

I hope he says yes. But if he does, then what will happen when Mommy finds out? Will she be mad because I want to spend time with someone else?

When Joyce's mother came back, she said, "It's okay with Doc."

Mommy said nothing when Joyce and I went to the rink every Saturday. Mommy even did half the driving. I could tell she thought Joyce wasn't quite good enough for me, but Daddy was the boss, and he liked Joyce's family just fine.

Joyce taught me to skate backward, hop on my toe stops, snap the whip, and shoot the duck. It took me a long time to get the hang of it with my awkward legs, and I never could skate as well as Joyce. But we became rink regulars.

Sometimes, I got to go to Joyce's house. Many years before, Mr. Becker had lost one of his legs when he was riding his motorcycle and was hit by a train, so he wore a wooden leg. He came home from work, took off his pants, then his leg, and sat in his chair. *What would Daddy think if he knew that Mr. Becker sat around in his underwear? I'm not telling. Daddy might not let me come to Joyce's house any more, and I like it here, a lot.*

The leg wore a sock and a work boot. The calf had lots of little holes, like they'd been drilled by a woodpecker. I told Daddy about seeing Mr. Becker's leg with all the little holes. Daddy told me that Mr. Becker —a mechanic—was a "character," and he liked to play jokes on strangers.

One day, two women were in the garage, waiting to get their car. Mr. Becker was sitting at a workbench working on a part. He stuck his leg out from the side of the bench, picked up an ice pick, and threw it into the bench where it stuck with a thwack. He did this— thwack. Thwack. Thwack. Until he had the ladies' attention. Then he "accidentally" threw the ice pick into his leg. He screamed. He grabbed his leg. He rolled out of his chair—onto the floor. One of the women fainted. In the end, Mr. Becker had filled his leg so full of holes, he had to get a new one. *I like people who are "characters," especially ones with a big sense of humor. They're just being themselves. I wish I could be myself. I wonder who that is?*

Mr. Becker didn't see my family as different from his. He said, "Doc Beare puts his pants on one leg at a time, like everybody else." *And that's how Mr. Becker takes his off, only in the living room.*

Joyce didn't think of me as different, either. She didn't envy all my stuff. *I think that's the big reason we get along. Maybe I'm not so different from the Beckers. Maybe I'm more like them than like Mommy and Daddy. If my first Mommy had kept me, I wouldn't have to pretend all the time to be someone else.*

Caught in the Middle

As I walked home from school one snowy, November Thursday, the dread of going out to dinner hung on me like a soggy wool coat. *Will it be Dayton, Lima, West Carrollton, or West Milton? Maybe Indiana —Fort Wayne, Berne, or Decatur? God bless America. What if it's Marshall, Michigan?* Held captive in the back seat, sucking up second-hand Chesterfields and Lucky Strikes gave me the heebie-jeebies.

I stepped inside the house-in-town. *Daddy's not home. I'd feel it in the air if he was.* The air moved different around Daddy than it did around everyone else. It had a stir to it. And the stir went through the whole house when he was in it. *It's easier to breathe without air-stir.*

Mommy was sitting in the kitchen. "Your father is at the hospital on an emergency. He'll be back any minute, and we'll go to dinner."

I ran downstairs and found Roberta feeding sheets into the mangle to iron them. I asked if I could go home with her. "If it's all right with Doc and your mommy," she said.

I visited with Roberta until I felt the air stir, and knew Daddy had come home. I found him and asked him. He thought it would be okay.

But the next morning, Mommy said, "Don't you ever again tell your father that you don't want to go out to dinner."

"Why not?"

"Last night he was mean all the way there and back because you didn't want to come. Don't let that happen again." *Daddy should like Mommy more than he likes me. They would get along better.*

24
Morning, Noon, and Night

I got my medical education at the house-in-town—morning, noon, and night. Every morning while I waited for Mommy to pack my toast for school, I saw the pad of paper on the kitchen table of Daddy's sketches of lungs, livers, bowels, and bladders.

At noon, I came home for lunch because IC didn't have a cafeteria. Daddy ate his sandwich while telling Mommy about his morning surgery. "I opened Mrs. So-and-So to take out her gallbladder and saw that her liver was full of cancer. Nothing I could do but sew her back up—is there another bottle of catsup? This one's empty."

At night, after the office closed for the day, Uncle Doc sometimes came into the kitchen and fixed himself a drink before going home. Then he stood at the counter and conferred with Daddy about the patients while we ate. This one had a stroke. That one had cancer. This one had a heart attack. That one had a deep vein thrombosis. This one had meningitis . . . and on and on.

After hearing about all kinds of terrible of diseases, I realized I had a lot of their symptoms. If I had a bad headache, it must be a brain

Dr. Ralph (R) and Dr. Paul (L)

tumor. A pain in my leg was probably a blood clot that would travel to my brain and cause a stroke. Short of breath after running—lung cancer. That dark freckle—melanoma. My toe hurt—gout. *Thank goodness gout isn't cancer. Or is it?*

The only disease I felt safe from was "old-age pension" because I was young. If cancer, diabetes, a heart attack, or a stroke didn't get you, and you lived to be old, then old-age pension would finish you off. I knew this because when a very old patient died, I heard Uncle Doc ask Daddy, "Did he have old-age pension?" The answer was, "Yes."

Sometimes my stomach hurt so bad that it just *had* to be an ulcer. *What if it's bleeding?* The worry was too much to bear, so I told Daddy I had an ulcer. I wanted him to poke my stomach and tell me that I didn't have an ulcer—that my stomach was just upset and I'd be okay. Instead he said, "If you want to know if you have an ulcer, go read about them in the medical dictionary and figure it out."

He thinks I'm imagining it. I'm not. The pain is real. "Can't you just tell me if I have one?"

"Hell, no. You can read, can't you? Go look it up." Then he marched me into the office, to the small, corner room with a desk and a shelf of medical books. He sat me in the chair, put the medical dictionary in front of me, and said, "Look it up." Then he left me alone.

I opened the book and flipped through it—1,344 razor-thin pages of diseases in fine print. I felt carsick. When I found the word *ulcer,* the definition included the words *cutaneous, mucous,* and *necrosis. I'm only ten years old, but Sister and the librarian say I read as well as any adult. I bet most adults don't know these words. Son-of-a-God-blessed America and damn it to Mexico and all the way back to Canada—he's going to quiz me on it.*

Daddy liked to give me an article from *National Geographic* or an entry in the *World Book Encyclopedia* to read and then ask me questions.

If I didn't know the answers, I got the "ignorant" lecture. If I knew the answers, I got a "Huh." Never a "Good job." I was beginning to feel hot all over, like a fever was spreading through me. *This is one more of his assignments.*

So I sat there, possibly bleeding from my ulcer, and looked up *cutaneous, mucous,* and *necrosis.* Each of those words had even more mystery words in their definitions and then those words. . . . It took almost two hours to get to the end of the word chain, and then work backward to *ulcer.* Once I got there, the entry went on to describe the different *kinds* of ulcers: *adherent, amputating, anamite* . . . and on through the rest of the alphabet for two-and-a-half pages. By the time I finished reading about ulcers, my eyes hurt, and I was exhausted. *And I still don't know if I have one. Daddy could tell me, but he won't. He thinks I'm imagining the pains in my stomach. I'm not, but since he won't believe me, I just have to leave my fate up to the wind and hope I survive.*

Because of the time I spent reading that dictionary, I learned a lot of medical words. If I hurt my ankle and it swelled, I told Daddy, "I have some edema." Or "Whoops. My patella slipped when I twisted my leg."

There was more wrong with me than my ulcer. One day I was in the kitchen hunting for where Mommy hid the cookies, when I felt a knife twist in my heart. It took the wind out of me. I sank onto the floor and called out, "Daddy, help!"

He came into the kitchen and said, "What are you doing on the floor? Get up."

I was lying still, trying not to breathe, because every breath made the knife dig deeper. "I'm having a heart attack! It gets worse every time I try to breathe."

Daddy bent down, took my pulse, and said, "You're not having a heart attack. You're making up that idea in your head."

This is NOT my overactive imagination. "It hurts something fierce."

"Don't think about it, and it will go away." With that, he stepped over me and went into the office, leaving me alone on the floor, waiting to die.

Why doesn't Daddy believe me? The pain is real. He thinks I'm crazy. He always believes his patients and some of them really are crazy. He would never leave one of them to die on the floor—not even the crazy ones.

The pain went away in a couple of minutes. It was just luck that I lived. After that, I had more heart attacks. When one of them hit me, I knew that no one was going to help me. I was gonna live or die—it was up to fate. After I lived through several "heart attacks," I decided they must be something else. And Daddy surly knew that. *But what are they, then?* I tried using the medical dictionary to find out, but didn't know what words to look up. *Daddy knows, but he says talking about something makes you think about it even more. NOT talking about it sure makes it worse for me.*

25
Leaning Toward Shiverdecker's

I loved Christmas because, for several days, our house became a lively place. The Celina florist decorated the living room mantle for the December parties. Roberta bustled about, cutting evergreens from the yard to make wreaths for the back door and the office porch. Together, we put Christmas lights in the shrubs. When we were done, Roberta and I lay in the snow and made angels. Then she got a big bowl that we filled with snow, took inside, and made into snow ice cream. *Roberta would be a great mother. Sometimes I wish she was mine.*

The next day Grandpa came, and we took the puddle-jumper (his old Ford) to get the tree. When we pulled into the parking lot of the P & B, he said, "This year, we're going to find the perfect tree." *He says that every year.*

We searched through all the trees on the lot—some too small, others too skinny, too short, or too bushy. Others had bare spots, broken branches, or a dogleg. When we found the best one of the lot, Grandpa said, "Not perfect, but good enough. We'll find that perfect one next year." *I hope we never do. It's such fun looking for it with Grandpa.*

When we finally got the tree up, Grandpa said, "It's leaning toward Shiverdecker's again." *That's his funny way of saying something is crooked.*

On Christmas Eve we went to Uncle Doc's, and I got to be with my cousins. I wished I was more like them. They had friends at school. *Uncle Doc wants his kids to be just like everybody else. But Daddy and Mommy need a princess.*

Uncle Doc always decorated their tree himself. This year, he flocked it to make it look like it was covered in lavender snow. It was his prettiest one yet. I said, "Do you think it's leaning toward Shiverdeckers?"

Uncle Doc said, "How do you know the Shiverdeckers? They used to be our neighbors back in Versailles."

We all had a good laugh. *Too funny, Grandpa.*

Aunt Ginny served eggnog, and Uncle Doc played Christmas songs on the organ. I played some carols on Uncle Doc's piano with my cousins. After a big ham dinner, Anne and I rushed to clear the table. We wanted to get the dishes over with, so my family would go home because both our families opened our presents on Christmas Eve. We had a great time in the kitchen washing the dishes and blowing suds on each other. *I love my cousins and the little bit of fun we have together. It would be a lot of fun if I could be with them more often.*

In the car going home, Daddy said. "When I hung up our coats at Doctor Paul's, I saw Janice's old high chair at the back of the closet. Doctor Paul borrowed it for his girls, but he never gave it back."

Why would we want it back? I adored Uncle Doc—he was always good to me, but Daddy had some resentment against him. Mommy said it was because Daddy had their mother all to himself until Uncle Doc came along, nine years later. *And that's why our families can't be together more often?*

Daddy age 10, holding baby brother Paul

A UFO

At home, Daddy tuned the Scott to a station that played Christmas music so we could listen while we opened our presents. I had just unwrapped a book from David when the radio said: "We interrupt this broadcast to report that an unidentified flying object has been picked up on radar over the North Pole. It's heading for the United States."

It's a Russian missile. A nuclear bomb!

Anxiety and anger danced the bunny hop in my chest. Everyone knew the Russians were trying to spread Communism. They hated our democracy, and they had the bomb. The TV news was always talking about the threat of nuclear war with Russia. *It's begun. We're all going to die!* The ruckus in my chest was causing arrhythmias. *There are lots of different kinds of arrhythmias, according to the medical dictionary. Some are benign and some are deadly. I wonder which kind these are?*

"I wonder what that unidentified flying object is?" Daddy said.

"It's a Russian nuke," I said.

Daddy said, "Be quiet, Janice, and listen to the radio."

Grandpa said, "Tut, tut, tut, Kiddo. Who flies around the world on Christmas Eve?"

The broadcast continued, "We have more information on that UFO heading our way. It appears to be a sleigh pulled by reindeer."

What? Why would they tell people there was an unidentified flying object coming at us? That's a mean joke.

"Janice, you had better go to bed," Mommy said. "Santa will be here soon." I took my arrhythmias to bed. It was a long time before they finally tired themselves out and let me fall asleep.

It Didn't Blow

That winter when it was time to go to Florida, Daddy had Roberta and Urb drive the T-Bird to Daytona so he could run it in the time trials of the Grand National to see how fast it would go. Mommy, Daddy, Grandpa, and I rode in the Tahitian Coral Iridescent Caddy. It was a great time having Roberta and Urb there. They played shuffleboard against me and Grandpa.

It was thrilling to watch Daddy roar down the measured mile on the beach. He hit 120 mph, and when it was over, he said, "I still had some left, but I learned that 120 was as fast as I want to go." *I'm very proud of Daddy. And the car didn't blow up.*

My wonderful suffleboard-playing Roberta (L) and Mother (R) in Daytona

'Doc' Beare Hits 120 At Daytona

DAYTONA BEACH, Dr. Ralph Beare, Celina, became a member of the NASCAR-sanctioned Century Club February 5 when he drove a 57 Ford T'Bird over the famous Daytona Beach measured mile course at 119.681 miles per hour. Century Club trials are not official records as they are limited to one-way runs only.

The Century Club trials are a feature of the Eighth Annual NASCAR International Safety and Performance Trials that will be climaxed with three days of racing; 125-mile Sportsman and Modified division, Friday, February 15, 160-mile Late Model Convertible division Saturday, February 16 and 160-mile Grand National Division Championship Sunday, February 17.

February 1958 *The Daily Standard* Reprinted with

26
HAL…LE…LU…JAH!

Check the Food

I was in the kitchen with Mommy while she was cooking dinner. Office hours were running late, and it was almost seven when she put the steak on to broil. A minute later, we heard a loud pop from inside the oven. Mommy pulled the door open. The light bulb had burst and spewed tiny shards of glass all over the steak. Mommy turned off the oven, took the steak out, and said, "Ralph will be here any minute." She took the steak over to the sink and was rinsing it off under the faucet. "I'll have to finish cooking this in a skillet."

"We can't eat that. There's glass in the meat," I said.

"I rinsed it off." She glared at me and said, "Don't mention it to your father. Just eat your dinner, and don't think about it."

How does she know she got it all? Maybe some of the sharp pieces are stuck down in the meat. My heart tripped over itself, and I rocked on my feet. *How can I not think about it?* I imagined taking a bite of the steak and chewing. I could almost feel a sharp piece of glass cut my tongue and embed itself in my gum. I could feel sharp shards scratch my throat on their way down. And my stomach—it would be cut to ribbons. Terror tore through me and filled up my every corner. *I'm going to have to eat that.* Then I realized an awful truth: *I can't make myself do it. I'm about to cause the biggest fight the house-in-town has ever seen.*

Just then, Daddy came in from the office and said to Mommy, "Why are you holding the steak under the faucet?" *Is she going to tell the truth? Oh, please. Tell the truth.*

"And why is the oven door hanging open?" Now Daddy was looking inside the oven. *Surely, he can see the broken bulb.*

She said, "The light bulb broke while I was broiling the steak."

Daddy walked over to the sink, took the steak, and shoved it down the disposal. Then he said to Mommy, "Get your purse. We're going out." *Mommy always tries to avoid trouble. I hope she doesn't find out that I'm different from her.* From then on, if I wasn't in the kitchen when Mommy was cooking, I checked my food carefully before eating it.

In the Middle Again

Our family dentist, Doctor Apfelbaum, was elderly and semi-retired. His stuffy office was up a long flight of narrow stairs above a store, and his equipment was probably the same stuff he'd started out with forty years before. He didn't believe in filling a tooth until the cavity was large, making it "worth filling."

I was terrified of him and his drill. Whenever he had a patient in his chair, he loudly played 78 LP records by the Mormon Tabernacle Choir. "They're wonderful, are they not?" he always said. "Just listen to that harmony."

This time, he said my cavity was big enough to be worth filling, and he brought out a syringe to numb my tooth. "Open wide," he said, with a kind smile. I couldn't sit still in the chair, let alone open wide. My body had a mind of its own, and it hopped right out of the chair.

"Janice," Mommy said.

I sat back down. My body hopped right back up. I saw the look on Mommy's face and threw myself back into the chair. This time she pinned my arms to the chair. Doctor Apfelbaum's syringe was headed for my mouth. I tried to open it for him, but my upper and lower teeth were glued together.

Mommy said, "Janice. You have to get your tooth filled. It's important."

I heard her, but my body wouldn't obey. Finally, Doctor Apfelbaum said, "I'm going to have to put her to sleep." He brought out a white mask and tried to put it over my face. Mommy still had my arms pinned, but my legs kicked wildly. A burly nurse appeared and sat on my legs. As the mask came near, I desperately jerked my head side-to-side.

Mommy said, "Janice, your eyes are as big as tractor tires. Hold your head still."

I couldn't do it, so the nurse gripped my head. *They've got me.* My arms—cuffed to the chair by steel fingers. My legs—flattened by a butt heavier than a boulder. My head—clamped in a vise of big iron mitts. My heart was pounding in my ears like a jackhammer busting up a sidewalk. I saw the mask come down. *NO. PLEASE NO. . . . Hmm. . . .* Mommy's nose was circling her face as if it were a telephone dial, dialing numbers; three . . . chuk, chuk, chuk, five . . . chuk, chuk, chuk, chuk, chuk, while the Mormon Tabernacle Choir sang, "Hallelujah. HALLE-LUJAH. HAL . . . LE . . . LU . . . JAH!" *Just, please. Let me wake up from this nightmare.*

On the ride home, I couldn't wait to tell Daddy about how they held me down and put me out, when my thoughts were interrupted by Mommy saying, "Don't tell Daddy that Doctor Apfelbaum gave you general anesthesia just to fill a tooth. Your father would run him out of town."

He should be run out of town. I'm telling.

"Why, people have died from general anesthesia."

Wait. What? How can Mommy be so careless with MY life? I'm telling for sure.

"Ralph would be furious with me."

Well, Goddamn-bless-it-to-hell-America. I can't tell because I have to protect her from Daddy. "Very well, MOTHER."

Every time after that, when I had to have a tooth filled, I told myself: *I don't want to die. And it's all up to me to make sure I don't.* I somehow forced myself to hold my mouth open to get the shot. Mother was proud of the brave way I behaved. *I'm sorta proud, too, because now I know I can do a hard thing to protect myself if I have to.*

27
Five Minutes Closer

In the school parking lot, I stood outside a classmate's mother's car and peered into the back seat. Three boys sat staring back at me. Sister moved past me, spread a white hanky on the middle boy's lap, and told me to climb in. The middle boy blanched and whisked the hanky onto the next boy's lap, who then looked like his friend had dropped a tarantula on him.

"Get in, Janice." Sister's voice was extra stern.

Me? Sit on Cooper? Son-of-a . . . God bless America.

It was spring 1958, and my fifth-grade class was going on a retreat to the Shrine at Maria Stein, some fifteen miles south of Celina, the home of more than a thousand Catholic relics.

Sister prodded me with her bony pointer finger. *I would rather eat fish than sit on Cooper.* I got in the car. I arranged myself on the hanky on Cooper. *I'm a fifth-grade statue. I feel nothing.*

The girls in the front seat chatted away. But in the back—not a word. Cooper and I had fused, our eyes locked in glary stares. I'm not sure we breathed all the way to Maria Stein. The other two boys had dancing eyes and twisted smiles, due to zipped lips.

At Maria Stein, we toured the relics chapel. Sister pointed out a gold reliquary and said, "This is one of our most precious relics. Saint Peregrine was born in 1260. He was a priest who had a cancerous growth on his foot, which needed to be amputated. He dreamed that

Jesus came and touched his foot. When he woke, it was healed. Saint Peregrine lived to be eighty. At his funeral, three people were cured of illness. There have been thousands of cures since. Saint Peregrine is the patron saint of cancer."

Imagine that. Saint Peregrine's relic can cure cancer. Why do so many of Daddy's patients die from cancer if they can just come here and get a miracle? I guess God decides who He will and won't save. That doesn't seem fair, somehow.

Then a priest gave us a talk. He told us that the fire in hell is real, and it is eternal. He said in a grim voice, "Hell BURNS without destroying —the AGONY NEVER ENDS." *Isn't dying bad enough? Does God then have to burn you up for all eternity, too? Just because you did something to make Him mad? I HAVE to love God, but I don't like Him much. He's a mean one.*

Father stopped talking abruptly. He leaned over the lectern and cast his gaze around until he held every one of us in anticipation. Then he pointed to his watch, and said in a deep, dramatic voice, "I've been talking to you for five minutes. You're now FIVE MINUTES closer to the GRAVE." He paused to let his words sink in. They sank all right. They slid down over my soul and coated it with fear. My hands were shaking.

Father went on, "You are all going to die someday. You never know when it might happen. Don't let it happen to YOU when YOU are in the state of SIN."

I hope I get struck dead by God right when I'm walking out of confession. It's the only way I'm gonna get to heaven. Why does it have to be so hard to please God? Why can't I please my parents, either? What's wrong with me?

I Can Do It

The following summer I turned eleven at the cottage. Karen took me out in the Chris to tackle my water skis again. At first, it was just like last summer, with me thrashing around, desperately fighting to get up on the skis. *I'm never going to get this. I'm just too uncoordinated.* I was done with trying, but Karen gunned the boat, and then—the boat pulled me up. *I'm skiing! Gangly old me can do it!* My uncoordinated body had finally figured out what not to do, and how to let the boat pull me up. Once I got the hang of skiing on two skis, I managed to kick loose one ski, put my free foot in the back binding of the slalom, and ski on one ski. *Skiing on one ski is easier than skiing on two skis. And more fun, too.*

The rushing air chilled my wet skin and tore tears from my eyes while I skimmed over the water. *I'm in charge . . . of me, the ski, the rope, and even the water under me. This is what freedom feels like.* I could zigzag side-to-side or make big, sharp turns. I could make my slalom cut across the water and throw a tall, beautiful line of spray behind me. I was proud of my accomplishment. *If I can learn to ski, maybe I can learn to do other things, too.*

While I was having a wonderful summer, Mother was struggling with driving her pink Cadillac. At lunch one day she told Daddy, "Helen said she was at the boathouse and heard someone say, 'There goes Mrs. Beare's pink Cadillac to town again. I just saw it at the P & B a little while ago. She must have forgotten her groceries.'"

Daddy gave a little snort.

Mother was just getting warm. "Carl told me that every time we leave the car at the boathouse to take the Chris out on the lake, some-one sees it and says 'Mrs. Beare must have been wanting a boat ride.'"

"Let 'em talk," Daddy said.

Yes, let 'em talk. Now she knows what it feels like.

28
Requiem

At a time when, according to one of Mother's favorite songs, grown women were supposed to be "five-foot-two with eyes of blue,"[8] this eleven-year-old, brown-eyed, redheaded sixth-grader had already reached five-foot-six. "She's tall, all right," Daddy said, "like me. I'm predicting five-foot-eight." *I already stick up like a weed in a garden of moss. Now I'm growing like one, too.*

It was late summer of 1958. When Mother took me to Goldstein's to pick out my new school clothes, Lil said to me, "You're all leg." She told Mother I'd outgrown her store. I'd have to see what Harriet (another member of the Goldstein family) had next door in the women's department.

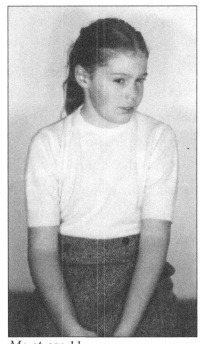

Me at age 11

When we came out of Goldstein's, two teenage boys were standing by the Caddy. One of them had his foot on the front bumper. He said, "Yessiree, Bob. When I grow up, I'm gonna get me a pink Cadillac, just like Mrs. Beare's."

That night at dinner, Mrs. Beare said, "Ralph. I know I'm not due for a new car until next year, but I can't take another year of this."

A few days later the Tahitian Coral Iridescent Cadillac had been replaced with a new one in Peacock Green. The pink one was never seen in Celina again. *I wish I could fix my problem with the kids at school that easily.*

~~~~

When school started, I changed my mind about being tall. I liked looking down on my classmates. I liked that the nuns had to look up to me. It had been quite a while since one of them had reached up to pat my head. Of course, my height gave the boys new ammunition. One of them decided my freckles weren't splattered cow dung, but the markings of a giraffe. For sure, a step up.

One April morning, when my sixth-grade class marched to Mass, a hearse was parked in front of the church. Whenever an old parishioner who had little family left to mourn him or her died, our school Mass served as their funeral Mass. Every child at IC school knew how to sing the funeral Mass. In Latin. By heart. After we took our seats, Father, wearing black vestments, stood below the altar to receive the casket as it was brought up the main aisle. The organ struck up, and we sang "Requiem Aeternum."

It was peaceful. It made me feel connected to all those ancient holy martyrs. I liked the feeling of being connected to others, living or dead. When I walked back to my pew after Communion, I noticed that among the handful of elderly mourners was my friend, Nora Fortman. A jagged rock slid down my throat and took a swipe at my heart on its way to my stomach. *I'm singing Joe's funeral Mass.* I hadn't seen Nora and Joe for a while and had no idea he had died. My rocky throat didn't want to sing, but I did the best I could for poor Joe.

A month later I attended another funeral, this time with my parents, and the church overflowed with mourners. Daddy's attorney and our good friend, Earl Dull, had died of cancer. He was forty-nine. *That's the end of the Short and Dull Law Firm. People die all the time, and everybody just goes on about their business like nothing's happened. Well, everybody except Mary Dull and her children.*

I asked Daddy what was going to happen to them. He said, "They just have to soldier on."

I guess when someone who's important to me dies and I feel sad, I'm supposed to hide it and just march on ahead like a good little soldier.

What About Poor Tommy?

When sixth grade was over, and I brought home my report card and gave it to Mother, she opened it, read it, opened her arms to me and said, "You're as tall as me now. Are you too big for this?"

No, Never. I sat on her lap, careful not to put my weight on her, and we had a big hug. *Right now she's more like "Mom" than "Mother." She tries her best to love me like her own. But she doesn't always see me when I need her.*

~~~~~

One day after school I picked up the upstairs phone to call Joyce about plans for going to the roller rink and overheard Mother and Aunt Helen talking. I was about to hang up when I heard Aunt Helen say, "Lou, did you hear about Tommy Smith?" Tommy was the only other kid in town that I had ever heard of who was adopted. He was sixteen —four years older than me—and went to public school.

When Aunt Helen said that Tommy had run away, Mother said, "Those poor parents! That adoption didn't work out very well for them."

What about poor Tommy?

Aunt Helen said, "Yes, you never know what you are going to get when you adopt. You and Doc were lucky."

"Yes," Mother said. "Janice would never disgrace us like that!"

I never would—that would be ungrateful times a million. Tommy's life must be terrible for him to run away. Either that or he's terribly brave.

29
WHOA!

Instead of a long road trip that summer of 1959, Daddy drove us to Gatlinburg, Tennessee. We checked into a motel, where he said we would be staying for at least a week. *Wow. A whole vacation in one place.*

Gatlinburg was a wide spot in the road, lined with restaurants, motels, and shops. The Smoky Mountain National Park lay just south of town. Daddy said we would be taking many long drives in the mountains to see the scenery. *I'll get The Pot.*

Just down the road from our motel was a riding stable, and I begged Daddy to let me ride.

"I don't know why anybody would want to ride a goddamn horse," he said.

He thinks a horse is a big dog. "Please, Daddy. It's important."

I was surprised when he took me to the stables where we met the owner, Mr. McCarter. Daddy let me go out with a group just leaving for an hour's trail ride. He stayed at the stable and got acquainted with Mr. McCarter.

To be up on a real horse was exhilarating. The minute I got back from the ride, I begged Daddy to let me go again, so he made arrangements for me to ride with another group in the afternoon.

The next day, Daddy bought me a sack lunch and dropped me off at the stables for the whole day. He, Mother, and Grandpa went to North Carolina to the Cherokee Reservation. When Daddy picked me up that afternoon, there were several cartons of Picayune Extra Mild cigarettes in the car. "I never heard of this brand," he said, "but they were so cheap."

The next day he dropped me off at the stables again. *Daddy comes through for me sometimes in a big way.*

My favorite horse was Ginger, a buckskin Tennessee walking horse. A trail ride at the stables was expensive. Since I was riding all day, every day, Mr. McCarter told Daddy, "It would be cheaper just to buy your daughter that horse and give it back to me when you go home."

Mr. McCarter (L) and me on Ginger—my very own horse for a week

So for one week, I had my own horse. *I never thought Daddy would do something like this for me. Especially since he doesn't like horses.*

One day when Daddy came to pick me up at the stables, he had his camera. Mr. McCarter said, "Get up on Ginger, Doc, and I'll take your picture."

Daddy looked surprised—like he had just unwrapped a present and found a dead muskrat inside. He cringed. "No thanks," he said, shaking his head.

"Ginger is a gentle horse," Mr. McCarter said, in an encouraging tone.

"Oh, please, Daddy. I'd love a picture of you on Ginger."

Mr. McCarter was all nods and smiles. "I'll hold Ginger for you. Janice can take the picture."

"Please, Daddy."

He looked unhappy, but Mr. McCarter led Ginger over to a crate, and said, "Just step up on the crate, Doc." Daddy looked at Ginger, then the crate. He backed up a step, then he stuck his neck out, stepped up on the crate, and grabbed the saddle horn. Ginger sideways-glanced at Daddy, rolled his eyes, and reared, almost knocking Mr. McCarter over. I swallowed hard and felt my eyebrows raise.

"Stand," Mr. McCarter yelled.

Ginger sidestepped away from Daddy. Daddy sidestepped away from Ginger. "I'll leave Ginger to Janice," he said.

Mr. McCarter scratched his head. "I've had this horse for ten years and put babies up on him. Never had him rear once." *Ginger must have felt the air stirring around Daddy.*

Wild Ride

One day I rode to Cherokee Orchard, an abandoned apple orchard high on the mountain. Our party fanned out to enjoy the views.

I stopped Ginger under an apple tree, stood in the stirrups, and reached up to pick an apple. I disturbed a nest of wasps. They were everywhere. Panic ran through me like a rampaging wall of water in a flash flood. The wasps attacked Ginger, who bucked and threw me. I landed on my back in the dirt. The flash flood smacked my heart and carried it up into my throat. With Ginger gone, the wasps set on me. Drowning in terror, I found my feet and charged wildly through the trees, while the wasps kept up their vicious attack. When they finally had their fill of me, I stumbled my way back to the trail, where the guide found me.

When he saw how badly I'd been stung, he put me up in front of him on Mix, a horse so spirited that only the guides could ride him. At the weight of a second person in the saddle, Mix pranced sideways and threw up his head, but he let me stay. The guide told the rest of our group that he would send someone back for them.

With one arm around my waist and his other hand on the reins, the guide kicked Mix into a canter. Mix sprang forward in a series of mighty leaps, and my heart leapt with him. Then he tore through the trees on the narrow, mountain trail. I clutched the saddle horn with both hands, leaning to and fro with the guide as we ducked and dodged overhanging branches. My heart hurt from being jerked from side to side while Mix navigated the twists and turns of the rutted and rooted trail. On my forehead, back, chest, hands, and arms were volcanos spewing fire—each one, a stab wound laced with painful poison. *I'm glad the wasps didn't drill through my pants.*

When we finally reached the road near the stables, Mix flattened out into a gallop. Galoomp, galoomp went my heart. The rushing air stabbed each of my stings with needlelike precision. Nearing the stables, I could see Daddy standing in the road with Mr. McCarter, who had called him when Ginger came back to the stables without me.

We flashed past them, into the stable yard, where Mix skidded to a WHOA. My heart banged back where it belonged, but it still hurt. The guide hopped down and lifted me off poor Mix, who was blowing hard and lathered all over. When the guide let go of me, I had trouble finding my feet, and I collapsed in the dirt. My volcanos were spewing fiery tentacles. They ripped along my nerves, carrying their inferno throughout my entire body. *I'm burning up from the inside out.*

Daddy knelt beside me, trusty shoebox in hand. He gave me a Benadryl and an aspirin to swallow, then he got down on one knee and painted my stings with an analgesic lotion. Finally, he pulled me to my feet and told me to get in the car. I was still wobbly, but I had to find Ginger. He had been unsaddled and turned into his stall. He had only a couple of stings and seemed okay.

"Janice! Where the hell did you go? Come back here."

In a minute. I have to do something first. I had to find Mix. He was being hot-walked to cool him down. I wobbled up to him, gave him a kiss on the nose, and thanked him for so bravely bringing me in.

Daddy snagged me, carried me to the car, and dumped me in the front seat. Back at the motel, I counted my stings. Twenty-three, each one a white welt with a hole in the middle, surrounded by an infuriated field of mottled red. Daddy brought me ice to cool them down. He said I was lucky not to have had a bad allergic reaction. In spite of the analgesic cream, the aspirin, and the ice, my stings screamed throughout the night. *The pain was almost worth it to get that wild ride on Mix. Horses are amazing. I'm going to ride like that again, someday.*

The next morning, at breakfast, I pocketed several cubes of sugar for Mix and Ginger. Daddy made me stay at the motel all morning, but finally got tired of hearing me beg to go riding and dropped me at the stables that afternoon.

Wife Doesn't Like 'Em

When vacation was over, on the way home, Daddy broke out the Picayune Extra Milds he'd bought at the reservation. He, Mother, and Grandpa lit up. The smog from those fags made the bouquet of aromas from Chesterfields, Old Golds, and Lucky Strikes smell like spring hyacinths. Mother choked, coughed a few times, and said, "These Picayunes are anything but mild."

Grandpa said, "They must have cut the tobacco with horseradish and cayenne pepper."

Daddy said, "Well, you get what you pay for, but we had better smoke them because I bought several cartons." *That means I'll be smoking them, too.*

A little farther down the road, they all had another one. In the middle of his second Picayune, Daddy said, "I have to say these are terrible." *They sure are.*

That night at the motel, Daddy put all the cartons of Picayune Extra Light in the trash can outside our door. *Good riddance.*

"Here now." It was the owner of the motel. "Why are you throwing out brand-new cigarettes?"

"Wife doesn't like 'em," Daddy said.

"I'll take them," the man said.

The next morning, when Daddy and I went into the office to pay our bill, the Picayunes were sitting on a table with a sign that said, "Free Cigarettes."

Daddy asked, "Why are you giving them away?"

"Wife doesn't like 'em."

As we drove off, Grandpa said, "Just think of all the people who are going to have a go at those Picayunes." *And they aren't going to be me.*

30
Get the Damn Show on the Road

Every Sad Melody

When I went back to school in the fall of 1959, my seventh-grade teacher was not another holy virgin; *he* was a young man. Mr. Kohnen was human, like us, and we were his first-ever class. He took some getting used to. He was patient. He told jokes during class. He didn't carry a ruler. We didn't fear him, yet even the boys behaved. *It's refreshing. That's what it is.*

~~~

In early December, Mother had a small dinner party. Uncle Rock and Aunt Helen, Uncle Charlie and Aunt Mildred, Uncle Paul and Aunt LaVaun, and Mr. and Mrs. Pogue. Mother put on a big feed in the dining room, and Roberta served. Uncle Charlie had eaten little when he said, "Excuse me," and went to lie down in the back room.

Aunt Mildred said, "Charlie hasn't been feeling well, and he doesn't eat much."

"How long has this been going on?" Daddy asked.

"Some time, now." Aunt Mildred looked worried. Then someone changed the subject, and the conversation went on.

After dinner, the guests moved to the living room for coffee, Roberta and I got busy in the kitchen, and Daddy went into the back room to see Uncle Charlie.

Late that night, I woke up in bed and heard distant murmurs. Sometimes when my parents went to bed, they talked softly about me behind their closed bedroom door. I called these conversations, their "what-are-we-going-to-do-about-Janice" talks. They didn't know that their soft-spoken words leaked under their door, drifted down the main hall, swept round the corner, and floated on along the back hall into my room, where they dissolved into mysterious whisps.

Whenever I heard these midnight whisps, I tiptoed to my parent's door and sat against it to listen. Some call it snooping. It was self-defense. If I heard they were disappointed in me for one reason or another, I could somehow figure out what they really expected, and I could give them that.

Their talks were not only about me. I also got big earfuls of office secrets and random other stuff. That particular night, I listened at the door because I was worried about Uncle Charlie.

Daddy: "I think Charlie is *really sick*."

Ice water gushed through me. *Sick* wasn't too bad. A person was *sick* with the flu, or strep throat, or chicken pox, or a bad bout of diarrhea. But a *REALLY sick* person wasn't going to get well. Please, God. *Don't let Uncle Charlie be really sick.*

A week later, when I came downstairs in the morning, Daddy was there, in the kitchen, instead of at the hospital. "Where's Mother?" I asked.

"I left her with Aunt Mildred." Daddy sat and pointed to my chair. I sat. He told me that Uncle Charlie had been sick in the night. My arms were tingling. Daddy spoke in the kind, gentle voice that he used to tell bad news to his patients. He went on to say that he'd sat with Uncle Charlie for a time, and then Uncle Charlie asked him to lift him (Uncle Charlie) up, so he could pass some gas. I was waiting for the rest of the story, when Daddy said, "You see, Kiddo, after Uncle Charlie passed some gas, he died while I was holding him."

The tingling turned into a twister that blasted my insides and made my head spin. *Uncle Charlie gone!* Twelve years old is too old to sit on anybody's lap, but I crawled onto Daddy. He held me tight for a minute while I hid my head on his chest. I wet his shirt with my tears. Then I looked up at him and said, "Do I have to go to school?"

"You don't have to go today."

I stood. "I want to go to Aunt Mildred's."

Daddy said, "That's not the place for you right now. I have to go to the hospital. I have surgery. You can come along."

I wanted to be with Aunt Mildred. To hug her. To cry with her. To . . . just to be with her because Uncle Charlie wasn't there anymore, but I knew Daddy wouldn't let me, so I said, "I'd rather just stay home, alone."

After he left, I cried some, then got my harmonica and played every sad melody I knew and then made up a new one.

From then on, every time I saw Aunt Mildred, I thought of how Uncle Charlie wasn't there anymore, and I'd never get to see him again. Aunt Mildred went on running the motel by herself. She soldiered on. What else could she do? She had to make a living. *Cancer took Earl Dull at forty-nine. Now it has taken Uncle Charlie, too. He was fifty-eight. Daddy is fifty-three. Life is so uncertain. You can't count on anything, really. The uncertainty of it all makes my ulcer hurt. Thank God it hasn't perforated.*

I Had to Beg

One Thursday afternoon when I got home from school, Daddy said, "Your mother and I are going out to dinner. Do you want to come along?"

He did this all the time now, asking me if I wanted to come instead of just telling me we were going. I knew better than to say

I wanted to stay home. Mother had made it clear that I was to go along, no matter what. "Yes, I'd like to come."

Daddy wouldn't accept my answer. "You know, Kiddo, you're twelve now. You don't have to come if you don't want to."

"I want to come."

"It's really fine if you don't."

"I'm coming."

"Now, look here, Kiddo. It's really okay if you want to stay here."

He seems to really mean it. Maybe now that I'm older, he thinks it's okay. "Well, I'll stay here, then."

My parents left, and I went to see what was in the fridge. When they came home, Daddy didn't seem mad at me at all. *How about that?*

Mother, on the other hand, was fuming. When she got me alone, she said, "Don't ever do that again. It was just awful."

After that, every Thursday I had to argue Daddy into taking me along. I had to insist at least ten times that I was just dying to go with them. Finally I had to beg, "Please, oh please, let me come," before he would give up and get the damn show on the road.

31
Some People

Somebody Let Janice Out

In March, Mr. Kohnen set aside a school day to have a carnival with games, contests, and a talent show—with prizes. There would also be a raffle to raise money for a class picnic in May. I decided to enter the talent show. The little voice told me to do it. *Sometimes I can't shut it up.* I couldn't believe my own daring. I had always been terrified of speaking in front of class, but now I wanted to prove to myself that I could get up there.

I had a record of a funny calypso song about a little donkey that was naughty and got put in jail. *I think I can sing it. I can dress up, too.* I remembered that I had a full skirt, printed all over with monkeys and bananas, from way back in fifth grade. It was too short and too tight, so I asked Roberta for help. She got some orange fabric and sewed a ruffle around the bottom of the skirt. She cut open the waistband and added elastic. With the skirt, I wore a fitted, white blouse. Roberta had a colorful scarf with tropical birds on it. I tied it around my neck. I dug out my sombrero, and popped it on my head. I thought my costume was perfect. I practiced singing the song in front of the mirror for hours, making up gestures and facial expressions to go with the song.

On the day of the carnival, when it was time for the talent show, I went into the girl's bathroom and put on my costume. When I walked back into the classroom, everyone stared, and some of the boys laughed. My legs got antsy, and I felt like running home. No one else was performing in a costume. That old familiar pain in my chest started growing. I walked on shaky legs to the front of the room, looked right at Cooper, and imagined he was Uncle Charlie smiling down on me from heaven. Adams became Roberta, waiting to see me perform in the skirt she'd fixed for me.

I started singing. My heart pounded in my head. The louder it pounded, the louder I sang. When I did my gestures, my arms shook. I sang louder. I wanted to make Uncle Charlie and Roberta proud. When I finished, my classmates clapped. *They're clapping for the giraffe!*

When the talent contest was over, Mr. Kohnen announced the winners. I didn't win third place, or second place, either. *Oh well, I didn't really expect to win.*

"And first place goes to . . ." Mr. Kohnen paused to add excitement . . . "Janice." Now my legs were kicking wildly under my desk. *I won the talent show! Not Doctor Beare's Daughter, or Beare. It was MY idea to sing that song. It was MY idea to dress the part. It was My idea to act out the words. It was all ME.* "It sure was."

First prize was a fifty-cent piece from Mr. Kohnen's own pocket. I used my prize money to buy two tickets for the raffle. The prize was a live puppy. When Mr. Kohnen called the winning number, I checked my ticket. *I WON.* My heart was beating in my throat when Mr. Kohnen handed me the puppy in a cardboard box. The little brown-and-white pup put its paws on the side of the box, stood up, and leaned against me, its tail wagging, its cute freckled face, looking up at me, brown eyes, shining. My heart was singing joyful music. *But Daddy will never allow me to have a dog.* My heart shut up and sank all the way down to my shoes, leaving a big hole in my chest. Sadly, I handed the box back to Mr. Kohnen. "Draw another ticket. I'm not allowed to have a dog."

Walking up the alley toward home, I couldn't hold off the tears. When I walked into the house, I was sobbing. Mother asked what was wrong, and I told her about the raffle. She said, "I know how much you've always wanted a dog. You should have taken the puppy. If you had brought it home, Daddy would have let you keep it."

He would? Daddy wouldn't allow me to have a dog, under any circumstances. Would he?

When he came out of the office that night, I told him what had happened. Then I asked, "Would you have let me keep the puppy if I had brought it home?"

He said, "If you had brought it home, that would have been different."

I had a puppy in my own hands and gave it back. Why, oh why, didn't I know enough to just bring it home? It's my own fault I don't have a dog. There were needles pricking me all over. I looked at Daddy and said, "Well, if I could have kept it, now can I get a different one?"

"We don't need a dog," he said, then added, "And don't you ever bring one home."

The needles became ice picks. *That's not fair.* "What's wrong with having a dog? Everybody has dogs."

"That's all right for *them,* but you're not everybody."

I know I'm not everybody. I'm Doctor Beare's Daughter. And SHE can't have a dog. "Why Daddy? Why can't I have a dog?" I tried to keep the whine out of my voice, but I was near crying.

"You don't need to know why. You only need to know that you can't have a GODDAMN DOG."

I snapped back at him, "Give me one GOOD REASON WHY THE HELL NOT." *Who said that? Did I just talk to Daddy that way?*

"How dare you speak to me in that tone of voice. Why, you love some GODDAMN dog more than you love your OWN FATHER."

How can Daddy think I don't love him just because I want a dog? "That's not true, Daddy. I love you. I just want to know why."

"There you go, again—thinking bad things about me. SOME PEOPLE don't have any respect for their father."

The ice picks were knives, stabbing me all over. "'SOME PEOPLE' just want to know why they can't have a 'GODDAMN dog.'" *What's got into me to yell at Daddy like that?*

"I'm not going to listen to any more goddamn nonsense about a goddamn dog. What a piss-poor way for you to treat your own father." His final words were, "If you want a goddamn dog so bad, then when you grow up, GET YOUR HUSBAND TO BUY YOU A DOG."

I ran to my room and cried until I ran out of tears. As I fell asleep, I realized that I had never told my parents that I won the talent show. *And I'm never going to tell them, either.*

I carried a grudge. If I couldn't talk to Daddy about getting a dog, I wouldn't talk to him at all. He seemed not to notice, but after about a week of my sulking, he put his hands on my shoulders and marched me into the half-bath off the kitchen. He stood me in front of the mirror and said, "Look in the mirror, and you'll see the person causing all your problems looking right back at you."

I looked in the mirror. The person I saw was Daddy, standing behind me. I felt my heart crack open like an egg, smacked with the handle of a knife. My heart ran, liquid through the rest of my insides, like the egg's guts onto a hot skillet. I ran straight out to the garage and climbed up on the JAMAs.

I don't want to live this life anymore. I'm not that perfect child who hates dogs and never gets crazy ideas, always says and does the right thing, loves eating fish, is a whiz at math, knows just what to buy her mother on Mother's Day, and loves going out to dinner with her perfect parents, who are so proud of her that they can't stop smiling.

I desperately wanted to run away, but Tommy Smith had tried it, and they found him and brought him back. *I'd rather be dead and burning in hell than be found and brought back. The disgrace. Now I know why people kill themselves. They must feel like this—trapped with no way out. No way out except . . .*

My eyes oozed single . . . slow . . . sad . . . tears. *We have lots of drugs. . . . I don't want to die! There HAS to be another way. . . . They're old. . . . I'm only twelve. So . . . that's it! I'M GONNA OUTLIVE THEM. Until then, I have to endure . . . somehow . . . I can do it. I'm a good actor.*

He Won't Be Back

Two weeks after the talent show I went to school, but instead of Mr. Kohnen, there was an older woman in our classroom. She told us she would be our teacher for the rest of the year. She explained, "Mr. Kohnen won't be coming back. For those of you who haven't heard, I'm sorry to tell you that he has died."

My gut grumbled. My heart heaved. My breath blundered. *This can't be.* After the gasps and outbursts died down, our new teacher said, "Mr. Kohnen had a heart attack."

Mr. Kohnen was twenty-three years old. He had been married less than a year, and his wife was pregnant with their first child. I thought about Larry, Joe, Earl Dull, and Uncle Charlie. Now poor Mr. Kohnen. I cried for all of them. The idea of outliving my parents seemed

DAVID L. KOHNEN

CELINA — David L. Kohnen, 23, died at noon Saturday at his residence at 110 N. Main, Celina. He suffered a heart attack.

He was born Dec. 12, 1936.

Mr. Kohnen was married Aug. 8, 1959, to Helen Edwards of Celina. She survives along with his mother, Mrs. Troy C. Armstrong; and two brothers, Henry of Fullerton, Calif.; and Donald of Celina; three sisters, Mrs. James Hart and Mrs. Ronald Wilkins both of Celina; and Mrs. Don Dondrell of Waverly, O.

He was a member of the Immaculate Conception Church in Celina, and a graduate of the University of Dayton. He was a teacher at the Immaculate Conception School.

Services will be at 9:30 a.m. Tuesday at the Immaculate Conception Church with the Rev. Marcellus Fortman officiating a' a requiem high mass. Burial will be in the church cemetery.

Friends may call at the funeral home after 7:30 p.m. Sunday.

The Lima News March 20, 1960 reprinted with permission

very real, and it scared me. More than usual. *But I am committed. Someday, I am going to outlive them and be myself.*

A few days after the funeral, I walked downtown and into the jewelry store on Main Street—the one Mr. Kohnen and his wife lived above. I wanted to feel close to him. I stood awhile, looking at the engagement rings in the glass case. These were modest diamonds compared to the ones in Mother's rings. *It's the old ones that wear the big rocks.* Any one of the small, solitaire diamond rings would look beautiful on a young woman's finger. I thought of Mr. Kohnen's young wife and how precious any ring that he had given her must be. Just then, the door to the store opened. Mr. Kohnen's pregnant wife walked past me and climbed the stairs to the apartment above. I felt a string of arrhythmias. *She's going to have to soldier on while she somehow takes care of their baby. God isn't fair at all.*

32
Proud to Be Doctor Beare's Daughter

Sabin Sunday

The first Saturday in April, Daddy and I went to the P & B where we picked up fifty, one-pound boxes of Domino sugar cubes—enough to vaccinate six thousand people against polio. *I'm going to be part of a big moment in history—people lining up all across America on Sabin Sunday to take the world's first oral polio vaccine. The vaccine could get rid of polio, just like that.* There had been an earlier polio vaccine that was a shot, but there was a bad batch that gave some people polio, and it was discontinued.

On Sabin Sunday, Daddy was in charge of vaccination at West Elementary School. I helped him and the nurses in the school cafeteria. On one side of the room, people checked in at one table and then went to another where nurses administered the vaccine. On the other side of the cafeteria, we laid out lunch trays on tables. The nurse in front of me filled the trays with paper dosage cups. I followed behind her and used tongs to place a sugar cube in each one. Daddy was next, dropping the pink vaccine syrup onto the cubes. While we worked, the parking lot was filling up, and a line of people was forming by the doors. When the doors opened, they gushed into the school and formed a line across the cafeteria, down the hall, out the doors, and into the parking lot.

Our team was in constant motion, refilling empty trays with new doses of vaccine. *This must be what it's like to work on an assembly line.* People all across America were vaccinated that day, and it put an end to wild polio virus in the U.S. I almost always felt proud of Daddy, but I was extra proud to be Doctor Beare's Daughter that day.

Heinz Ketchup

One time I wasn't proud of Daddy was shortly after Sabin Sunday when I was twelve and won a basket of groceries worth fifty dollars in a drawing at the P & B. When Daddy took me to pick up my prize, I asked him if he knew someone who needed food that I could give it to. He seemed surprised at my request, but said he would think of someone.

When we got the basket home, and it was sitting on the kitchen counter, Daddy looked at it and said, "There's Heinz Ketchup in there . . . and Del Monte peaches. We like those." He maneuvered them out from the cellophane and replaced them with a couple of store-brand items from the cupboard.

Poor people might like Heinz Ketchup and Del Monte peaches too. I guess if you're poor, you can't choose. You have to take what you can get. I couldn't have been more disappointed in Daddy if he had left an accident victim lying in the middle of the street.

The next evening, Daddy drove me and the basket to a small run-down house in the not-nice part of town. I stayed in the car while he took the basket to the door. When Daddy came back, a man came with him, shook my hand, and thanked me. *I should thank him because I got to help. I like helping others, and when I feel scared and alone, I wish other people would help me. That's not the way of The Three Beares. Daddy's rule is: "God helps those who help themselves." Only it seems to me that He doesn't do it either.*

33
Run!

Smack! Smack!

At the cottage, on my thirteenth birthday (1960), Daddy handed me a key attached to a red-and-white bobber. "Happy birthday, Kiddo." My mouth fell open, and I gulped air.

"I have a boat?"

Daddy explained, "I bought myself a new hydroplane runabout, so I fixed up the Penn Yan for you to have fun with."

My hand flew to my chest. My eyes strained to stare at the key in my hand. *I have my own boat. I can go out on the lake whenever I want and drive it all over.*

The Penn Yan was built for a small trolling motor, but Daddy had hung a new 35 HP Johnson outboard on it. To handle the heavy motor, Daddy had a woodworker reinforce the transom and build a splash well in front of it. He installed a fin on the boat's bottom for making sharp turns. Daddy had transformed a fishing boat into a hotrod. "Well, go try her out, Kiddo." I putt-putted away from the shore and looked back at Daddy. He yelled, "Give it the gun."

I shoved the throttle all the way forward. The Johnson screamed and dug into the water, causing the flighty nose to stand straight up in front of me. *I can't see where I'm going. I have to get that nose down!* I somehow managed to stand, keep my hands on the wheel, and lay forward over the deck. The nose dropped. *Thank God.* Then it

It only looks like a fishing boat.

smacked the water and bounced back up in the air. Again and again. Smack! Smack! My heart was beating wild. *This thing is dangerous.* I hung onto the wheel so tight I thought I might rip it out of the shaft. I pictured myself flying out of the boat with the wheel in my hands. I hung on as the Penn Yan bucked a few more times, then settled into —ZOOOOM. She flew over the water. The air tore at my face, and I felt a burst of elation. *I can drive this crazy thing. She's faster than the Chris. Being Doctor Beare's Daughter is amazing.*

When I finally slowed down, water rushed over the transom into the splash well and slammed against the back of my seat. Once she settled back into putt-putt, the water calmly drained out.

After I got used to handling my crazy boat, Daddy ran alongside me in his hydroplane. He made up signals so we could change directions together or slide in front or behind each other. He was proud of how I could handle the Penn Yan and even taught me to drive his hydroplane, which was probably the fastest pleasure boat on the lake. I felt proud of me, too. *That doesn't happen very often. And when it does, my ulcer feels better.*

Daddy rented dock space over on the channel for the Penn Yan and had a cover made to keep out rainwater. Almost as an afterthought, he lashed an inner tube to the ribs of the boat, just under the small front deck. "There. If she ever sinks, the front end will bob to the surface," he explained.

The Three Beares have three boats. A hydroplane for Papa Beare, an inboard for Mama Beare, and a hotrod for Baby Beare. That's The Three Beares for you. They do things in a big way. It's fun doing things in a big way, especially if it involves boats on the lake. Then I heard that little voice again, "Sometimes I'd like to do my own thing in a small way."

Mom Had It In Her

One day I'd driven the Penn Yan to St. Marys and had just started home when a storm came up. The wind whipped the water into whitecaps, the rain lashed my eyes, and lightning flashed everywhere. *I have to get off the lake!* I headed for shore and drove into the first little bay I saw. There was a lake patrol station there, so I tied the boat to the dock, went inside, and called Mother to tell her I was safe and I would stay at the station until the storm was over. Then I'd bail out my boat and go on home.

Twenty minutes later, Mother showed up in the height of the storm. My eyes were locked on the boat cover in her arms. To get it, she would have had to drive over to my dock and lug the wet, heavy thing into the car—in the storm. *I didn't know Mom had it in her.*

That Huge Patch of Asphalt

The first day of school, when I got off the bus for eighth grade, Nora's house was gone. My eyes wandered over empty space where her house had been. *Nobody told me that she'd died. But then nobody knew she was important to me.* The lot where Nora's house had stood and the empty lot next to it where the furniture store once stood were paved over. Now the house-in-town was right next to the new church parking lot. Staring at that huge patch of asphalt, it was as if my old friends, Clyde, Nora, and Joe, had never lived. My throat felt raw and my eyes grew watery. *I wonder if the church will gobble up the house-in-town, too, someday.*

Feeling Safe

In October, school was buzzing about the upcoming presidential election. John F. Kennedy promised to put a man on the moon and stop the threat of Communism. *Now that's really something.* I wanted our country to be safe. Feeling safe was something I wanted to do more often.

BOOOOOM

On an April Sunday afternoon, Daddy and I were on our way home from the drag races, driving that long, straight stretch of Kettlersville Road where there was usually no traffic. Daddy reached across and tugged my safety harness, and I knew what was coming. He put his wingtip down. The car jumped, then barreled ahead. The T-Bird ate up the road like a starving pelican gulping down fish after fish. The fields streaked by, and I was flattened against the seat as the Bird accelerated. My heart was a spider that scurried up my throat. I looked at the speedometer. 95 . . . 99 . . . 105 . . . BOOOOOM. The spider in my throat bit me in my Adam's apple. Metal parts came flying out from the engine everywhere. A big chunk flew right through the hood. I screamed.

Daddy, fighting to get the Bird under control, somehow reached over with one hand and slapped me. "QUIET!" *He slapped me. Does he even know he did that? Is the car going to catch fire?* The T-Bird slowed, and Daddy steered it to the shoulder. As it came to a halt, he reached over and released my harness. "OUT. NOW!"

He hadn't had to tell me. I shot out of the car. Daddy yelled, "RUN!"

My legs ran. My arms pumped. My heart sped. I bounded over the ditch into a plowed field, tripping over the ridges and furrows. When I was a good piece away, I turned to look back. The T-Bird sat there, smoking. Beyond the car and across the road, Daddy was standing in the ditch. He motioned for me to stay put. After a few minutes, he went over to the car. "It's not on fire," he called.

I walked back. A jagged hole in the middle of the hood spewed smoke. Chunks of metal littered the road.

We hitched a ride to a pay phone, and one of the men at the gas station came to take us home. He took one look at the dead Bird and said, "I told you that you couldn't run that much compression, Doc."

Daddy said, "Well, it was fun while it lasted." He didn't buy a new car. He put a new engine in the Bird and got a new hood. Then he went to work on the new engine, determined to make it even faster. *I hope he knows what he's doing this time.*

34
Can't Wear That in Celina

Knit One, Purl Two

It was May 1961, and Aunt Mildred had sold the motel and moved into the little pink cottage, three doors down from ours on Harbor Point. I was thrilled she was so close by.

That same month, I graduated from eighth grade. *I'll be in high school next year. High school is supposed to be fun. But it's not going to be any fun at IC.* So I began my campaign to go to Celina High in the fall. I told Daddy, "Celina High has a football team and a marching band. They have dances, every Friday night. They have a choir and an orchestra. IC has none of that. Please, may I go to Celina High?" *I could be with Joyce. I could make even more friends there. I could get lost in the crowd.*

Daddy wouldn't hear of it. We were Catholic. The nuns and priests were Daddy's patients. Uncle Doc was on the school board, and on and on. *I'm stuck at IC. The whole student body is 150 kids. My freshman class will be the same thirty-two kids I started with in first grade. And I'm never going to be asked out on a date.*

That summer, I visited Aunt Mildred every day. She taught me to knit a dishrag out of string. David thought knitting was silly, but knitting took my mind off everything else. If I didn't give it my full attention, I would knit when I should purl, and three or four inches later, I'd see my mistake and have to rip backward to fix it.

For some reason, Daddy didn't like to see me knitting. "There you are again, going like this." He twisted his hands together, imitating me. One time, when he saw me knitting, he said, "I know what you're thinking."

Knit one, purl two, knit one, purl two . . .

"You shouldn't be thinking like that about me."

"I wasn't thinking about you, Daddy. I was thinking about knitting." *Knit one, purl two, knit one, purl two . . .*

"I know better. You were plotting something against me." *Oh, oh.* "Why do you think bad things about me? SOME PEOPLE have no respect. My patients have more respect for me than you do. You don't give a tinker's damn about me, do you? There's something wrong with you."

I know. There's always something wrong with me.

"You should be ashamed of yourself."

I AM ashamed of myself. Even when I don't think I did anything wrong.

"It's wrong to think bad things about your father. MY." He grabbed his fly-rod and marched out the front door to the lake.

I wasn't doing anything wrong, but there's still something wrong with me. I know there is because I can feel it. It's always there, like a bad horror movie running in the background.

"I've Known It All Along"

I never before cared about what I wore when Mother was picking everything out. But now that she was letting me make my own choices, I discovered *Seventeen* magazine for teens, and suddenly style was important. I saw a pair of sandals in the magazine that I wanted so badly that I decided to make a pair just like them out of an old pair of leather loafers. I cut the body of the shoes into strips with a razor, leaving just the very fronts of the toes and backs of the heels intact. They looked nothing like the sandals in the magazine, but I wore them anyway, because they were my design. *I love style. Who knew?* "I've known it all along."

On Thursdays in Dayton, I got to shop at Rike's. They had fashions that weren't sold in Celina—pieces that were featured in *Seventeen*. I loved putting separate pieces together to create my own look. The one problem I had was that now, at five-foot-eight, pants that should have ended at my ankle stopped at my calf. I had to buy pants with big hems that could be let down. Even that wasn't always enough.

Sometimes I picked out pieces that made Mother say, "We're not buying that." When I asked her why not, she said, "You can't wear that in Celina." *I've lived my whole life in Celina, and I still can't figure out all the rules.*

I was looking at a one-shouldered dress on the rack, wondering if it could be worn in Celina, when a woman's voice behind me said, "Crystal. I didn't know you shopped here." I turned to face her, and she said, "Sorry. I thought you were one of my daughter's friends. You look quite like her."

My head spun and made me dizzy. Before I could get my bearings, the woman, obviously embarrassed, had hurried off. I wanted to run after her, pelt her with questions, but I didn't. I was afraid to know the answers. "I came from a Home in Dayton." *Was Crystal a member of my first family?* Afterward, whenever we were in Dayton and I saw a woman with red hair, I would look closely at her face to see if I could find any resemblance to me.

35
Tarred and Feathered

In September 1961, I was fourteen. At the kitchen table of the house-in-town, I gave my freshman schedule to Daddy to be signed. IC High offered two curriculums: College Prep and General. I would be taking College Prep, but home economics was a requirement for *all* freshmen girls. I was thrilled because they taught sewing. *I can learn to sew my own pants and make them long enough. I can choose colors and patterns and fabrics to make one-of-a-kind pieces to go with the things I find at Rike's.*

Daddy crossed out home economics and wrote, "study hall."

"But, Daddy. I want to learn to sew."

"We can afford to buy your clothes."

"I want to make some of my clothes myself."

"No daughter of mine is going to sew her own clothes."

"Home ec is on the schedule of all freshman girls. It's required."

"It's not on your schedule anymore." I wondered what Sister Paulissa, the principal, would say to that.

She said nothing. While all the other freshman girls were in home ec, I had two periods of study hall in a row. At the back of the study hall, was the school library. Sister Wilhelmine, the librarian, thought I didn't have enough to do and asked if I wanted to be a student librarian. *Yes. I love books.*

Sister trained me, and for two periods every day, I sat at the reference desk, checked books in and out, and directed students where to find the materials they needed for their projects. I had to talk to everyone who came to the desk—including my classmates. *Maybe they will learn to like me if I smile at them and act friendly.* I drew a smiley face on a note card and taped it to the desk to remind me.

~~~

The first Friday night after high school began, I went to a dance in the gym for freshman initiation. I sat next to one of the girls in my class and said, "If a boy asks me to dance, what should I do?"

She gave me an odd look. "Say, 'I'd love to,' then dance with him."

I don't know how. While the other girls had been getting together over the summer, learning how to dance, I had been out on the lake. *No worry. No boy in my class is going to ask me.* A low, raspy voice said, "Would you like to dance?"

My body twitched. *I was right about one thing. He's not in my class.* He was tall with dark hair slicked back on one side. While most of the boys wore khakis, he had on tight, black chinos. While most of the boys wore white dress shirts, his was pink. And the top two buttons were open. I could see his curly chest hair. I had to pull my stubborn eyes off his chest. *YIPES.*

It was a slow dance. All I could do was stumble along. He told me his name was Jax, and he was a junior. His deep-green eyes were the color of the lake during a thunderstorm. They made a hole in me. My eyes darted from his—looked away, over his shoulder, but I couldn't see anything but him. At the end of my stumbling act, he walked me back to my seat, thanked me, and walked off. I felt a strange mix of relief and longing. *I'm glad that ordeal is over. A boy asked me to dance!*

No one else asked me to dance, and a short while later, the senior boys rounded up all the freshmen and told us to line up in the hall outside the gym. We were blindfolded and led, one at a time, onto the stage of the auditorium. At center stage, we were tarred-and-feathered in front of the whole school. They smeared "tar" on my arms and dabbed it on my head. Then they added feathers. One of the girls started to cry. But I wasn't worried. *No one would dare harm Doctor Beare's Daughter.*

After they were done with me, I took off my blindfold and went to the girls' bathroom. The other tarred-and-feathered girls in my class were there. Everyone was laughing at how strange we looked in the mirror with our arms and heads covered in feathers. And for once, I was one of them—just a regular kid. I saw myself smile in the mirror. I smiled inside, too. The "tar" was honey. It washed right off my arms. My hair, on the other hand . . .

That night when I went to bed, it was hard to lie still. I tried lying on my side. *A boy asked me to dance.* I remembered the way he looked — the tight, black chinos—the open-neck, pink shirt. Those lake-green eyes. The sound of his voice, deep and raspy, when he asked me to dance. I heard myself say, "I'd love to." *Why did I say "LOVE?" It made me sound overeager. I should have said, "I'd LIKE that" or "Okay" or "Sure." "Okey Dokey?" "All righty?" Why, oh why did I say "I'd LOVE to?"*

I rolled onto my back, remembering the way his hand felt against mine while we danced—cool and strong. I could see those eyes poking holes in me. I turned onto my stomach. I remembered the way he smelled—spicy—like a warm pumpkin pie. *Why, oh why did I say, "I'd LOVE to?"*

I replayed the scene where he asked me to dance, and I said something different each time. Then I imagined I hadn't stumbled all over him and I looked into those lake-green eyes instead of over his shoulder. When I finally fell asleep, the scene played on in my dreams.

When I woke Saturday morning, the slide show in my head stayed with me. It was Sunday evening, and my brain still hadn't moved on.

On Monday, in English class, Mrs. Klein was explaining iambic pentameter. "An iamb is a metrical foot made up of one unstressed syllable followed by a stressed syllable. Pentameter means—"

"Mrs. Klein." *That voice—deep and raspy. Jax. What's a junior doing in freshman English?*

"Yes, Jackson?"

"So, the syllables are ten centimeters instead of twelve inches?" Jax asked.

A couple of girls giggled. *Can Jax be that dumb? Is that why he's in freshman English? He's wearing a red shirt today. Red.* The other boys always wore white. Jax's red shirt stuck out like a red flag waving at a lake-green-eyed bull. I noticed a small patch sewn on the front pocket.

Mrs. Klein shook her head. "'Metrical foot' refers to the *meter* or *rhythm* of poetry." She continued, "A pentameter is a line of five metrical feet."

"So we're talking about a line of poetry that is fifty centimeters long." Jax gave her a handsome smile. His lake-eyes glowed. *He's playing with her.*

Mrs. Klein sighed. "Iambic pentameter is a line of poetry whose rhythm goes, da-DUM, da-DUM, da-DUM, da-DUM, da-DUM. Now who can give me an example?"

Jax jumped to his feet. "I can." *He's wearing black leather boots. In school.* They looked worn out, but had been polished so they shined.

Mrs. Klein rolled her eyes, but before she could say anything, Jax said, "i-DON'T like-ENG lish-CLASS to-DAY at-ALL." He smiled brightly.

Everyone watched Mrs. Klein. *Jax is walking the edge of the Grand Canyon in those boots.* She said, "Good example, Jackson. Let's move on."

In the days that followed, freshman English became a contest between Mrs. Klein and Jax. Mrs. Klein—trying to teach us something while Jax got in her way with his outrageous, innocently-posed questions. Mrs. Klein treated him kindly. On the other hand, the "smart" kids made fun of him—branded him a "hood" for the way he dressed. I had a hard time falling asleep nights for thinking about Jax. His black boots. The colored shirts. Those tight chinos. He dressed how he wanted and laughed with his eyes. He mocked the "smart" kids who made fun of him, without them knowing it.

IC didn't have a yearbook, but the photographer gave everyone a booklet with all the student pictures. I took it to bed with me and kissed Jax's picture. Longing surged through me and hollowed me out. My stomach clenched. Then I cried because I loved him and knew I could never ever be with him. He was a bad boy. A greaser. Mother would say, "Not our kind." Daddy would say, "Not good enough for my daughter." *Why do they assume that I'm their kind? I could come from a big family of greasers or, God forbid, a long line of criminals.*

I couldn't get Jax out of my mind until one night after dinner, when President Kennedy came on TV and urged Americans to build fallout shelters as soon as possible in case of fallout from a nuclear bomb.

"Are we going to build a fallout shelter, Daddy?"

"No."

"Why not? President Kennedy wants everyone to build one."

"Russia isn't going to drop a bomb on us because if they do, we'll annihilate them."

"But what if there's a nuclear accident."

"Don't worry about it." Oh, but I did. Now, instead of Jax keeping my stomach churning, it was the Russians.

36
I'm Not a Soldier

In October, Grandpa came for a visit, and after a couple of days, he had a series of strokes. He died, with Daddy, Uncle Doc, and a priest at his bedside. I couldn't cry. My sorrow was too heavy and thick to squeeze its way out of my eyes. It suffocated me, like many layers of wet, wool blankets. It made it hard to walk or even hold my head up. It was a tremendous burden to bear. The only way to carry that feeling was to numb it and soldier on.

At the funeral home in Versailles, I looked at Grandpa in his casket. Like Larry, Uncle Charlie, Earl Dull, and Mr. Kohnen, Grandpa had fled his skin, leaving behind his shell. *When they go, they just go. I didn't get to say goodbye to any of them. That's sad, but I'm numb.*

~~~

Christmas was coming, and Mother soldiered on by ordering an artificial Christmas tree from the Celina Flower Shop. When Roberta and I opened the box, it was silver. The trunk was a wooden pole, covered with aluminum curlicues. The branches were covered with spiky aluminum needles, ending in feathery whorls. Roberta and I fit the branches into the trunk and stood back to see the result. Voila —an aluminum-foil Christmas tree so bright, it made us blink. It came with a color wheel that turned and made the tree, red, green, gold. Roberta and I had assembled a spectacular spectacle the likes of which Main Street had never seen. I could hear Grandpa say, "Never mind, Kiddo. We'll find the perfect tree next year."

Well, this year we have a perfect tree. There wasn't a single dogleg, bare spot, or broken branch. I was looking at our perfect tree, when I noticed it was leaning toward Shiverdecker's. A wild wind whipped off the numb cloak I had been wearing and left me shaking and shivering in grief. I ran upstairs to Grandpa's room, opened the bureau drawer, grabbed his pajamas, and sobbed into them until my eyes turned red and dry and Grandpa's pajamas were sopping wet. "I'm not a soldier."

The spectacular spectacle that leaned toward Shiverdecker's

37
This Isn't a Dog

As January wore on, I dreaded February. Riding all the way to Florida without Grandpa was unthinkable. There'd be no stories to take my mind off throwing up in The Pot and gasping for a non-existent breath of smokeless air in the back seat. Worse yet, Daddy would feel free to go off on a rant that might last hundreds of miles.

One night at dinner Daddy said, "Now that you're in high school, you'll miss too much if I take you out of school to go to Florida. Aunt Mildred will stay here while your mother and I are gone."

I felt as relieved as I did the time I stepped on a snake in the woods and realized it was more afraid of me than I was of it.

"We'll be gone for two weeks."

"You always spend the whole month in Florida," I said.

"I don't want to leave you behind for that long," he said.

Oh, don't mind me.

"We'll miss you, Kiddo," Daddy said.

"I'll miss you, too," I said, fighting down the corners of my lips that were trying to get to my eyes. Aunt Mildred didn't get mad for no reason and go off on tangents like Daddy. She didn't get her feelings hurt easily like Mother. She listened to me, and she *heard* me. She didn't think the things I had to say were crazy.

For the next two weeks, Aunt Mildred and I did things my parents never allowed. We ate in front of the TV every night. Sometimes

Aunt Mildred picked up a large pizza and a big bottle of Coke at the Celina Beer and Wine Store, and we ate while we watched *The Mickey Mouse Club*. I loved that show but never got to see it because it was on at dinnertime, and I always had to eat at the table. The next day Aunt Mildred and I had cold pizza for breakfast. Other times, she heated up frozen TV dinners. I'd never had a TV dinner before, so we tried all the varieties. *I feel like this is my first real vacation.*

A few days after Aunt Mildred came, I was walking home from my piano lesson when an orange tabby cat came up to me and meowed. I bent down to pet it. It was wearing a collar with an address on the other side of town. *That cat is a long way from home. It's lost. Like me, except I don't have a collar that says where I really belong.*

I picked up the cat and carried it all the way across town to its address. I could feel it purring next to my cheek. The owner thanked me and said she had too many cats, and would I like to take this one?

I'll take the cat. I'll adopt it! But . . . I can't. Daddy won't let me keep it. Then I heard Mother's voice in my head, saying, "You should have taken the puppy. If you had brought it home, Daddy would have let you keep it." Then I heard Daddy's words, "And don't you ever bring home a dog." *This isn't a dog.*

"I'll take good care of him," I promised the woman. She took the collar off the cat, and I carried him home. "I have a cat," I told Aunt Mildred.

"That's nice," was all she said.

I named my cat "Tinker." As in "don't give a tinker's damn." I knew Daddy wouldn't let me keep him in the house, so I fixed up a bed for him in a corner of the garage. Tinker was a loving cat. I let him in the house in the evenings while Aunt Mildred and I watched TV. He climbed in my lap and purred while I scratched his ears. It made my stomach hurt less.

When my parents came home from Florida, I told them, "I have a cat. Aunt Mildred let me keep him."

"Well, hell," Daddy said.

I got to keep Tinker. I made sure to never let him in the house when Daddy was home. I asked Mother why Daddy didn't like animals. And why did he especially hate dogs?

She said, "When Ralph was a small boy, he made friends with a stray dog. One day, the dog was rabid and bit him through his coat, breaking the skin. Ralph's mother watched him for signs of rabies for months, afraid that he might die. So you see, Ralph doesn't hate dogs—he's afraid of them."

My hero Daddy, who drives like a demon and looks death in the face every day at the hospital, is afraid of dogs. I wonder what else he's afraid of?

38
A Scrap of His Big Toe

It was late March when I sprang awake in the middle of the night. *What's happening?* I heard Daddy yell, "I'll save you. I'll save you!" Then "THUMP!"

A thundercloud rolled through me. I jumped out of bed, raced along the halls, then stopped at my parents' door. I heard Mother say, "You had your hands on my neck. You tried to strangle me!"

He wouldn't. Would he? He wouldn't. Mother sounded shook up, but she was alive and talking, so I sat down at the door to listen.

Daddy: "I had a dream that you were choking, and I had to save you. Then I woke up on top of you on the floor, and it was me who couldn't breathe."

Mother: "I thought you were going to choke me to death."

Daddy: "I've been waking up at night not able to breathe. There's a mass growing in my throat that's choking me. I can feel it."

Sparks crackled through my veins.

Mother: "Oh, Ralph. You need to see an otolaryngologist."

Daddy: "I wasn't going to, but now I have to."

I felt something lodge in my heart—a stick of dynamite, whose fuse had just been lit in some distant place in my body. *Daddy has cancer. What else can it be? Cancer got Earl Dull and Uncle Charlie and now it's going after Daddy. Like the fuse slow-burning its way to my heart, cancer creeps through you until . . . Bang! You're dead.* I wanted to run to Daddy and hug him, but I knew that wasn't a good idea. So I went back to bed. Now I was burning inside and freezing on the outside. I made myself into a ball around my heart and hugged the covers to me. I shook with the cold until it was time to go down to the kitchen in the morning.

As always, Daddy was already gone, and Mother acted like nothing had happened. She smiled when she handed me my packet of toast. *What's going on? If I ask her about it, she'll know I was listening at the door.*

As I walked to school I wondered if what I had heard had been real. *Maybe it wasn't Daddy who had a nightmare. Maybe it was me and my overactive imagination. No. I was awake. I know what I heard. You sure? You sure about that? No. Yes. I know what I heard. Do you? Do you, really? Maybe not. . . .* The argument played inside my head all day. The back-and-forth was the only thing that kept the burning fuse from reaching my heart, blowing it up, and shattering me.

That night at dinner, my parents gave no clue that something was wrong. *Are they acting? They couldn't be this calm if it were true. Still . . . I know what I heard.* I lived in fear—the kind of fear that eats you alive, like a fish nibbling at a live minnow on a hook.

It was four days later—four stretched-out, dragging-their-feet, unbearable days of back-and-forth in my head, painful-suspense-in-my-heart days—when I finally got the answer. When I came home from school, my parents were in the back room, sitting, waiting for me. "Sit down, Janice," Daddy said.

My feet hardened into cinder blocks. My legs hauled them over to the couch where I sat next to Mother.

Daddy looked straight at me and said in the same gentle voice that he had once used to tell me that Uncle Charlie had died, "I have cancer of the larynx, Kiddo." His face looked like he had just read the grocery list. The fuse finally burned all the way to my heart and blew it up. I had an immense pain in my chest.

Daddy went on, "I have a mass in my throat. I went to the otolaryngologist over in Lima—the one I refer my patients to. The mass is cancer. I have to have my larynx removed."

"But . . . how will you talk?"

"I will have a hole in my throat—a stoma. After it heals, I will have to learn to talk by forcing air through the hole."

A stoma . . . like Mr. Mueller down at the newsstand. He had his larynx removed and wears a metal plate over the hole in his throat. He opens it to talk in low-pitched grunts. "When is your surgery?"

"I don't know yet. I want the best surgeon I can find—one who only does laryngectomies." Daddy got up and went into the office.

I snuggled up to Mother. She put an arm around me, and I cried. She said, "There's nothing we can do about it. I'm going to start supper. You go do your homework." She got up and went into the kitchen.

Now I felt like my stomach had been kicked by a horse. *I'm supposed to do my homework like nothing's wrong.* I tried, because Doctor Beare's Daughter would just go do her homework, but I couldn't think about the assignment. *What will it be like for Daddy to lose his big booming voice that fills our house and the office? Will he be able to work after his surgery? What will happen to us if Daddy can't work? What if the cancer has spread? What if it's already too late?*

During dinner, my parents acted like nothing had happened. It was clear that I was supposed to act that way too, but near the end of the meal, I started to cry. *I'm so scared. Please, somebody tell me everything will be all right.*

Daddy snapped, "Stop that, Kiddo. I have enough to worry about right now. We can't be dealing with you, too. I don't want to hear anything more out of you."

I wiped my tears with my napkin and held my face stiff. Then Daddy added, "I don't want you talking to anybody else about it either. Not Roberta. Not anybody."

My father has cancer. He's going to lose his larynx. He might even die. Why can't there be somebody for me to talk to? Why do I have to act normal when I'm so scared inside? I have to carry it all inside of me for them. That's why.

The next day, the front doorbell chimed. Mother answered it, and a nun from the Shrine at Maria Stein handed her a gold reliquary. "What's this?" Mother asked the nun.

"It's the relic of Saint Peregrine, the patron saint of cancer. We want Doctor Beare to keep it until after his surgery. We're all praying for him." The nun turned and left.

Uncle Doc must have asked one of our nuns for prayers for Daddy, and she must have told the Maria Stein nuns. Even holy virgins gossip among themselves.

Mother handed Saint Peregrine to me and said, "Put this on the chest of drawers in the guest room."

I looked at the heavy, golden object in my hand. *Saint Peregrine's relic is maybe the most important one at the shrine. Imagine bringing it here. What about all the other people with cancer who want to be in its presence and pray for a miracle? I hope Saint Peregrine has a miracle for Daddy.*

Whenever I couldn't stand acting normal another second, I went into the guest room,

Photo reprinted with permission from The Shrine at Maria Stein, Ohio

The relic of St Peregrine

sat on the bed, and stared at the relic in its ornate, gold case with its small round window. Since I couldn't talk to anyone, I could sit with a saint. *What is that tiny thing in there? A sliver of his rib? A fragment of his skull? A scrap of his big toe? The one that had cancer?*

~~~~~

Daddy chose a surgeon in Chicago. We drove there and stayed at Aunt Vida's (Mother's sister). Uncle Harold drove my parents to the hospital. Daddy's surgery would be the next morning. I waved them off. *I've heard Daddy's voice for the last time.*

A couple of hours later, I was in Aunt Vida's front yard and saw Uncle Harold's car pull in the driveway. Mother was with him . . . so was Daddy. *The cancer has spread, and they can't operate. Daddy is going to die.* When Daddy stepped out of the car, he was smiling. I ran to him. "What happened?"

"The doctor examined me and found that I have a contact ulcer on my larynx, caused by the loud way I talk. It's not cancer."

My knees buckled, and I swayed.

"I have to rest my voice for six weeks, and the ulcer should heal."

Not cancer? Did the otolaryngologist in Lima make a mistake? Or did St. Peregrine work a miracle? Everyone assumed that the diagnosis had been a mistake. I wondered what the nuns thought. I didn't know what to make of it. After we got back home, someone from the shrine came to get Saint Peregrine, and Daddy never referred another patient to the otolaryngologist in Lima.

For six weeks, my father stayed home from work and had to write what he wanted to say on a pad of paper. It made him so frustrated that he would stop writing, throw the pencil across the room, and tear up the paper he had just written. *Six whole weeks without a rant—unheard of.*

~~~~~

One day, after Daddy was back at work, I asked him about something that had been bothering me. "What happens to me if you and Mother are both gone?"

He flinched, then said, "That's not going to happen. One of us will always be here to take care of you."

"But *what if?* I want to know."

"Well, you would have to go live with Uncle Doc, but then—I'd have to put him in charge of my money, too." That idea seemed to upset him. He thought a minute then looked at me and said, "I could fix it so Uncle Rock down at the bank would manage your money. Then you could go on living here and hire a housekeeper."

He doesn't want Uncle Doc to have me. I'm only fourteen. He thinks I can live here by myself with a housekeeper. Every kid I know has some family somewhere who will take him or her. Mine disappeared when I was adopted. Mother and Daddy think they are enough for me—that I don't ever need anybody else. If they die and leave me, I'll have to take care of myself. "I do a lot of that already."

39
Dropped Stitches

When I turned fifteen in June 1962, Mother took me to the Bureau of Motor Vehicles to get my learner's permit. She sat in the small waiting area. The clerk gave me a form to fill out: name, address, and so on. I came to place of birth and realized I didn't know where I had been born. I walked over to Mother and said, "I have to write down where I was born."

She gestured for me to lean down and whispered in my ear as if revealing a dark secret, "Cincinnati."

Cincinnati? I thought I came from a Home in Dayton. Somewhat stunned, I went back to my seat and wrote "Cincinnati." Then came Father's occupation. I wrote down Doctor. Then Mother's occupation. I knew the right answer was Housewife, but that seemed an over-statement—Roberta took care of the house. I started thinking about what Mother really did. She cooked. She played bridge. She guarded Daddy when he took his naps. But the thing she did the most was sit. This struck me as funny, and I wrote "Sitter." *On second thought, she's a pretty good lier, too. If she's not sitting, she's probably taking a nap.* I checked my weird sense of humor, erased "Sitter," and wrote, "Housewife."

When I handed in the form, the clerk said, "I need to see your birth certificate."

It never occurred to me before that I even had one. *Of course I do. Everyone has one.*

I went back to Mother and said, "I need my birth certificate." She pulled a piece of paper from her purse and gave it to me. Invisible hands grabbed me by the throat and squeezed. *I'm holding my birth certificate. I'm not supposed to know what's on it.*

I slowly walked back to the clerk's window. I didn't want Mother to see me looking at the paper in my hand, but my eyes scanned it before I could stop them. "Certificate of Birth Registration." The only information was my name, date of birth, and place of birth. The invisible hands let go of my neck. I gave the certificate to the clerk.

She read it, then showed it to another clerk and said, "This isn't an actual birth certificate. Can we accept this?"

The second clerk looked at it, then at me, and said, "That's Doctor Beare's Daughter. We'll take it."

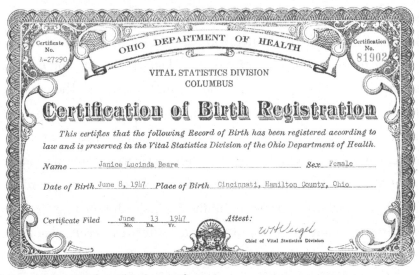

My poor excuse for a birth certificate

After we got home, Mother was drinking iced tea in the living room. I was in the chair opposite her, knitting a sleeve. Mother didn't mind my knitting like Daddy did. I had graduated from dish towels and was knitting my first sweater. I had chosen sky blue for the body, but was working the sleeves in the exact shade of navy that matched a skirt I had. Casually, Mother said, "You were born in Cincinnati because that's where Catholic Social Services in Dayton sent your birth mother away to have you."

My knitting needles jerked wildly, and I dropped a bunch of stitches. *They sent her away?* I knew from listening at my parent's bedroom door why girls were sent away to have their babies. They were "in trouble." I heard Daddy tell Mother about some of the girls he had "sent away." The cover-up stories told in Celina to hide these shameful pregnancies were amazing. One girl went to boarding school but didn't like it there, so after a semester away, she came back to Celina High. Another girl's father got transferred to Paris for a year. While the family was in France, the girl's mother had a late-in-life surprise baby. Yet another girl's predicament leaked out, and the whole family had to move away from Celina.

Mother was talking again. "She was just a young girl who got herself in trouble. I saw her in the hallway of the courthouse in Dayton when we went there to sign the adoption papers. I felt sorry for her. I don't think she saw me or knew I was there."

Mother SAW her? Did she have red hair? Was she tall? Don't tell me. Once I know it, I can't un-know it. It would make my coming from another mother real. Why is she telling me this? It's supposed to be a secret. My body was thrumming now—I was running for my life inside, but sitting still on the outside. I thought I might implode. I concentrated on picking up my dropped stitches, one at a time, as if I hadn't noticed what Mother just said. *Is she going to tell me more?*

She sipped her tea, then said. "I thought maybe you were curious."

It's a trap! If I say I'm curious, it will mean that I acknowledge that Mother isn't my REAL mother. I don't think she could stand that. "I'm not curious." The little voice said, "I want to know."

Mother said nothing more. My gears ground to a halt. I felt exhausted, but kept on knitting as if I hadn't the slightest interest in anything Mother had said. I made the sleeve two inches longer than the other one. *So that's why my first mother gave me away. Getting "in trouble" is the worst thing a girl can do to her parents. Worse even than running away.*

The next day, I saw Daddy sitting in the living room at the cottage. He was intently sewing up a ripped seam in one of Mother's dresses with a curved suture needle and a length of catgut. I sat down, and said as casually as I could manage, "Where was I born?"

"Why are you asking that?" His voice had a tone I didn't like.

"Sometimes I have to fill out a form that asks for my place of birth. I don't know what to write."

"If anyone asks where you were born, you say: right here in Mercer County." Daddy tied off his work and put the dress down. I could tell that was the end of the conversation. I had already stuck my neck way out. I sat there in silence a few minutes in case he said something else. He tucked his left hand behind his back and turned his attention to using the thumb and forefinger on his right hand to throw a line of perfectly spaced knots down a long length of catgut.

Daddy just lied to me. He thinks the fact that I came from somewhere else isn't of any importance—that the whole thing was over and done a long time ago. It's best forgotten. And he doesn't want me thinking about it, either. "I can't forget."

Sorry, Mrs. Bachinger

That summer, I spent a lot of time on the lake. *A good way not to think about things I'm not supposed to think about.* One day when I slowed my boat, water rushed past my feet. I told Daddy, "The Penn Yan has a leak somewhere."

"You swamped water over the top of the splash well."

"I didn't. There's a leak."

Daddy said, "I'll hear no more about it."

The next time I went to get my boat, a couple inches of water stood on the floor. I bailed it out. That night at dinner, I told Daddy, "There was water standing in the Penn Yan. Then, when I was running on the lake, more water rushed in when I slowed down. It's coming in from up front."

"You're swamping it."

"I'm not swamping it. The Penn Yan has a leak. It's going to sink."

"It's not going to sink. I'll hear no more about it."

I felt my shoulders tense. *I'll be in big trouble out on the lake if the Penn Yan sinks.*

A couple days later, when I went to the dock, the Penn Yan wasn't there. I thought it had been stolen. Then I saw the ropes. The stern rope was taut and disappeared straight down into the water. The bow rope had a bit of slack. I could see the tip of the Penn Yan's bow, just breaking the water. *The inner tube has done its job.* I ran home and called the office. When Daddy got on the phone I said, "The Penn Yan sank at the dock."

"The hell it did," he said. "Don't bother me with your nonsense. I'm busy with a patient."

He doesn't believe me again. In the background I heard a female voice say, "Doc. Your language." Daddy's good Catholic women patients took exception to his cussing.

"Sorry, Mrs. Bachinger," Daddy said.

"Daddy. It sank."

"SONOFABITCH sorry, Mrs. Bachinger."

When he got home, we used the Chris to drag the Penn Yan across the bay to the boathouse. Once we got the straps under my boat, it took two days of pumping to raise her. Daddy brought the boat to the cottage and placed it upside down on a pair of saw horses in the front yard by the lake. While he took the engine apart in the shop, he set me to patching the boat bottom with fiberglass. I had never worked with fiberglass before, so I didn't know to wear gloves. Even worse, I didn't wear a mask when I sanded the patch. I coughed and itched all night.

Pumping out the Penn Yan at the boat house

The next morning I had a bad sore throat and red bumps up both arms. Daddy said, "Why didn't you protect yourself?"

I felt heat rising like a fountain in my stomach. "I didn't know I was supposed to."

His eyes grew hard, locked on mine, and held them. "Some people don't have the common sense they were born with. Who would have thought that my daughter, who's been around boats all her life, could be so goddamn ignorant? MY."

I know I have no common sense, but I wish he wouldn't tell me over and over.

After Daddy left the house, Mother said, "It's Ralph's fault. He should have given you gloves and a mask. He's mad because he can't admit that—even to himself." *She's just trying to make me feel better. We both know it's my fault because I'm stupid.*

A Clue

In July, Aunt Reva and Aunt Vida came for a visit. Mother smiled a lot when she was with her sisters. When I was alone with my aunts, I asked them what it was like for them growing up. Aunt Reva said, "We were poor but didn't know it because we had love."

Mother never wants me to be friends with any of the poor kids. Now I find out she was poor herself.

Aunt Vida said, "We had fun growing up. Lou was adventuresome and always up for a good time." *That doesn't sound like Mother.* "After Mama and Poppy died, Lou struck out on her own and surprised us by marrying a doctor. She seemed very happy at first, but then she changed."

Mother told me it was Daddy who had changed. So they both changed. I wonder who changed first? Was it Mother because she didn't

have any children, and then Daddy got tired of her being sad all the time?
Well, now they have me. Why can't I change them back to happy?
That's my job.

Mother and her sisters when they were younger L to R: Nell, Vida,
Lou, Reva

40
They Look Alike

*W*hen I started sophomore year in the fall (1962), Jax wasn't in my English class. He wasn't in school at all. Word was, he had quit. *What's going to happen to him? It seems like the world is stacked against him just because he's different. I'm different, too. If you're going to be different, then let it be rich-different, not poor-different.*

About two weeks after we moved back to the house-in-town, Tinker went missing. I knew if I couldn't find him, Daddy would never let me get another cat. I begged Mother to let me put an ad in the paper. She said I could offer a five-dollar reward, but not to publish our name. The ad read: "Lost—orange male tabby cat. $5 reward. Call 2110."

The day after the paper came out, one of the patients offered to give Daddy a kitten. Another said, "I see Janice has lost her cat." Still another said, "For five dollars you can pick out any of our barn cats." Some of the patients may have recognized our phone number. But being that this was Celina, some people were curious enough to know who had lost a cat that they scanned the entire phone book to find out.

A couple days after the ad ran, a lady called and said an orange male tabby cat was hanging around her yard. Mother and I went to the lady's house and saw the cat.

"Is that Tinker?" Mother asked me.

That's not Tinker. "It's him," I said.

Mother gave the lady a five-dollar bill, I grabbed the stranger, and we went home. I kept the stranger locked in the garage a few days and fed him, so he wouldn't stray. I felt guilty about deceiving Mother, but I knew if I didn't keep the stranger, I'd never get another pet. The stranger didn't have Tinker's cuddly personality, but he took to me in his own way.

A couple of weeks went by, and Mrs. Wilson came to our door. She said, "I came to tell you that Tinker has been staying at your cottage, and I've been feeding him."

Tinker's okay. . . . Oh, OH.

"JANICE," Mother said. "You pulled a fast one." Then she smiled. *Thank Goodness she isn't really mad. But Daddy is not going to be amused.*

The cottage was two-and-a-half miles from the house-in-town, and the cross-country route was through woods, fields, and bogs. *How did Tinker manage that?*

Mother drove me out to Harbor Point, and there he was—my sweet Tinker—sitting on the cottage step. *I have two cats.*

When Daddy found out he said, "You couldn't recognize your own cat?"

"They look alike," was all I could say.

"MY."

I named the stranger, "Winker." My two male cats didn't like each other, but learned to tolerate each other's presence. It wasn't long before Tinker went missing again. It took him three days to

You probably can't tell them apart, either.

show up at the cottage. Mother and I brought him back to town. He went right back to the cottage, so I gave him to Mrs. Wilson. About a month later, she stopped in at the house-in-town to tell me that Tinker had gone missing. This time, he was never seen again. I missed him dearly. Unlike me, Winker was glad to be an only.

41
She Told Him

That summer, Mother let me chauffeur her around in the Cadillac with its automatic transmission to practice driving. In the fall, Daddy insisted that I learn to drive his new 1963 Corvette Sting Ray. It was a split-window coupe. I loved the style of that car. The flow of the front fenders, and the spine that ran between the rear split windows and on down the tail of the car, just like a stinger, made the Vette look very much like a sting ray. *I like style in everything, not just clothes. That must be part of who I am. The real me.*

Learning to drive the Corvette

"Step on the clutch, put the car in first, let off the brake, and step on the accelerator as you let up the clutch," Daddy said.

Say that again? I flooded the engine. I ground the gears. I made the Vette hop down the road like a toad. I drove it across the center line and onto the opposite shoulder. I gritted my teeth waiting for the yelling and cursing to begin. Instead, Daddy just said, "Well, at least we aren't in the ditch. Try that again."

I tried again. And again. And again. When I finally got it, I fell in love with driving the Vette. It responded to the slightest tap on the gas pedal or twitch of the steering wheel. *Being Doctor Beare's Daughter is amazing. Being her can almost drown out that little voice that lives deep inside that sometimes says,* "I'm here."

How About That?

I'm too stupid to understand equations. I got a D on my first algebra test my sophomore year. Daddy looked at my test and said, "MY." Then he tried to explain the logic behind each problem to me. When I didn't understand his explanations, he threw up his hands and started yelling, "SHIT. I'm trying to EXPLAIN this to you. How can you NOT UNDERSTAND?"

I'm not smart enough to do algebra. I'm not even smart enough to follow Daddy's logic when he explains it to me. Every one of our sessions ended with Daddy disgusted, and me terrified I'd never be able to get it. *Doctor Beare's Daughter would get it.*

Finally Daddy threw up his hands and said, "I'm done."

He's giving up on me.

Then he said, "On Saturday morning, you're to take your algebra book and go see Mrs. Brady." Mrs. Brady was one of Daddy's patients and a retired math teacher. She lived a few blocks north of us.

On Saturday, I walked to her house under the big elms that lined

North Main. It was a beautiful fall day, and the air was filled with the acrid smoke coming from the heaps of burning leaves along the curb. I would have enjoyed it all, except for the weight of failure that lay on me. Mrs. Brady met me on her porch, and we sat outside at a small table. She began by walking me through a problem. It seemed very simple and . . . it was exactly the way Sister explained it in class.

"That's not correct," I told her.

"I assure you that it is," she said.

"But . . . it can't be that easy."

"Why not?"

"Because algebra is hard, and I'm not smart."

Mrs. Brady patted me on the hand and said, "You're very smart. The problem is that you don't seem to know it."

I felt my eyes widen and my jaw drop. I hadn't been able to solve algebra equations because I thought the correct answer couldn't be so easy. So I *made* it complicated and then guessed. Mrs. Brady worked with me for an hour, then said, "We're done. You don't need to come back. You'll be fine."

I was fine—I could solve equations easily, and aced all my algebra tests. *If I'm so goddamned smart, then why do I still have trouble adding columns of numbers?*

I'm Going to Be Expelled

Then came Latin II. I hated that class because Sister Adelmar had it in for me. If I made the smallest mistake, she made me stand in front of class. She said, "Either you're too busy to study, or you just don't want to learn. Now which one is it?"

Why does she do that to me? I'm not even failing, and there are other kids in the class who are. She doesn't embarrass them.

I had a few mistakes on a writing test one day, and she made me stand while she read every sentence on my paper and then called on the other students to tell what I did wrong. She handed me my test and said, "If you can't do better tomorrow, I'm going to expel you from this class."

A razor-sharp pain in my chest spread down my arms. The other students looked shocked. I think they felt sorry for me. *I need two years of Latin to get into college. If she expels me from class, I'll never get in. That would be a disaster for Daddy.*

When I got home from school, I went straight to my room and got out my Latin book. The pain in my chest and arms was getting worse, but I kept going until Mother called me. "I want you to go count the cars," she said.

I ran outside, counted the cars, and headed back to my room.

"Wait a minute," Mother said. "You haven't set the table."

I practically threw the dishes on the table, then said, "I have to get back to my books."

"What have you been studying for the last two hours?"

"Latin. If I make a mistake writing sentences tomorrow, I'm going to be expelled from the class."

"You won't be expelled from class for making a mistake."

"Oh yes, I will. Sister Adelmar said so. I have to study."

When Mother called me for dinner, I ate as fast as I could and asked to be excused, so I could get back to the Latin. A few minutes later, she came into my room and said, "I wouldn't study too hard at that if I were you."

"I have to learn this by tomorrow."

"Don't worry about it," she said and went back downstairs.

A while later Daddy called up to me, "Come down here. I want to talk to you." The pain in my chest and arms ran up my neck into my head. *My God. She told him.* I had to walk my hands down the railing to keep myself from falling down the stairs. Daddy was sitting in the living room waiting for me.

"Sit down, Kiddo." I sat. "You're no longer taking Latin II. Tomorrow you will be in Sister Wilhelmine's German I class. Then, next year, you'll take German II."

"But I can't get into college without two years of Latin."

Daddy slapped the table like I was trying his patience. "I just talked to Sister Paulissa and Sister Wilhelmine. They assured me that while two years of a foreign language is a requirement, most colleges no longer require that it be Latin. You're two weeks behind in German class, but Sister Wilhelmine will help you catch up."

Daddy went over to the convent. At night. Were the nuns in their nighties? Did Daddy see them with their veils off? "But Daddy, Sister Adelemar . . ."

Daddy's blue eyes turned to grey steel. "You won't be having any more classes with Sister Adelmar. Now go watch TV with your mother."

Sister Wilhelmine

I felt the pain drain away. *Daddy is powerful, and he uses that power to protect me.* At school the next day, when I passed Sister Adelmar in the hall, she looked the other way. Doctor Beare's Daughter stuck her nose in the air and pranced on down the hall.

42
A Wonderful Idea

I Wish We Had Built that Bomb Shelter

On the evening of Monday, October 22, 1962, Daddy called Mother and me into the living room and turned on the Scott. "President Kennedy is going to address the nation."

Daddy settled in his chair, Mother sat on the sofa, and I plopped down on the carpet. We listened to Kennedy, in his Massachusetts accent. "Within the past week, unmistakable evidence has established the fact that a series of offensive missile sites is now in preparation on Cuba. The purpose of these bases can be none other than to provide a nuclear strike capability against the Western Hemisphere."

My heart was playing tiddlywinks.

He went on to say that the Soviets had been lying to the United States about the buildup.

My heart was playing hopscotch.

Kennedy continued, saying that the United States was going to blockade Cuba to prevent the Soviets from bringing in any more military equipment. He said that any missile launched from Cuba would result in "a full retaliatory response" on Russia.

My heart was playing leapfrog. *We're on the brink of nuclear war with Russia.*

At school, everyone tiptoed through the day. The nuns began each class with a prayer that Russia would back down. No one in the entire country felt safe. *Now they all know what it feels like to be me.*

Two days later, Khrushchev called the U.S. blockade an act of aggression and said Russian ships would proceed to Cuba. It seemed that only a U.S. attack on Cuba would remove the missiles. The news, that night, listed places in the U.S. that Russia would likely target, including Wright Patterson Air Force Base in Dayton. My heart was doing jumping jacks. *That's only eighty miles from here. I wish we had built that bomb shelter. Please, God. Don't let me die before I can grow up.* The entire world perched on a cliff until October 28, when Khrushchev announced the missiles would be removed. Only then did my heart reset itself.

Muriel

One November Sunday afternoon while Mother napped, Daddy said we were going for a ride in the country. I was curious because there were no drag races that late in the year. We drove out west of town and turned in at a barn next to a field of Hereford cows. There was no farmhouse, but next to the barn stood a shed with a door and one small window. Smoke swirled out of a stack in the roof. I followed Daddy up to the door, where he knocked. *Who's living in this little shed?*

Jerry, the butcher from the IGA grocery down Wayne Street where Daddy bought our meat, opened the door. Daddy and I squeezed into the shed with its wood-burning stove, two chairs, and a small desk. Rosettes, and photos of Arabian horses adorned the walls. Daddy asked Jerry to show me his Arabs, and he took us to the barn. Three box stalls held two elegant mares and a magnificent stallion. Jerry asked me, "Have you ever ridden English?"

"Only Western."

"Would you like to try an English saddle on Muriel?" He gestured to one of the mares.

Yes, yes, YES. "Please."

Muriel had a sleek dapple-gray coat and the refined dish-face of an Arab. Jerry tacked up Muriel and rode her around the barnyard to settle her down. Then he hopped off and boosted me onto her. I felt like I was ascending into heaven. The English saddle was small and light, and there was no horn. I had to rely almost completely on my own balance. I rode Muriel around the barnyard and then up the road a ways. On the way back, I kicked Muriel into a canter. When I got near Daddy and Jerry, I pulled her up. She hopped into a halt so suddenly that my left foot, which wasn't secure in the stirrup, flew up over her back, and continued on down to the ground, causing me to lose the right stirrup and land on both feet in a flying dismount. *Wow. That was fancy, even though it was an accident and could have ended badly.*

"Told you she could ride," Daddy said, proudly.

Back in the barn, Jerry whispered to me, "I suspect that next time you will keep both heels down in the stirrups."

There's going to be a next time! I adored Jerry for keeping our secret from Daddy. After that, on winter Sunday afternoons, Daddy sat with Jerry in the tack room, talking and drinking coffee, while I meandered over Jerry's acres on Muriel. No one watching. No one judging. It gave me the same precious feeling of freedom as when I explored the wild places along the lakeshore alone in the Penn Yan. *I wish I could ride horses every day, far away from my parents' eyes and all those other Celina eyes, too. I got a wonderful idea.*

The next day, I told my parents I wanted to go out West that summer to a camp where I could ride horses. Mother got that hurt look in her eyes and said, "You want to go away and leave me? How can you stand to do that?"

I thought she was going to cry, but Daddy ended the conversation by saying, "Your mother and I will talk about it."

A few days later, I asked him, "Did you and Mother talk about camp?"

"What camp?"

"I want to go to camp out West and ride horses this summer."

"Your mother and I will talk about it."

Days later, I asked Mother, "Did you and Daddy talk about camp?"

"Oh, we assumed you forgot all about that."

"Oh please, Mom." *She likes it when I call her that.* "I'll be sixteen in June. I'm old enough to be away from home. And I love riding horses." I was watching her closely, expecting her to be hurt. She said nothing and left the room. *Well, that's the end of that.*

A couple of days later Mother handed me a brochure. The headline said: Teton Valley Ranch Camp, Jackson Hole, Wyoming. There were pictures of boys and girls riding horses and hiking in the wilderness. The first five weeks of summer were for boys, and the second five weeks for girls. *Five weeks out West, riding horses where nobody knows me.*

I threw my arms around her. "Oh. Thank you, Mom! This place is perfect."

"I'll show it to your father, and we'll talk about it tonight." She looked like she might cry, but then she didn't.

Poor Mother. I wish she was happier.

That night, I crammed myself against my parents' door. *What about camp?* I listened to Daddy's description of amputating the arm of a farmer who had fallen into the corn picker. *But what about camp?* Then came a discussion of a patient whose lungs were filling up with sawdust from working on the sander at the furniture factory. *But what about camp?* I had to hear the shocking truth about a classmate of mine who had a venereal disease before Mother finally said, "What are we going to do about Janice and camp?"

Daddy: "It would be educational."

Mother: "She'll miss me too much. She'll be homesick."

Daddy: "That's a very expensive camp. She'll be with girls from the wealthiest families in America. She could make lifelong friends with some of those girls. Those girls have brothers. Send in the deposit."

I hopped, skipped, and jumped back to my room. *I can't wait until summer.*

43
A Fresh Mound of Dirt

Aunt Mildred was staying with me in February (now 1963) while my parents were in Florida. Late afternoon on a Monday, I fetched *The Daily Standard* from the porch. It was soggy from snow, so I opened it flat on the kitchen counter to dry. I caught the words: "Harold Putoff." "Killed." "Accident." My hands shot to my face and covered my eyes. *NO. Not Harold. Not my grade-school hero who always saved me a seat on the school bus.* I peered through my fingers at the paper. *It's true.*

Harold had been on a date with his girlfriend. While driving home late at night, he had gone off the road. He wasn't found until the morning, when a motorist saw the wrecked car about four hundred feet from the road in a field. Harold had been thrown twenty feet from the car. His skull was fractured. It was thought he'd fallen asleep at the wheel. Harold was eighteen. *Did he die instantly? Or had he lain there for hours, knowing he was dying and there was no one to help?* That old familiar feeling of something precious lost seeped into my bones. I knew it would lay there a long time.

Some days later, I walked downtown to the flower shop and bought a rose. When I came out of the shop, it was snowing. I pulled up the hood of my carcoat, then walked a mile up North Main, across Summit Street to the Catholic cemetery. I wandered around, looking for a fresh mound of dirt. I found one, almost snowed over. There was no marker yet, but it had to be Harold because there were other Putoff graves there. I laid the rose on the mound in the snow and said, "Goodbye, and thank you, Harold."

Before I left the cemetery, I had a quick visit with Joe, Nora, Uncle Charlie, Earl Dull, and Mr. Kohnen. I thought of Larry, lying in the cemetery in Neptune, and Grandpa, in his grave in Versailles. *A ripped-out chunk of my heart lies with each of them.*

44
Oh, Shush

Mrs. Eby, the music teacher from Celina High, came to IC High to teach music. We had never before had any extracurriculars except for boys' basketball. I loved to sing, so I tried out for choir. Mrs. Eby told me I had a lovely voice and gave me little solo parts. A tingle ran through me. *I'm good at something.* Mrs. Eby went to see Daddy and told him she wanted to train me. He agreed to private lessons. I jingled inside.

I adored Mrs. Eby. She was a very large woman who dressed flamboyantly and wore spike heels covered in peacock feathers and very unusual hats. Everyone called her a "character," but at the same time, they seemed to like and respect her. I envied her being able to be her odd self in front of everybody and be liked because of it. *I think that I might be a "character," too, but The Eyes of Celina want Doctor Beare's Daughter, so that's what I have to give them. Doctor Beare's Daughter is special and she gets to do special things, like drive her own boat, go away to camp with horses, and take private voice lessons.* That little voice inside me whispered, "But all that doesn't make up for having to give *me* up." *Oh, shush.*

Mrs. Eby entered me in the solo and ensemble competition in Lima. I rode there on a public-school bus with her other vocal students and the band class from Celina High. Everyone was in high spirits, and some of the band students got out their instruments and played us down the road. I tapped—hands and feet—to the beat. *I wish I could go to Celina High and be part of all this. When I go to college, I'm going to a big university to make up for what I'm missing in high school. I'll study music or fashion design. Oh, right. Daddy won't let me learn how to sew. And God forbid! that Doctor Beare's Daughter would want to be a musician.*

I was very nervous to sing in front of a judge, but I gave it my best. I earned an excellent rating. *It's not as good as a superior, but I'll take it.* On my evaluation sheet, the judge wrote many suggestions to work on, then praised the quality of my voice. I got home just as Mother was putting dinner on the table. I put my evaluation sheet down on the counter and sat down to eat. Daddy said, "Did you have a good time with Mrs. Eby today?"

"It was a competition," I explained. "I got an excellent rating." I grabbed my evaluation sheet off the counter and gave it to him.

He glanced at it, put it aside, and said, "I'm proud of you Kiddo. I'm glad you're having fun."

Daddy thinks music is something to do for fun. It's fun, alright, but it's much more than that, too.

45
Tall, Colorful Flags

One May afternoon, when I came home from school, I saw a sporty, white convertible with the top down parked in the alley behind our house. I hurried inside to find out who was visiting, but it was just Mother and Daddy. "Whose car is in the alley?"

Daddy said, "Isn't it a beauty?"

I nodded.

He went on. "It's this year's model, and the Cadillac dealer got it as a trade-in. He brought it over to see if you might like it." He tossed me the keys.

My heart rode up an elevator. *I have my own car? I don't even have my driver's license yet.* I looked at the fancy keys in my hand, then at Daddy.

"Go on, Kiddo. Have a look at your car."

I raced out to the alley and jumped in the car. It had a red-leather interior with low-slung bucket seats and a center console. It was dazzling. It was an Oldsmobile Starfire. I had never seen one in Celina before. *Who buys their fifteen-year-old kid a snazzy convertible before they even have their driver's license? Daddy, that's who. He buys it for Doctor Beare's Daughter.*

~~~

On my sixteenth birthday, Mother went with me in the Starfire so I could take my driving test. The written test was easy. The driving test was easy. The parking test was impossible. I had to parallel park the Starfire in a space between four tall, colorful flags without touching them. The Starfire was almost the size of the space itself. I had three tries. I failed all three. When Daddy came home to the cottage that night, I had to tell him that I flunked my driver's test.

"THE HELL YOU SAY. I taught you to drive myself. You can drive hell out of the Vette, the Cadillac, and the Olds. How did you manage to flunk your goddamn driver's test?" His neck grew stiff as he leaned toward me. His eyes hardened into stone cannons that had me in their sights.

I felt like ducking. Instead I said, "I didn't flunk driving. I flunked parallel parking—I couldn't park between the flags."

He pulled his neck and eyes off me and said, "Hmmm."

The next day, when he came home to the cottage for lunch, Daddy said, "You're going to drive me to the office this afternoon in the Starfire."

"What am I supposed to do at the house-in-town all afternoon?"

"You'll see." When I was driving up Main Street, Daddy said, "Drive on past the house and turn left on Wayne."

After I made the turn, I saw ahead of me four tall, colorful flags marking out a parking space next to the curb—in front of the office, right across the street from the convent, and in direct view of the high school. Daddy gestured for me to pull up at the curb. He said, "While I'm working, you will practice."

My heart was a buckeye being thrown in the lake. *He's making me practice parallel parking in front of the patients as they come and go. In front of the nuns at the convent. In front of anyone who happens to drive by on Main Street. In front of everyone coming or going to the high school. The boys are in there practicing basketball.* "Can I practice out at Harbor Point? Can I practice in the alley? Can I take the Vette for my next parking test?" *The Vette is so small, parking it would be easy.* Daddy didn't answer me. He had already disappeared into the office.

I put the top up on the car, thinking that might somehow make me less noticeable. *That's dumb. I have the only Starfire in town.* Then there were those colorful flags waving in the breeze. *They look exactly like the ones at the Bureau of Motor Vehicles. Of course. He borrowed them.*

I parked my car. And parked my car. And parked my car. Then I parked my car. I knocked over the flags. I backed up onto the curb. I kept at it until the engine overheated and died. The high school boys laughed and pointed at me. The patients gaily waved. Even the nuns came out on the front step of the convent across the street to watch for a few minutes. I was used to the Eyes of Celina watching me, but they were boring in that day. I was devastated by my public humiliation— at first. But as I learned how to maneuver my car between those flags, a feeling of pride came creeping over my shame. I got so I could park that car in between those flags in the blink of an eye. I would wait until one of the boys from school drove by, then whip the car in between the flags. *I bet he can't do that.* When I went back for my parking retest, Doctor Beare's Daughter passed on her first try.

46
Barrel Racing

On the day I left for camp, we got up very early. Mother and Daddy were taking me to Toledo, where I would catch a train to Chicago, then another train to Wyoming. I dressed in my jeans, western shirt, cowboy boots and hat. I picked up my duffel and looked in the mirror. A cowgirl looked back at me. *Is that me? It sure-as-shooting is, pardner.*

At the train station in Toledo, Daddy had a pinched smile on his face, and Mother was crying. I gave her a big hug and told her I would miss her. The sparks of joy I felt at leaving home were near extinguished by Mother's tears. Not only had I hurt her by wanting to go away, I was leaving her at the mercy of Daddy. The guilt I felt was almost enough to make me get back in the Cadillac instead of on the train. *Almost.* She was still crying when I waved to her through the train window as it left the station.

In early afternoon, I arrived at Union Station in Chicago, a palace with soaring pillars and statues of Greek goddesses. The enormous waiting room was filled with rows of wooden benches like church pews. *How will I find the other campers?* I walked into the great hall. There, a barrel-vaulted skylight soared a hundred feet overhead. The sun's streaming rays shone down on a group of cowgirls, perched on a pile of duffels, causing all their western hats to give off a golden glow. It was a breathtaking sight. *I'm living a dream—a golden dream.*

When I joined the group, I was about to tell everyone my name, then hesitated. *Do I want to be stupid, sad, lonely "Janice" who has no common sense and crazy ideas? Would I rather be smart, rich, "Doctor Beare's Daughter" who drives a hydroplane and a flashy car and has traveled the entire U.S.? . . . I don't really like either one of them.* "Hi. My name is Jan."

When I got to the ranch, I was assigned to a cabin and got a top bunk. After lights out, I rolled over, the springs let loose, and my mattress, with me on it, landed on the girl below me. My arms and legs were everywhere. I could feel squirming from underneath my mattress, so I rolled onto the floor. Then I picked up my mattress to see the small blonde girl struggling to sit up. *Thank God she's alive.* Daddy had been right about one thing. Donna Yordy and I would become lifelong friends. Daddy had been right about another thing. There were girls at camp from some of the wealthiest families in America, and they had brothers. However, none of those girls had the bunk underneath mine.

With Donna on the front porch of our cabin.

One of the girls at camp had a guitar, and I would go to her cabin to listen to her play and sing. At our evening campfires, the counselors played guitar while we sang camp songs. *I want to play guitar.*

I learned to throw a lariat and compete on a roping team. I also learned how to ride the barrels. I competed in both events at the Sunday rodeos. *Dreams can come true.*

Slept with a Skeleton

The best thing I got to do at camp was a five-day pack trip on horseback, deep into the Teton Wilderness. We rode all day, through lodgepole pine forests, aspen groves, and across steeps covered with sage and Indian paintbrush. We saw moose, elk, pronghorns, mule deer, big-horn sheep, marmots, eagles, and other wildlife in their habitats. We were so deep in the wilderness that there were no sounds of cars or planes, just the music of the mountains—the bellow of an elk, the breath of the wind sliding through the aspens, the whoosh of a fast-flowing creek, the howling and yipping of a pack of coyotes. To this we brought our own sounds—the creaking of saddle leather, the hollow plodding of our horses' hooves, the crackle of a campfire, the sizzle of bacon in a cast-iron frying pan. *This is what peace sounds like.*

In the evenings, we cooked over a campfire and washed our dishes in a creek. The water was so clean, we drank and filled our canteens from the mountain streams. *The water and the air taste cleaner than in Celina.*

We slept on the ground in our sleeping bags, and I drifted asleep to the rustle of the night creatures in the bushes. One night I couldn't get comfortable in my bag. It was as if I was sleeping on rocks. When dawn came and I rolled up my bag, I saw that I had slept on top of the skeleton of a moose. *How many girls from Celina have slept with a skeleton? The Eyes of Celina can't see me here.* Sometimes I felt so free that I forgot that I had abandoned Mother.

In the Teton wilderness with the buckskin horse I rode for five days

When I was back at the ranch, I wrote to Mother every other day. She expected it. She wrote me daily. Even though I didn't like being reminded of home, I found myself looking forward to reading what she had to say. *It can't be that I miss her, can it? Yes, I miss her.*

At the final campfire, I cried. I was leaving behind "Jan," who dressed like the other campers, said anything she felt like saying, and no one told her, not even once, to be quiet.

When my parents picked me up at the train station in Toledo, the first thing Mother said was, "Did you miss me?"

"Yes." *Now I miss camp.*

The first thing I said to Daddy was, "I want a guitar."

47

Maybe Something Like...Jones

One Friday afternoon near the end of summer, I was sitting in front of the cottage, trying to figure out how to play chords on my new guitar, when a boy came walking down the seawall and said "hello." His name was Theo. He was fifteen—a year younger than me —and played guitar in a band in Dayton, where he lived. His family were weekend people on Harbor Point. He stayed to talk a while and show me some chords until Mother called me for dinner. *I met a boy in my own front yard.*

After dinner, Theo came to the door. Mother let him in, and he sat on the couch, next to me. I thought he wanted to play my guitar, so I got it out and handed it to him. He played a couple of songs but was acting nervous. He kept looking up at me while he was playing. After maybe ten minutes, a knock sounded on the kitchen door. It was Theo's mother. She came into the living room and said to him, "What are you doing? I've been waiting in the car for you."

Waiting for what?

Then she turned to my mother and said, "My son came over to ask your daughter to go to the movies with him." A thrill-chill ran up my frame. "I've been waiting to see if Janice could go, because I was going to drive them to town." Then she turned to Theo and said, "Well?"

You're kidding.

Theo put down the guitar, looked at the floor and muttered, "Would you like to go to the movies?"

I'm going on a date. What will Daddy say about this? "I'd like that." I tried to toss off my words nonchalantly, as if I was asked out on dates all the time.

Theo's mother drove us into Celina to the theater and dropped us off. Midway through the film, Theo took my hand and held it for the rest of the movie. It felt nice. For a little while I felt like my own person. When the show was over, Daddy was waiting in the Caddy to take us home. *I've been on a real date.*

Lying in bed that night, my last thoughts before falling asleep were: *Somewhere in America, a boy, my age, is growing up. He has no idea that someday he will meet me and we will get married. I wish I knew who he is and where he is. I wonder what his name is—the name that he will give me? Maybe something like . . . Jones. It would go really well with Jan.*

I dated Theo the rest of the summer. Since he was still fifteen, I drove us in the Starfire. *It feels wonderful to have a boyfriend.* I wondered what my parents thought about my dating, especially Daddy, but they said nothing about it. Like it wasn't happening. Maybe they were amused and didn't take my dating Theo as anything important. When summer was over, Theo's family closed their cottage for the winter, and I moved back to town. Theo and I agreed to write. *I grew up a little this summer.*

48
Wallflowers

September 1963. I had just started my junior year and decided to go to the school dance on a Friday night. I wore my A-line skirt of sage speckled wool and matching vest with corded leather seams. I pulled my hair up on top of my head and took care with my makeup —just light touches to set off my eyes and lips. I looked in the mirror and saw the result of everything I had learned from *Seventeen* magazine and from watching the popular girls at school.

The girl looking back at me had her own style—tailored and trim— the leather cording adding a bit of edge that was distinctly *me.* I had even learned to love my hair. Mostly because a Harbor Point woman asked me for a lock of it, saying, "I always tell my hairdresser that I want hair the color of Doctor Beare's daughter. She never gets it right. Now I'm going to take her a sample of the real thing."

I stand out because of my hair and my height. Since they're always going to look, Doctor Beare's Daughter is going to give them something worth looking at. I went off to the dance, hoping a miracle would happen and a boy would ask me to dance. I should have known better. It turned out like all the other school dances—I sat on the lowest bleacher while the popular girls in my class danced with the boys. I was that thing that every girl dreaded being: a wallflower. There were other wallflowers there—a line of them, also sitting on the lowest bleacher, but I didn't feel welcome to sit with them, so I sat several yards away. *High school is passing me by while I sit on the sidelines, watching everyone else have fun. What do the other girls have that I don't? I guess that smiling at the other kids in the library isn't enough. I'm going to have to make myself speak to them at other times, too. I don't know if I can do it.*

Always Lurking

On Monday morning, the halls of IC High were swarming with students getting books, but there was no slamming of locker doors, no chatter, and no shuffling of feet. Everyone moved as ghosts— the silence was shocking. Senior David Fisher was dead. His cousin, freshman Bob Braun, lay in a Lima hospital with massive head injuries,

and my classmate Tom Link was in the hospital with multiple injuries.

David had driven out in the country to pick up Bob and Tom to drive them to the dance. The boys were heading back to Celina on Mud Pike after dark. A semi was backing up across the pike onto a side road. The trailer

Celina Youth Dies In Crash; Shelby Countians Unhurt

CELINA — An 18-year-old Celina youth was killed and two others injured, one critically, when the car in which they were riding collided with a tractor-trailer outfit west of here Friday evening.

Dead at the scene of the accident was Dave Fisher, son of Mr. and Mrs. Clifford Fisher, of 117 South Buckeye street, Celina.

In critical condition at St. Ritas hospital at Lima, with serious head injuries, is Paul Robert Braun, 16, of R. R. 5, Celina.

In Gibbons Hospital here, with less serious injuries, is Thomas Link, 16, also of R. R. 5, Celina. Both Braun and Link were passengers in the car driven by Fisher.

Mercer county sheriff's deputies report that the accident occurred shortly before 7:30 p.m. at the intersection of Mud pike and Fleetwood road, approximately two

miles slightly northwest of Celina.

The tractor-trailer outfit was being driven by Donald Bernard Sharp, 51, of Houston. The outfit was owned by Norton Kirk, of Anna, Shelby county. Neither was injured in the accident.

According to investigating officers, Sharp was westbound on Mud pike and had stopped at the Fleetwood road intersection, and preparing to turn around, had started to back across the highway into the latter road.

The auto carrying the three youths was eastbound in Mud road, heading toward Celina.

As the tractor-trailer outfit swung across the highway the passenger car plowed into it, passing under the larger vehicle between the wheels of the tractor and trailer portion.

The auto was completely demolished by the force of the impact.

Sidney *Daily News* September 21, 1963 Reprinted with permission was blocking the pike, but the cab's headlights were beaming straight ahead. To David it must have looked like the truck was approaching in the other lane. David drove under the trailer and was killed instantly.

I, and many other students, attended David's funeral on Tuesday. Tom Link recovered quickly and we learned that Bob Braun was going to live. *Death pounces when you least expect it.*

49
Can't Believe What I'm Hearing

Fire Drill

All that fall of 1963, Joyce and I went to the Celina High football games on Friday nights. I loved sitting in the bleachers and cheering on the Bulldogs. When they scored a touchdown, we waved pompoms and screamed. Screaming was something I seldom got to do, and often, before the game was over, I'd screamed myself hoarse.

One night at an after-game dance in the fieldhouse, a boy named George asked me to dance. Somehow, I managed to follow him, and he asked me for another dance. *This would never happen at IC.*

The next afternoon, as I drove down Livingston Street, I noticed in the rearview mirror that a boy on a motorcycle was following me. It was George. His motorcycle stalled out at every stop sign. He had to get off and run, while pushing the motorcycle to get it going, then hop back on. I felt amused and admired. He was trying so hard to keep up that I drove slowly. When I lost him at Main Street, I was disappointed.

Then it started happening more often; a boy in a car would see me in traffic and follow me for a while. He would eventually give a honk and a wave and go his own way. I enjoyed this game and always waved back. They were Celina High boys and boys from other parts of Mercer County. *They see Doctor Beare's Daughter in her convertible. The boys of IC never follow me because they see Beare, the snob.*

I met a new friend at the football games. Eleanor went by the nickname "Leo." I envied her because, even though she was Catholic, she went to Celina High. She was a petite girl who weighed ninety-five pounds. She had a goal to weigh 100 pounds. For several weeks she had two chocolate milkshakes a day plus all the French fries she could stuff herself with and made it to 101 pounds. She couldn't hang onto it, though. All that rich, fatty food made her sick. She was soon back to ninety-five pounds. *Leo's such a character.*

Leo introduced me to her friends: Frieda, Dana, and Jim. They took me into their fold, and we were an odd gang of four girls and one boy. I was drawn to Jim because he was funny and had red hair like me. On Saturday nights, the five of us cruised Main Street in the Starfire to see who else was out and about. We drove through downtown, turned around at the lake, drove back through downtown, passed the house-in-town, and turned around in the parking lot of the bowling alley, only to head back downtown.

When we stopped for a red light, Jim might yell, "Fire drill." Then we jumped out of the car, ran around it, and jumped back in before the light turned green. Whoever jumped into the driver's seat would end up driving the car. Sometimes four of us ended up in front, which was hilarious because of the Starfire's bucket seats. If the light changed too quickly, a couple of us had to jump on the trunk as the driver pulled out. Once, I drove off, leaving Jim in the middle of the street. *I love being silly. I wish Jim would ask me out. Two redheads. Boyfriend and girlfriend. Wouldn't that be something?*

Drag Race

I was sitting at a red light in front of our house one Saturday afternoon, when a car pulled up beside me and revved its engine. Excitement rose in me. I got a lot of challenges from boys who wanted to see if their cars could get off the line faster than the Starfire. I knew what to do. I stared straight ahead and revved my engine back at them. The light turned green. I peeled out, laid rubber, and shot through the intersection, but the other car wasn't with me. I saw it in the rearview mirror. It was a police cruiser. The exhilaration of racing soured in my mouth. I stomped the brakes, then crept slowly up the street. The patrol car passed me. The officers were having a big laugh. I felt a surge of relief. *I'm not going to get a ticket. Of course not. The police officers know Daddy. He takes them for rides out in the country in the Vette.*

The following day at the dinner table, Daddy said, "The next time you want to race the cops do it out in the country, not in front of the house." *He's proud of me for being like him. Next time I'll look before I race.*

Can't They Show a Soap Opera?

On Friday, November 22, 1963, I was taking a biology test in Sister Hilaria's class when Sister Paulissa's voice came over the PA. "President Kennedy has been shot." My whole body turned cold. Sister went on. "He was riding in an open car in a motorcade through Dallas, Texas. Governor Connally, who was with the president, has also been shot. They were taken to a nearby hospital. That is all we know at this time."

There were gasps, and the sounds of pencils hitting papers or the floor. *I can't believe what I'm hearing. This can't be true.* Sister Hilaria said, "Let's bow our heads and pray for our president and the doctors who are taking care of him."

I bowed my head, but I couldn't pray. *Who shot President Kennedy? Why?*

Then Sister said, "Finish writing your tests until we learn more. It's best to keep occupied."

How can I write a test when I'm freezing? Poor Mrs. Kennedy. She has two small children. She lost another baby in August that only lived two days. Now this. When time was up, Sister Hilaria collected the test papers. I hadn't answered a single question since the announcement. Now, the PA again: "Two priests just came out of the Dallas hospital and talked to reporters. The priests said they had given the president the Last Rites. They told the reporters that President Kennedy has . . . he has . . . just . . . just . . . died."

I felt like I had turned into an ice sculpture *NO. PLEASE, GOD, NO.* After a few seconds of silence, the PA said, "This has not yet been confirmed by the hospital. School is now dismissed for the day, so you can go home to be with your families. Students who ride the bus will please go to the auditorium to wait for your busses. Father will be there leading the rosary while you wait."

In the halls, students were milling about crying or praying out loud or saying things like "How could this happen?" or "Is our country safe?" One nun was passing out tissues.

I walked down the hall toward my locker to get my coat when the PA came on again. "It is now confirmed that President Kennedy has died."

My coat would be useless to warm me up. I walked on past my locker, out the back door of the school, and into the afternoon grey-ness that threatened to spit snow. I ran across the alley and into the house, where I found Mother and Aunt Mildred in the back room, watching Walter Cronkite on TV. I sat between them, hoping to get warm, and we watched as Walter Cronkite told us that the president had been shot in the head and the neck, and Governor Connally in the back. Governor Connally was expected to recover. Walter Cronkite was matter-of-fact in his reporting, but I could tell he was shaken as he kept taking off his glasses and putting them back on. He went on to report that Vice President Lyndon Johnson had been taken to a safe place.

This is just awful. What's happening to our country? Daddy came out of the office to watch with us for a bit. He said that some of the patients had left without seeing him, and others were gathered around the TV in the waiting room. We continued watching, and the report came in that a man named Lee Harvey Oswald had fired the shots that killed Kennedy from the Texas School Book Depository, where he worked. He had also shot and killed a policeman while trying to escape. He was finally caught in a Dallas theater. Oswald was a communist. *Is he part of a communist plot to take over our government? Is Russia behind this?*

Aunt Mildred stayed for dinner, but none of us were hungry. When we watched the evening news, we saw Lyndon Johnson being sworn in as president on Air Force One as it flew Kennedy's body back to Washington, DC. Standing next to Johnson was the president's wife, Jacqueline, who had been sitting next to her husband when he was shot. Her suit was splattered with her husband's blood and brains. She said, "Let them see what they have done to him." She spoke her mind in front of the whole world. *She's so brave. That's something I don't know how to be.*

The only thing on TV the entire weekend was the live coverage of Kennedy's flag-draped casket lying in state in the rotunda of the Capitol. Every time I turned on the TV, there was the casket and a long line of people walking past it. *Two whole days of looking at Kennedy's casket. This is all too much. Can't they show a soap opera or a sitcom or something? For just a little while?*

50
Let Me Have the Truth

Now Sing, Damnit

In December, our choir was giving a Christmas concert. Mrs. Eby said I was ready to sing an entire number by myself (this news raised the baby hairs on the back of my neck) and accompany myself on guitar (this news made my whole scalp tingle). I hoped that when my parents saw that I had been chosen to perform, they would be proud of me.

The auditorium was packed with parents when we filed in and took our places on the choir risers. I heard Mother's soft cough and located my parents in the audience. That cough had been with her so long now that it had become part of her.

After the choir sang some Christmas carols, Mrs. Eby announced my solo and gave me a nod. My legs grew shaky, but they managed to step down from the riser. I even managed to pick up my guitar and walk, front and center. Now my hands were shaking, too, and if not for the shoulder strap on my guitar, I would have dropped it. *I HAVE to perform well. My parents are sitting there. I would rather die than embarrass them in front of everyone. The first chord is C. Strum a C. Okay, now go to F. Now G. Now sing.* My whole body was trembling, my heart was running wild like a mouse being stalked by a cat, but my voice was steady and carried the rest of me along as I sang on. When I finished, there was much applause. I looked at my parents. Daddy was smiling wide, clapping, and nodding his head. He was proud of my singing and how I could play guitar and piano. There were other things I did that made him proud, too, like how I could ride a horse, how I could handle the corvette and the boats, how I could beat the boys at drag racing, and the way I dress when we go out. On the other hand, Mother was only sorta smiling, her hands in her lap. I couldn't think of anything that would make her truly proud of me.

Despises Catholics, but Loves Doctor Beare

It was my parents turn to host the annual New Year's Eve party to ring in 1964. Mother told me I could invite a friend. I knew instantly who I wanted to invite—gregarious, funny, and charming Jim—leader of the girl-pack. This was the perfect way to get a date with him. He was thrilled when I invited him. He said he'd never been to a big party before, and he'd heard that the parties at Doctor Beare's house were really something.

The night of the party, Jim came all dressed up and brought flowers to Mother. He mingled, talking to the adults, especially my "aunts." Then he whispered things to me like, "My word! That's the wife of the man who runs the furniture factory." or "I've never seen so many bottles of liquor before." or "Your Uncle Rock runs the bank!"

While Jim was bending the ear of one woman, she kicked off her high heels, saying, "These shoes are killing my bunions."

Jim said, "My Grandma has bunions. She soaks her feet in Epsom salt. You should try that."

Aunt LaVaun pulled me aside and said, "Your friend is quite the live wire." *That's Jim, all right.*

When the party was over in the wee hours of the new year, Jim thanked me for inviting him. He didn't have to say he had a wonderful time.

The following week Jim asked me out. He took me to Lima for dinner and a movie. Now it was my turn to be thrilled. We had a fun time together, and I hoped he would ask me out again. He didn't. He continued to hang out with me and the other girls like always and sincerely seemed to like me. I was puzzled and asked him about it.

He said, "I like you a lot, but I'm not allowed to date Catholics. You see, my grandma lives with us. She rules the house, and she despises Catholics."

"Then why did you ask me out?"

"Grandma said I had to take you out to pay you back for inviting me to the party at your house."

"Why did she let you come to the New Year's party in the first place?"

"Because you invited me to Doctor Beare's house. Grandma loves Doctor Beare. He saved her life—twice."

My.

I'll Do Anything.

In early January 1964, the surgeon general reported that smoking was the main cause of lung cancer and also caused heart disease. Daddy threw out his cigarettes. He told Mother that she had to quit, too. He said, "You need to get over that cough, and smoking is making it worse."

Mother stopped smoking—in front of Daddy. She only pretended to quit. Then I noticed that Daddy was pretending, too—pretending not to notice the smoke rolling out from under the door of the powder room when Mother was in there. He turned his head away from the glowing butts in the ashtrays. He ignored the stench in the Caddy that was getting worse instead of better.

Over the winter Mother's chronic cough got worse. She became so short of breath that she had trouble getting up the stairs. She was taking longer and longer naps and was still exhausted. She hid her symptoms the best she could from Daddy, which only worked because he was still looking the other way. I heard her crying through her closed door when she was "lying down." I overheard her telling Aunt Mildred that she thought she had lung cancer and was going to die. Then they both lit one up. *Mother is sick—maybe REALLY sick, and Daddy doesn't seem to want to know about it. Why do people turn their eyes away from the truth? I want to see trouble coming, so I can figure out how to make it miss me. I'm a hawk, my eyes constantly casting about from a high perch. My parents are ostriches with their heads in the ground. Sometimes they're such scary people to love that I wish they'd chosen a different "special" baby and left me in the Home for whoever happened by next.*

I think Mother would have gone on pretending she wasn't sick until she dropped dead, but Daddy finally had enough because one night at dinner he casually said to Mother, "I'm taking tomorrow off from the office and you and I are going to Dayton early in the morning." Then he looked at me and said, "And you're going to school as usual. Since we won't be back until evening, you will have dinner at Roberta's."

Mother opened her mouth to say something, but Daddy cut her off. "I've arranged an all-day consult for you with a specialist at the Dayton hospital. You will be having a lot of tests."

"Tests? I don't want any tests!"

"After the tests, we will see the specialist for the results."

"I don't want to go, Ralph." Mother said.

"I have it all set up. We're going to find out exactly what is wrong with you. All in one day."

"I don't want to die!" Mother cried. "But if I'm going to, I don't want to know about it." She started to sob. Then she looked at Daddy, tears flowing, eyes, beseeching, and said, "I'll do anything, Ralph—anything if I don't have to die. I'll quit smoking. *Anything!*"

My poor mother! I don't want you to die, either.

I couldn't pay attention in school the next day, and even taking Betsy for a walk at Roberta's didn't help. I was terrified that I was going to lose my mother. It was almost seven p.m. when my parents finally came to Roberta's to get me. Mother looked weary, but Daddy was smiling. He said that Mother had emphysema. If she stopped smoking, her lungs would clear themselves and her cough would go away. She also had prediabetes. She could prevent becoming diabetic if she followed a special diet. She had been given a second chance as long as she stuck to the program. *I'm not losing my mother.* I was so relieved that instead of riding home with my parents, I joyfully ran all the way across town.

Mother was so relieved. She followed the diet, and took a long walk every day. *She's trying hard.*

51

What Are We Going to Do About Janice?

But It's Sunday

Every Sunday after Mass, the popular girls in my class gathered in a circle on the church steps. On one particular Sunday, Mother said, "Go over there and join them. I'm tired of always being embarrassed because you aren't one of the popular crowd."

I felt like there were ants crawling up my neck. *What will they think if I do that?*

Mother got hold of my arm and her nails dug in. "Go on."

I'd rather jump into the sewer than go over there, but I can't disappoint Mother. I approached the girls and hovered just outside their circle. They saw me and clammed up, but after a few wide-eyed looks they went on talking about their plans for later. They decided to meet at the bowling alley at noon for lunch, then walk downtown to the movies. Then one of the girls said, "Janice, will you come with us?"

I can't believe it. My campaign to be friendlier in the library must be paying off. I want to go. "I have to check with my mother." *She's going to be so pleased.* I went over to her and said, "The girls are going to have lunch at the bowling alley and then go to a movie. They asked me to go along."

She looked like I had slapped her. "You know we always go to Koch's in St. Marys to eat at noon on Sundays."

I felt like kicking Mother in the shin, then felt guilty for having such a thought. I went back to the girls and told them I couldn't come.

Algae and Man

Sister Hilaria, my science teacher, said that every junior taking science had to create a science project, so I asked Daddy for suggestions. He pointed out that space travel was a hot topic. John Glenn had just become the first man to orbit Earth that February, and now the National Aeronautics and Space Administration was launching Project Apollo to put a man on the moon. Daddy said, "Man's ability to travel in space is limited by his ability to sustain himself in a spacecraft for long periods of time. Solve that one, Kiddo, if you can."

I called my project: *Algae and Man for Space Life.* I made a display showing how humans and algae could be a self-sustaining ecosystem aboard a spacecraft. My project earned a superior rating, which meant I would advance to the district science fair, held at Celina High.

My project was on display in the fieldhouse with the winners from all the high schools in Mercer County. My parents came that evening and strolled the fair. *I'm going to make them proud—especially Daddy, since he thought of the topic.* The judges were impressed with my project and gave me another superior rating. Now I would be presenting my project at the state science fair in Columbus, at Ohio State University. *I have a great project. Daddy was so smart to suggest it.* A win in Columbus would mean advancing to the national level in Washington, DC.

That night, I listened at my parents' door, hoping to hear them talk about how proud they were of me.

Mother: "What are we going to do about Janice? I suppose we're going to have to get her to Columbus."

That's a problem? Well, tit-and-shit banana split! It's not really blasphemy and it's a lot stronger than stupid God bless America. And I thought it up myself.

Daddy: "I have office hours on Saturday. I'll get Roberta and Urb to take her."

The idea of Mother driving me or Daddy leaving the office to Uncle Doc for the day didn't come up.

At the science fair in Columbus, there were proud parents everywhere. *My parents had to PAY someone to bring me.*

When the judges came to talk with me, I realized that if I won again, my parents would have a new "What-are-we-going-to-do-about-Janice?" problem. *Who are they going to pay to take me to Washington, DC?*

It was evident that the judges had a great first impression of my project. And so, on my presentation, I looked down instead of at them. I answered the questions with less than complete explanations. I made sure that I didn't advance. *I just solved the next "What-are-we-going-to-do-about-Janice?" problem.*

All Girls and Run by the Nuns

In the early spring of my junior year, it was time to decide where I would go to college. I wanted desperately to go to Ohio State, study fashion or drama, and get lost in that big and busy campus. But Daddy gave me the terrible awful news that I had to go to a Catholic, all-girls college, run by the nuns. Disappointment sprang up inside me like a geyser. *GOD, NO. PLEASE, NO. I didn't get to go to Celina High. Now I'm not even going to get to go to a co-ed college. He might as well send me to a convent.* I was determined not to let him see me cry, even though I was crying all over the place inside. I felt powerless over my life. *Daddy owns me and there isn't a damn thing I can do about it.*

I chose Marygrove College in Detroit because it was far enough from Celina that no one there would know me, and because it was right down the street from the University of Detroit that had boys and social events. Daddy said I should be a nurse or a teacher because they could always get a job if their husbands died. Not for me. I decided to get a degree in social work. It was not as good as fashion or acting, but at least it wasn't nursing or teaching. Daddy reluctantly agreed, and I knew it was all I was going to get away with. *I have the rest of my junior year and all next year before I go to Marygrove. If I have to sequester myself with the nuns at Marygrove, at least I will be living away from home and can say what I think while I'm there.*

52
The Streets of Celina

*C*ruising with Leo on Saturday nights was a good way to meet boys. Driving the Starfire with its top down along Main Street was like dragging a silver minnow lure through a school of hungry bass. Sometimes boys followed us for several blocks; other times we pulled over and talked to them in the parking lot of the bowling alley under the big lights.

They see me as Doctor Beare's Daughter—the redhead who drives the flashy car. They want to meet me, but they don't ask me out. Why not? And how am I getting away with meeting them? It's like The Eyes

The silver minnow lure

of Celina are too sleepy to pay attention to Doctor Beare's Daughter on Main Street after dark on Saturday nights. Being chased by boys is fun. I feel pretty and part of life. I feel like I'm dipping my toes in the rolling ocean, when I only dangled them in a stagnant pond before.

One night, a couple of guys in their twenties followed us into the bowling alley. Henry from St. Marys asked me out. I told him I couldn't date older boys, but that didn't stop him from becoming a friend of sorts. Leo and I would bowl with him and his buddies, or park next to him for a burger at the Willow Drive-in. Another night Leo and I were followed by another Starfire—a red convertible.

The driver waved me down in the bowling alley parking lot, and we admired each other's cars. We were both surprised to see another Starfire. His name was Ed and he asked me out. He was twenty-four —eight years older than me. When I told him I couldn't date him, he still stuck around. He became a sort of big brother. Sometimes we followed each other around town to parade the cars together, and Ed taught me about boys. He said, "Most boys your age don't have a lot of confidence with girls yet—I sure didn't when I was that age—and well, a stylish redhead in her flashy car is kind of, well . . . unnerving."

Stylish? It must have been Seventeen *magazine. They're more afraid of me than I am of them? I'm going to have to learn to be a lot friendlier.*

Ed, and Henry, watched over me on the Saturday-night street. There were all kinds of chances to get into trouble. I met girls who smoked, drank, did drugs, went to bonfire parties in the woods by the lake, and had sex with their boyfriends. I learned of one girl who had been gang-banged and gotten pregnant, and then her girlfriends gave her an abortion with a wooden spoon. *I don't believe how trusting my parents are to let me out in my car at night. I'm like a pet cat that isn't allowed to sit on the kitchen counter and has to eat dry kibble all day, then is let out at night. Now the cat can hunt mice, get in fights, and mate with other cats while its owner thinks it's sleeping on the back step. Weird.*

Daddy and Mother had no idea that I cruised for boys with the top down. That I hung out with Henry and Ed, who were old enough to buy liquor. I could have gotten in lots of trouble, but instead, I earned myself a new reputation on the streets of Celina: GOOD GIRL. *Doctor Beare's Daughter will NEVER be sent away to a Home.*

A Grave Mistake

One Saturday night, Leo and I went to a dance out in the country. After driving back to Celina with the top down, our hair was wildly blown. We were at the north edge of town and didn't want to drive down Main Street looking like that, so I turned onto Summit Street to find a place to stop so we could comb our hair. My oddball sense of humor came over me, and I decided to spook Leo out and have a laugh. I drove on down the block and pulled into the cemetery.

"Why did you turn in here?" Leo said.

"Cause our hair's a fright," I said.

Instead of laughing at my silliness, she said, "Don't stop. Look behind us."

In my rearview mirror, I saw a carful of boys—five of them, all strangers. *Oh oh. There are no other people around.* I thought I could drive on through the cemetery and back out to the street, but the boys circled around a loop and were facing us. *YIPES.* I couldn't back up —the lane was so narrow, I'd surely hit a gravestone. My only escape was to turn an angled corner in the wrong direction. I was very nervous now, and I was having trouble hanging onto the wheel. I didn't manage the turn and I drove my car against a post. *What a grave mistake. My sense of humor never leaves me.* I tried backing up, going forward, and turning the wheel, but I only put the Starfire tighter against the post. Afraid that I would damage the car, I threw my hands in the air and gave up.

One of the boys hopped out of their car . . . *Yipes* . . . and came right up to me. He said, "I can drive it away from there for you."

I didn't know what else to do, so I got out of my car. Leo eyed him suspiciously, but stayed in the car when he got in the driver's seat. As he maneuvered my car away from the post, I realized he could just take off in my car with Leo, and I'd be at the mercy of the others. I was about to loudly announce that I was Doctor Beare's Daughter *(no one would dare hurt HER)* when he got out of my car and said, "You should stay out of cemeteries at night—especially when you're being followed." Then he paused, looked down at his shoes and said, "Er . . . do you have a boyfriend?"

"No." *I did once, but Theo met a girl in Dayton and stopped writing.*

The boy looked up and said, "I'm . . . Mark." Then he told me he was a junior, like me, and lived with his family above their restaurant in St. Marys. Then he looked away at his buddies in their car and said, "Would . . . would you go out with . . . with me . . . next weekend?" My stomach lurched. He looked up at me, then glanced away again.

YES, YES, YES. As casually as I could manage, I said, "I'd like to go, but I have to make sure it's okay with my parents."

As we drove off, Leo said, "Imagine getting asked out on a date by a stranger in a cemetery."

"He's probably a ghost," I said. *Like my first date with Theo, this one just dropped out of the sky for no reason. He's real, all right. Oh Damn. My car.* I drove to the bowling alley parking lot where I could look at my car under the big lights. There were only a few light scratches on the aluminum side panel. *I can rub them out. Thank God, I didn't dent it. If I had, I would have to explain to Daddy how it happened. Now that's really scary. . . .* And I never did comb my hair.

I Tried

Daddy knew who Mark's family was, and they were good Catholics, so I could go out with him. Mark took me to a movie and then to the coffee shop for a milkshake. He was easy to talk to and had a good sense of humor. He seemed shy—didn't look at me directly—but I caught him staring when he thought my attention was elsewhere. When he walked me to the front door of the house-in-town, he looked over at the cars at the traffic light on Main instead of at me when he said, "Will you go out with me again?"

I thought of the junior prom. I never dared dream that going was possible. But now . . . I said, "My prom is in two weeks. Would you go with me?" *Girls aren't supposed to ask boys out.* I held my breath.

"Yes. I'd like to take you."

My heart gave a giggle. *I'm going to prom!* I somehow managed to keep myself from shouting, but there was no keeping the huge smile off my face. *This will make Mother happy, too. She can tell her friends that her daughter is going to prom, like all the popular girls at school.*

The prom was for juniors and seniors, and it was tradition for the juniors to decorate the gym. The popular girls in my class were the prom committee, and they were meeting at Aileen's house to work on decorations. *Here's another chance for me to be friendly.* I went up to Aileen and said, "I'd like to help with the prom decorations."

She was so surprised that she choked like she had swallowed a jawbreaker, then got a grip on herself and said, "Come over to my house tonight. We need all the help we can get."

At Aileen's, we made flowers out of pastel-colored tissues. I worked quietly while the other girls nattered on about their dates for the prom, until one of the girls said, "Janice, do you have a date for the prom?"

She's sure I'm going alone, and she wants to point it out to everyone. "I'm going with my boyfriend." *She didn't see that coming.*

Hands stopped folding tissues. Mouths dropped open. Wide eyes were on me. It was so quiet you could have heard a worm spit. Finally one girl said, "What's his name?"

"Mark. He's from St. Marys."

The chatter began again, and this time, I joined the conversation. *This isn't as hard as I thought it would be.*

The next day, I found a beautiful, long formal gown at Goldstein's. It was white moiré with an applique of a single pink rosebud on the bust, the green stem of which flowed all the way down the skirt to the floor. I loved the dress, but it was strapless, and girls at IC weren't allowed to wear strapless gowns. So Harriet had her seamstress make a pair of straps from matching fabric and sew them to the dress.

I overheard Mother talking to Aunt LaVaun on the phone about prom. I thought she'd be bragging that her daughter was going to prom. Instead, she said, "It just burns my butt that they put the prom the night before Mother's Day. Why would they do such a thing? Janice will be out late and too tired to spend any time with me."

She thinks the prom will interfere with me giving her attention on Mother's Day. It's always the same— Mother's Day—the worst day of the year for her—and for me. It's the day that reminds her that she had to adopt a child in order to get one.

Dressed for junior prom

The night of the prom, Mark and I entered the gym, walking under an arch made of a thousand pastel tissue flowers. The walls of the gym were hung with strings of white lights. Little tables with tablecloths and candles were scattered around the edges of the dance floor.

Mark and I sat at our own little table for two. I could feel the curious eyes of my classmates on us, and I threw back my head and laughed, so they could see what a wonderful time I was having with my boyfriend. It wasn't an act.

Mark was a good dancer and, shy or not, he wasn't afraid to get out there. While we were dancing, I looked over his shoulder and saw the wallflowers in their prom dresses, sitting in a line on the bottom bleacher, tapping their pumps in time to the music. When we went back to our table, I said to Mark, "How would you feel about asking one of those girls to dance?"

He looked stricken. "I only want to dance with you—you're so beautiful."

His words sent a thrill through me so big that I had to grab the edge of the table to keep from falling off my chair. I gave him a big smile. I glanced at the wallflowers. *I tried.*

When the dance was over, we went to the after-party at the bowling alley. I sat next to Mark and felt like we were part of the couples-crowd.

When he finally brought me to the front door at two a.m., he found the nerve to kiss me good night. I blushed all over—inside. *My face is not a blusher, thank God.* I went to bed feeling valued— WANTED. I felt WONDERFUL.

I got up early the next morning, dressed, and put on makeup to look extra nice to go to church with my parents. After Mass, I gave Mother a sentimental card and a beautiful scarf. She looked at the scarf and set it aside with a pained face. She gave me a weak thank you, while she stifled a tear.

I'm standing right in front of you, Mother. Why can't you be happy that I'm here? I wish I could say that to her out loud, but she would just say that she was lucky to get me, and it doesn't ring true.

At noon, we went out to eat at Koch's. I chatted to Mother about school and acted like I was having the most wonderful time in the world because I was with her.

Later, at home, after she got up from her nap, I went for a long walk with her. I told her how proud I was of her for sticking to her diet and exercise program. She had lost weight, and bought all new dresses from Harriet in a smaller size. I could tell that her new figure pleased her. I went to bed thinking that I'd done everything I could to give her a good day.

Monday, during dinner, Daddy said to me, "The next time you let your date kiss you good night, have him do it in the car." *Whoops! Even at two a.m., Celina had opened her sleepy eyes for a brief moment.* Then Daddy told me that dating boys was fine as long as I didn't get serious about anyone. "You are not to go steady," he said. "Play the field."

That's okay with me. I'd like to know lots of boys, so I can understand them better. But the boys of IC don't like me, and most of the others are afraid to ask out Doctor Beare's Daughter.

Going to Hell for Sure

It wasn't long after Daddy gave me his "boy talk" that Mark got his class ring. In the car, he slipped it on my finger and said, "Will you wear my ring?"

A sparkler lit me from the inside out. *He's asking me to go steady.* Some of the popular girls at school wore their boyfriend's rings, wrapped in bright mohair yarn so they would be noticed and fit on their fingers. The ring said to other boys, "I'm taken, but go ahead and look at what you're missing." The ring shouted to the other girls, "Lookee here. I've got a boyfriend." It was like a game and part of me wanted to play. *I'm not allowed to go steady, but I could wear Mark's ring on a chain under my clothes and show it off in school. . . . I could . . . but . . . I won't. I'm not like them. I can't let Mark think I'm committed to him, just so I can show off at school.*

Mark's face looked hopeful. I took off the ring and put it in his hand. His face changed to sad. I said, "I'm not allowed to go steady with anyone, but I do like you a lot." *That's the truth.*

I dated Mark all summer. When we were out together, he watched me intently. I didn't feel judged, but treasured. *He's wonderful, and I love him.*

We shared lots of sinful but thrilling kisses that gave me a lot of sinful thoughts. The nuns taught us that you're not responsible for having an impure thought, but acting on an impure thought is a mortal sin. *So if a kiss gives you an impure thought, you'd better find something else to do, right now. But if you kiss again, then you're going to hell for sure—unless you get to Confession before you die. That's why all the popular kids go to confession on Monday mornings.* Every time I confessed to the sin of acting on impure thoughts, Father gave me absolution, then told me to "avoid the near occasion of sin."

That means avoiding Mark. I'm not giving up my wonderful boyfriend. But I don't want to burn in hell, either. Going to bed at night was torture. I was terrified of dying in my sleep, and waking up in hell for all eternity.

The longer I dated Mark, the more Daddy reminded me, "You should go out with more boys than just Mark."

"No one else has asked me," I told him.

As I continued to date Mark, Daddy often made remarks like, "You never want to marry a boy who lives over a restaurant," or "That boy's not going to college."

I imagined that Daddy's head had grown a pair of antennae tuned to pick up signals of how I might feel about Mark. *I have to be very careful what I say, or there might be interference.*

All summer long, Mother stayed on her diet, and she walked around Harbor Point several days a week. Her '65 Cadillac was the first one that didn't reek of cigarettes.

53
Cowed

That fall of 1964, on my first day of senior year, I was given my schedule and saw that one of my classes was home economics. I went to see Sister Paulissa, the principal, and told her, "I need a different class. My father won't let me take home ec."

She said, "Home economics is a graduation requirement for all girls in the archdiocese of Cincinnati. You didn't take it as a freshman, so you must take it now."

"You mean I can't graduate if I don't take home economics?"

"That's right."

I must have looked gobstruck because she elaborated. "If you don't take home economics, you may still go through the graduation ceremony, but you will get an empty diploma cover. The archbishop won't sign your diploma if you don't meet the requirements."

I had trouble containing my glee until I got out of the principal's office. Out in the hall I laughed out loud and ran all the way to my locker. I didn't even care that the other students were staring at me. *Yippee! I'm going to learn how to sew. And Daddy can't do anything thing about it.*

At home, I smugly handed Daddy my schedule. He saw home economics, let out a sigh, drew a line through it, and wrote in "chemistry."

I was ready for him. "Daddy, I *have* to take home ec. It's a graduation requirement for girls. If I don't take it, I can't graduate. The archbishop won't sign my diploma."

Daddy said, calmly, "No daughter of mine is going to sew her own clothes."

My heart did a deep dive. *Now what's going to happen?*

What happened was that the next day I found myself in chemistry class. My heart hit my heels. *Daddy has been over to the convent again and cowed the principal. But what about the archbishop way down in Cincinnati? Come spring, I might not be graduating from high school. I wonder what Daddy will say about that?*

54
It Wasn't My Hems

At dinner one night in October, Daddy said, "Sister Wilhelmine came to see me today."

I'm in trouble. What can it be? I aced my last German test.

"She's taking a few of her students to study German language and culture in Austria for six weeks this summer. It's a program run by the Foreign Language League (FLL) with side trips to explore many places in Europe. I signed you up. You'll leave in mid-July and be back before you go to Marygrove the second week in September."

Do I want to go to Austria? I don't know. I just know I'm going. It could be fun, though, and it will take me away from being home with my parents for most of the summer. I wonder if I'll still get to go if I don't graduate?

My senior year was sliding by quickly. It was a Friday night in February, and I went bowling with Leo. She knew one of the boys in the next lane, and we joked with them as we bowled. *I'm making a point of being friendly.* One of the boys was Randy, who had a creative wit and seemed very nice. During the rest of the game, I felt his eyes on me. *There must be something off about my appearance. It's my pants. They're an inch too short. If only I could sew.*

It wasn't my hems. When I was leaving the bowling alley, Randy stopped me and asked me out for the next Saturday night. I was delighted and said "yes." *Thank goodness it's for Saturday because I have a date with Mark on Friday.* Dating two boys in one weekend! I felt grown-up and sophisticated.

I came out of the Big Boy on Friday night with Mark and someone driving by honked and waved. It was . . . Randy. *Yipes.*

The next night when I was out with Randy, he said, "I was surprised to see you with a boy at the restaurant."

I'm not gonna lie. "I usually go out with him on Friday nights."

"I'd like to take you out again," he said.

I was ecstatic. We made a date for the next Saturday. And then the next, when Randy said, "I wish you would stop going out with Mark."

"I'm not allowed to go steady." Now that I was dating two boys, Daddy had lowered his antennae. I didn't want them to go back up.

Will You Marry Me?

I was having a great time dating two boyfriends at once, and I was especially enjoying Daddy no longer making remarks about my dating life. In March, Mark took me to a party at his family's restaurant to celebrate his parents' anniversary. I wore a long-sleeved, green-wool dress, fitted, with a twist of the fabric at one side of the waist. I loved the drama of the dress, but it didn't drape as smoothly as I would have liked. *If I knew how to sew, I could adjust that twist and make the fabric flow better.*

The mom-and-pop restaurant was crowded with extended family. We sat to eat with some of Mark's male cousins. The talk was about Vietnam and the new draft. Vietnam was a divided country. Communist revolutionaries in the North were determined to unite the country by forcing the South into communism. The U.S. had been helping the South by bombing the North, but now the South Vietnamese government was losing the war. President Johnson had just committed the United States to a full-scale ground war. Hundreds of thousands of boys over eighteen would be drafted and sent to fight in the jungles of Asia.

The young men at the party who were eighteen, or turning eighteen soon, had received their draft cards. A feeling of doom hung over the conversation. One of the boys said that if he was called up, he was going to Canada. I thought of my cousin John, who was a sophomore at university. *He's safe—for now.* Boys who went to college could get deferments until they graduated. Still, no young man was completely safe from the draft. *I hope this war is over quickly before all these boys have to go.*

After we ate, Mark asked me to go outside to look at the full moon. He held my hand and walked us to the back of the parking lot. Then he pulled me close and kissed me. I could smell his aftershave. It was spicy, musky. He held me, reverently, like I was the most important thing in the world to him. He said softly into my hair, "Will you marry me?"

My breath ran out of my lungs. My heart tumbled over itself. My head spun. *What? . . . I . . . What? . . . I'm . . . seventeen . . . in high school.* I felt as confused as if someone had whopped me on the head.

He put his hand under my chin and tipped it up so I was looking into his eyes. They were soft, shiny, honest. *He means it. He's waiting . . . for my answer.* I stammered, "We're still in high school. . . . I . . . I'm going away to college next fall. I'm not going to get . . . married for a long time."

His eyes held mine. "But will you marry me . . . someday?"

"I don't know," was all I could say.

He gently nudged my head back against his chest and held me close, his chin resting on top of my head. I heard him say, "It's okay. I'll wait."

I love Mark, but I don't think I'm in love with him. And Daddy would never stand for me to marry a boy who works in a restaurant. I broke up with Mark. I felt terrible that I had hurt him.

Randy was very pleased. I invited him to be my date for my senior prom. I had to beg the priest for permission to bring Randy because he wasn't Catholic.

The week before prom, I heard Mother talking to Aunt LaVaun. She said, "The prom is the night before Mother's Day. AGAIN. Janice didn't spend any time with me on Mother's Day last year. She slept all day because she was too tired from staying out all night. It will be the same thing this year."

My stomach acid boiled and my ulcer burned. *Mother doesn't remember a thing I did for her last year. Honoring her on Mother's Day is my most important job, and I'm a failure. Well, I'll not fail again.* I had already bought her a present—a bottle of her favorite perfume. I went shopping again and bought her two more gifts. I would give them to her throughout the day. I learned a song to sing and play on my guitar about how my mother was the most wonderful mother in the world. *I'm gonna give her a Mother's Day she can't possibly forget.*

Prom with Randy was a magical night. The juniors did a bang-up job of decorating the gym, and there was a live band. At one point, one of the boys in my class came up to me and asked me to dance. I couldn't have been more shocked if I had stuck a fork in an outlet. *How did this happen? Why have they changed?* Then I realized it wasn't the boys in my class that had changed. It was me. I was friendly. *Ed was right about boys my age. They can be shy and need encouragement. I wish I'd known a long time ago.*

I got up early the next morning to give Mother one of her gifts before church. I gave her the second one after we got home from Koch's, and the last gift at dinner that evening. She was surprised at getting three gifts, and said, "What did you do that for?"

"Because you're a wonderful mother, and I love you." After dinner, I sang my song to her. Then I sat with her and watched TV. I was feeling pretty smug.

It was only a week later when I heard her complain to Aunt Helen, "I still don't understand why the school held a prom the night before Mother's Day. Janice was tired and didn't spend any time with me. It spoiled Mother's Day."

Her words clubbed me on the head and made my knees wobble. I felt like slapping her and crying at the same time. *I absolutely, positively, unequivocally, and utterly DESPISE Mother's Day. And right now I can't stand Mother, either.*

55
Congratulations Janice

The week after prom, I got an invitation from a civic club to their banquet for Celina's senior honor students. The other girls in my class who got invited made plans to carpool and sit together at the dinner. I thought about asking if I could sit with them, but it seemed like begging and made me feel pathetic. I shrank from the idea of showing up at a formal dinner by myself and having to find an empty seat somewhere while all the other honorees would be in their little clusters, noticing that "Beare" had to come alone. I decided not to go. This did not please Mother. She said, "You HAVE to go. I already told my friends that you're going."

Tit-and-shit banana split, Goddamn-bless America, and son-of-a-bitch from hell. I wish I wasn't an honor student. Now I also have to go to confession. I was dreading the ordeal ahead of me, when Owen Pogue called. He said he was a member of the civic club and would like to escort me. My feet did the Watusi, and I dropped the receiver.

On the evening of the banquet, I dressed to be seen. I arrived at the banquet on Owen's arm. From my place next to him at the head table, I could see the girls from IC among the crowd that lined one long table. And they saw me. It felt like a little revenge for twelve years of being an outcast, and I felt like I had scored a victory after a grueling triathlon. *God bless Owen Pogue.*

Owen Pogue, God Bless him

Certainly Extravagant

Right after the honors banquet, we moved to the cottage. The first
Saturday in June, Mother answered the door to the florist delivery
man, who handed her a box of a dozen roses. "I wonder why Ralph
is sending me flowers," she said with a big smile. When she read the
card, she said, "Why, Janice. These are for you, from Randy." Her
upper lip curled toward her nose and she said, "That boy is certainly
extravagant."

That boy is certainly romantic. That was just the first of many
deliveries. Every Saturday afternoon, the florist delivered more roses
from Randy.

"That boy isn't just extravagant, he's crazy," Mother said.

*I feel like Mother slapped me. So—only a crazy boy can love the
real me. Randy is not crazy and he does love me. I'm crazy about him,
too.* Daddy's antennae were all the way up now. He made remarks
like, "That boy isn't Catholic," or "That boy isn't going to college," or
"You'll want to marry a doctor . . . or I suppose a lawyer would be
okay. Remember that, Kiddo—a doctor or a lawyer."

I was very careful not to talk about Randy in front of Daddy, but all those flowers kept him on Daddy's radar. I nabbed them as soon as they were delivered and put them out of sight in my bedroom.

Spent on the Sidelines

The whole student body was assembled in the gym for the annual end-of-school awards ceremony. I was expecting a certificate for being on the honor roll and a librarian pin, when it hit me. *Goddamn bless it —banana split shit. I'm going to get The Archbishop McNicholas Memorial Award. Back to confession—damn.* Only one of this special medal was awarded in each high school in the archdiocese of Cincinnati to the graduating senior who had made the most personal growth in four years. I had started as a freshman, so shy that I walked with my head down, kept to myself, and was unable to talk to my classmates. Now I walked proud of my sixty-eight inches, my auburn hair, and my own style. I had finally managed to talk to my classmates in the halls. No one else in my graduating class had changed so much. *I'm getting that award. I don't want it. I don't want to walk up on that stage in front of everyone and accept an award just for growing up.* The Archbishop McNicholas Memorial Award was the last to be presented. I held my breath. Up on the stage, Sister Paulissa said, "This year's award goes to . . . Janice Beare."

Even though I knew it was coming, my gut felt punched. "Congratulations Janice," Sister Paulissa said, as she gave me the medal on a red ribbon. A photographer from the paper took my picture, and the student body clapped. I smiled, but inside I was crying— crying for the loss of my high school years spent on the sidelines. All because I didn't

The Archbishop McNicholas Memorial Award

know how it was done until it was too late. I hadn't known that the problem was me and not all the other kids.

Karl J. Alter

My classmates and I were gowned and lined up to receive our diplomas. I stood between Adams and Cooper for the last time. Will my diploma cover be empty? What will Daddy do if I don't graduate?

"George Alan Adams." Adams walked forward and took his diploma.

Will I be going to Marygrove in the fall? Or taking home ec at IC with the new freshmen?

"Janice Lucinda Beare."

I walked across the stage, got my diploma, walked back to my seat, and sat down. I looked down at the fancy cover I was holding. My hands quivered, and my mouth felt parched. I opened the cover. There it was. My diploma. And there was the signature: Karl J. Alter: Archbishop of Cincin-

nati. *I'm the only girl who has ever graduated from IC without taking home economics. Of course, I am. I'm Doctor Beare's Daughter. And Doctor Beare can manage an archbishop any day.*

Graduation day at the cottage with Daddy and Mother

Things Are Different Now

The night of my graduation, I saw Daddy sitting alone in the living room, staring at his hands. He looked up at me and said, "I was just thinking about all the people these hands have helped, about how many lives they've saved."

Daddy's hands had broad nails—short and neat. His skin was worn thin from scrubbing for surgery—so thin that his fingers picked up splinters easily and they went deep. It had always been my job to remove them. I had become an expert at probing for the hard ones under the magnifying light in the ear, nose, and throat room of the office. Daddy looked up at me and said, "Now that you've graduated, I'm retiring. I want some time to do what I want while I still can."

I can't imagine Daddy not practicing medicine. He's fifty-eight. Most doctors work until they're much older. However, he's practiced medicine for more than thirty years and deserves to do what he wants.

When he told Mother he was going to retire, she said, "Now we can sell the house-in-town and build our new house on Johnson Avenue."

Daddy said, "Doctor Paul isn't ready to retire. I'm keeping the house and renting the office to him."

"But, Ralph, you promised that . . ."

"Things are different now. Charlie is gone. And Mildred doesn't live there anymore. Part of our dream was to live next to them."

"Well, I still want my dream house," Mother said.

"Maybe when Doctor Paul retires and I sell the house-in-town, we can build a new one."

Poor Mother. Daddy gets to decide everything for her and for me. I hope she gets her dream house someday. At least I'm going to be able to run my own life while I'm at Marygrove.

The Thursday after graduation, we went to Dayton for shopping and dinner. While we were in Rikes, Daddy took me to the jewelry department and pointed out a display of diamond cocktail rings. "Pick out your favorite," he said. "A graduation gift from Mother and me."

The ring I chose was beautiful, all right, and Doctor Beare's Daughter wore it well. *Being her is amazing.* The little voice said, "I'm still here . . . waiting." *Oh, shut up.*

I had a date with Randy on the Fourth of July. It was our last time together before I left for Austria. He asked me if I loved him. I told him I did.

56
Lucky to Be an American

Rot! Rot! Rot!

Two days later, I left for Austria with Sister Wilhelmine and six other students. We stayed in Seefeld, a village high in the Alps, and I lived in a *gasthaus* (guest house) with two other girls. We studied German language and culture at the local school with teachers from the University of Innsbruck.

Me on the balcony of my gasthaus and my Haus Herr and Frau below

Doing my laundry on the balcony

I soon learned that the German boys of Seefeld thought red-haired American girls were wild. I was chased down the street a few times by boys yelling, "*Rot! Rot! Rot!*" (Red! Red! Red!) I had to run into a shop to get rid of them. One German boy came right up to me and asked me out with the promise of "a good time." Another one suggested I sneak out and meet him in a beer garden. There was one other redheaded American girl studying in Seefeld with the FLL, and she had the same problem. We had lunch together sometimes to compare our experiences.

Every weekend, we took a tour bus to other places throughout Europe. In Munich, we saw the German Museum and had lunch at the Hofbräuhaus. In Venice, we went to Mass at St. Mark's Square and rode the streets that were canals in a gondola. In Switzerland, we stayed on an alpine farm that had the barn connected to the house so the people didn't have to go outside in the winter to milk the cows. The chickens and pigs made themselves at home in the kitchen.

The FLL had advised us to bring Kennedy half-dollars from home, and I found that one of them would buy most anything, anywhere. *Daddy is right when he says travel is educational. I'm learning a lot about many different cultures living next to each other. Celina has just one culture, and I feel suffocated by its rules—at least by its rules according to Mother.*

One of my most memorable experiences was meeting Anka, a girl from East Berlin who was staying at my *gasthaus* visiting her relatives. It was rare for East Berliners to be allowed to visit the West. Anka told us about her life behind the Iron Curtain. She said the government censored the news and monitored peoples' activities. One didn't dare speak against the government, even to close friends, for fear of cruel punishment. I asked her why she didn't just stay in Austria with her relatives and not go back. She said if she didn't return to East Berlin on time, her parents would be harmed or killed. *We have such freedom in the United States and take it for granted. I'm so lucky to be an American.*

Brad, one of the other FLL students from South Carolina, asked me to a movie. It was in German, and we had fun figuring out what was going on. Brad brought his guitar with him to Seefeld. The hotel where my group ate lunch and dinner every day was also a nightclub, and Brad took me to a talent show there. I borrowed his guitar and sang in the show. It didn't matter that I didn't win a prize. What mattered was that I had the guts to perform in front of a large sophisticated

Performing in the talent show at the Klosterbrau nightclub in Seefeld

audience with other musicians. And it was such fun. When it was time to go back to the states, Brad asked me to write to him and suggested I fly to his university in South Carolina to visit him, where he would be studying pre-med. *He's going to be a doctor.* I said auf Wiedersehen to Brad.

I had learned a lot during my time in Seefeld. I could speak German fairly well, and I had earned a few college credits from the University of Innsbruck. Best of all, I had learned how to yodel—lay—e—O. *Oh, that was bad. Sounds like I'm calling pigs in German.*

Bigger than The Three Beares

When I came home from Austria to the cottage, I noticed that the stir in the air was more intense than I had ever felt it before. Daddy was retired now, and he filled his time by playing golf, tinkering in his shop, fishing, and serving on the hospital board. When he was at home, he drove Mother crazy. He supervised her cooking, telling her how to do differently the things she had been doing for thirty years.

Mother was no longer going for walks, and her new slimmer dresses were getting a bit tight. Sometimes I saw her finish off food left on Daddy's plate when she cleared the table. Daddy didn't notice. I wanted to say something but knew better. The best I could do was invite her to take a walk with me. But she always had something else to do.

The first weekend I was home, I went out with Randy. Afterward, Daddy said, "I thought you would forget about him while you were in Europe."

I gritted my teeth. *So that's why I went to Austria. Doctor Beare's Daughter would forget.* "But I won't."

Then Daddy said, "Either marry him and forget about school, or break up with him."

I felt like an ax had fallen on my neck. *Did I hear him right? I'm not ready to get married. And it should be my decision, whether or not to end my relationship with Randy, not Daddy's. I'm not ready to break up with Randy.*

"Do you hear me, Kiddo?"

I wanted to yell at him. Tell him how I felt, but decided not to. It would cause a huge "discussion" that wouldn't end until he had stripped me down to a mere puddle of tears. *Lots of girls go off to college and have boyfriends back home. I'm going to let my relationship take its course and see where it goes.* "I heard, you, Daddy," was what I said. I didn't say I agreed to his ultimatum.

The day before leaving for college, I'd been on an errand for Mother and was driving from town to the cottage. It was my last ride in the Starfire. Daddy was selling it because freshmen couldn't have cars on campus. I loved that car and wanted to keep it to drive next summer, but Daddy's mind was made up. The turnoff to Harbor Point was just ahead. *I'm not ready to go home yet.* I barreled on past the truck stop and took the Starfire up to 80 mph. *Celina is the only home I've ever known, and all I ever wanted was to belong. But glamorous Doctor Beare's Daughter was above it all. And poor, pathetic Janice was beneath it all.* I put my foot down harder. The wind whipped my face, lashed my eyes, and made them tear. *Someday my life will be mine. And it will be bigger than Celina and The Three Beares.*

57
Marygrove

It was the fall of 1965 when my parents left me in Detroit, at Marygrove. Before they drove off, Daddy reminded me, "Remember Kiddo: a doctor or lawyer."

A doctor? Never.

Liberal Arts building at Marygrove

At Marygrove, I lived in a suite—two dorm rooms with a bathroom in between. My roommate, Mary Lee, was a beautiful girl, artistic,

and had a flair for fashion. And she thought I was exotic—that my lifestyle was glamorous and sophisticated. *Doctor Beare's Daughter is impressive, all right. Daddy made her that way.* The little voice whispered, "I wonder what I'm really like?"

My suitemates were Mary Beth and Joan. They and Mary Lee were always ready to have fun. I was always ready to instigate. *This is what it must feel like to have sisters.*

I had brought my guitar and harmonica to school. At night when I practiced the guitar and

sang, some of the girls gathered around to listen. When it was time for bed, I went into the bathroom, opened both connecting doors, climbed up on Mt. John (the toilet seat), and solemnly played taps on my harmonica. Sometimes, early in

(top) My roomie, Mary Lee (L) and me (R) wearing our freshmen "Dinks"

(left) L to R Joan (lying down), Mary Lee, Jan Mary Beth

the morning, I scaled Mt. John and played
my roomies awake with a burst of reveille.
I think the music and the silliness is part of the
real me. "I like that part a lot."

Life at Marygrove was like walking with
one foot dragging along in the upper-class
world of my parent's generation and the other
foot springing ahead into the world of tomorrow. The old traditions dictated that all students wear academic dress (cap and gown) to
the monthly assemblies. Heels and hose were
required at dinner, which was served by wait-
ers in white jackets. Pants were never worn
off the dorm floor. In contrast, our learning
focused on racial equality, social justice, and
women as leaders. I learned that some of the
things you couldn't do in Celina were just fine

Playing taps on Mt.
John

to do in the outside world. I felt the Celina city limits falling away.

While I didn't miss Celina, I did miss Randy. We wrote often. In
one letter he asked about coming up to one of my school dances. I
couldn't wait to see him.

Fury and Fear

While Mother wrote to me every other day, Daddy had *never* written
me a letter. So I was surprised to find one from him in my mailbox.
I ripped it open. It *looked* angry—words pressed hard into the paper
in the blackest of ink, underlines slashed onto the page, and massive
exclamation points. My hand trembled as I held it and read:

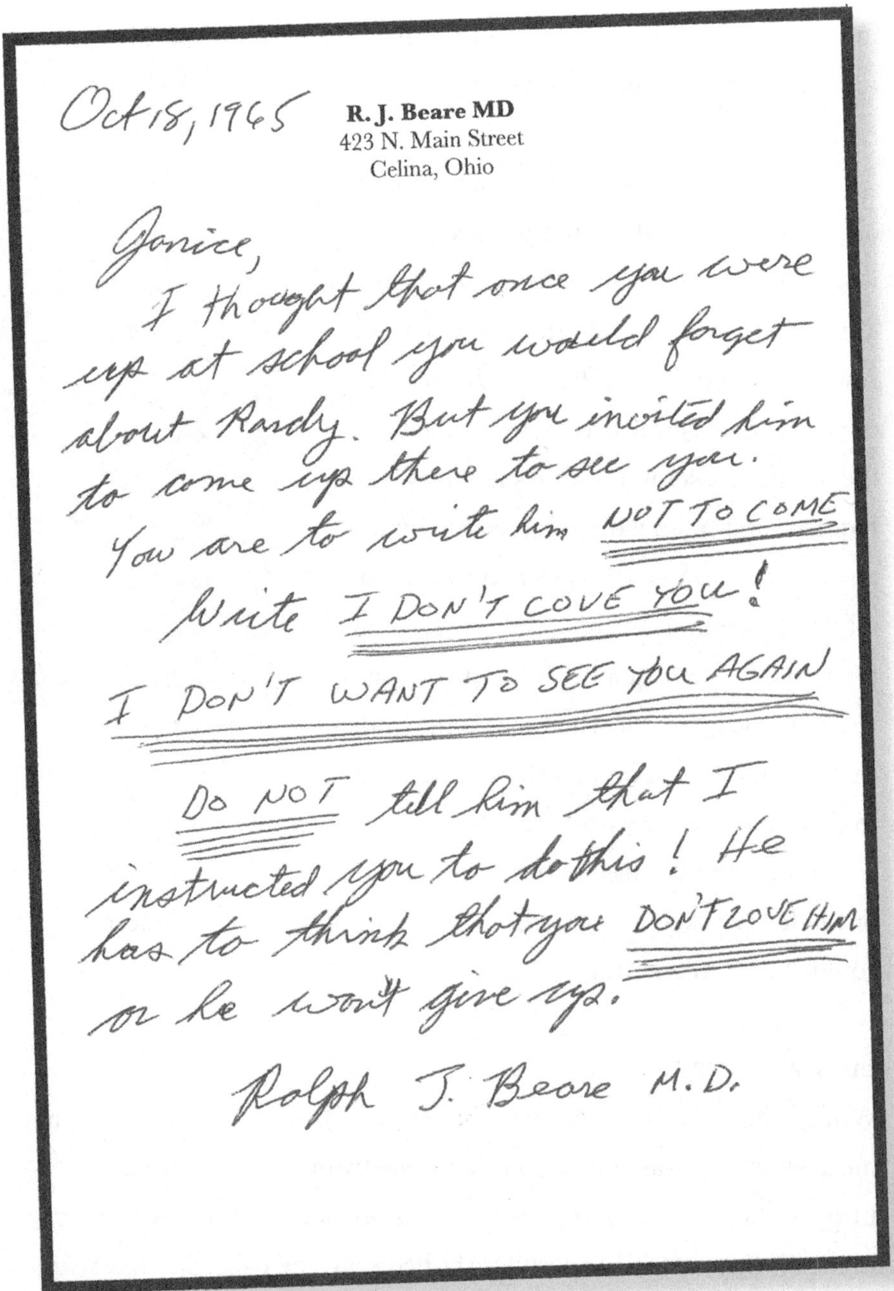

Oct 18, 1965

R. J. Beare MD
423 N. Main Street
Celina, Ohio

Janice,
    I thought that once you were up at school you would forget about Randy. But you invited him to come up there to see you. You are to write him NOT TO COME

Write I DON'T LOVE YOU!

I DON'T WANT TO SEE YOU AGAIN

Do NOT tell him that I instructed you to do this! He has to think that you DON'T LOVE HIM or he won't give up.

Ralph J. Beare M.D.

Daddy's letter

Fury and fear twisted themselves inside me like two towels wound together and wrung out hard. Fury demanded I rebel against Daddy. Fear reminded me of Daddy's ultimatum: "Marry him and forget about school, or break up with him."

If I don't break up with Randy, I won't be able to go home again or stay in college. I won't have any way to support myself, and I'm not ready to get married. Randy isn't ready either. And he's facing the draft. Daddy is forcing me to choose while I'm still dependent on him and he has all the power. It's not much of a choice, really.

First, I cried myself sick. Then, I wrote Randy the letter. I knew my heart would ache for the longest time.

I didn't want to go home for Christmas break. When Daddy came to pick me up, he said nothing about the letter. At home, I learned that

Randy was in the army, and I hoped that he would survive Vietnam. Leo's boyfriend had not survived it—killed just one month after he got there. Leo was devastated, and my heart hurt for her.

Roberta had made all kinds of treats for the holiday. My favorites were her mini pecan tarts and her chocolate chip cookies. I ate quite a few, then later my upper right side under my ribs became tender and painful, and I felt nauseous. I asked Daddy about it and he said, "If you were 'fair, fat, and forty,' it would sound just like a bad gallbladder, but you're much too young to have that kind of trouble. If you don't think about it, it will go away."

This is in my belly, not my head. At least he didn't make me read the medical dictionary.

While I was home, I noticed changes in Mother. She never went for a walk. She had gone off her diet and developed type II diabetes. Daddy had her on medicine to control her blood sugar. When I opened her purse to get some money to go grocery shopping for her, I saw a pack of cigarettes. *Here we go again.* I couldn't sleep at night, thinking about her smoking. *Why does she do that when she knows that this time she probably won't be so lucky?* The next time I was alone with Daddy, I said, "Mother is smoking again."

"She knows better than that."

I tried again, "Daddy. Haven't you smelled the smoke in the bathroom after she's been in there? There's two burn holes in the front seat of the new Caddy. She smokes."

"If she does, I've never seen her."

He knows! "You have to do something."

He gave me a stern stare and said, "If I don't see her smoking, then I don't know about it, and I can't say anything." The tone of his voice said our conversation was over. Any more out of my mouth wasn't going to convince him to do anything.

The next day, Mother and I were sitting in the guest room, wrapping Christmas gifts. I said, "When you thought you had lung cancer and were going to die, you said you would do anything if you could get well. Then you did everything right. You were feeling good and looking wonderful. You weren't diabetic. Why won't you stick to the program? Why are you doing the things that you know will probably kill you?"

She said, "I don't like being hungry all the time. And I like to smoke. It makes me feel good. And why would I want to walk when I have a Cadillac to drive? What's the point of living if I have to give up everything I like?"

She cares more about her damn cigarettes than she does about being here for me. That hurts.

The first week in January, Daddy walked into the house and said, "I just sold the lots on Johnson Avenue. Got a good price, too."

Mother burst into tears.

Daddy could have made Mother's dream of a new house come true—if he had wanted to. He should have built her that house a long time ago.

He Won't Be Back

On a Friday night, with just three weeks left of my freshman year, I had studied all day and was tired. I just wanted to go to bed. But Mary Lee wanted to go to a U of D mixer. We would have to walk six city blocks to get there, and we weren't allowed off campus after dark, except in pairs. So if I didn't go, Mary Lee couldn't go either. She begged me. I finally gave in saying, "Oh, all right. If I don't go, I'll probably miss meeting the boy I'm going to marry." *I don't really mean that. It's just something silly to say.*

The dance was in the foyer of one of the dorms and had gone on for some time when a young man took my hand and walked me onto the dance floor. He was dressed in filthy wheat-colored jeans and a grime-splotched sweatshirt. He had at least a day's growth of stubble. *Why do the grubby ones always want to dance with me? And why didn't he ask me instead of just taking my hand and pulling me out here?* It was a slow dance. The song ended, another one began, and he kept on dancing with me. *He still hasn't said anything. Not even his name.* At the end of that second song, he continued to hold my hand and finally spoke, "Come on. I'll show you my car."

This guy is weird. So how come I'm letting him lead me right out the door to the parking lot? I'm more curious than cautious right now.

He led me to a Corvair convertible. "There it is," he said. "And look." He pointed in the driver's window. "It has a record player."

Yep, the car had a 45-rpm record player mounted under the dash.

Still holding my hand, he said, "Come on. I'll show you my room."

He really did want to show me his car. I guess I'll go see the room, too. The nameless, grubby boy led me along the side of the building, where the basement dorm rooms had ground-level windows. He pointed in one brightly lit window and said, "There's my room. And that's my roommate."

There was a passed-out-drunk young man lying spread-eagle amid a huge pile of dirty laundry on the floor of a squalid dorm room. *Why would he want to show me that?*

He led me back into the building, and— still holding my hand— he finally told me his name was Jeff Jones, and he was from New York. He was a mechanical-engineering student in his junior year. The dance being over, Jeff asked, "Can I drive you back to Marygrove?"

Whenever a Marygrove girl went to U of D for a dance, her goal was always to find a boy with a car who would drive her back to school and bring along other girls who needed a lift. I said, "Yes, and my friends need a ride, too."

So Jeff, Mary Lee, and I, and five other girls crammed ourselves into the Corvair and drove down Six Mile Road with Jeff's record player blasting.

At Marygrove, Jeff walked me to the door. The other girls went on inside, but he had my hand again and stopped me on the steps. "Can I take you out next weekend?" he asked.

"I can't," I explained. "I'm going home for the weekend."

He studied me intently for a moment. I think it was then that I realized that in spite of his grubby state, or maybe even because of it, Jeff Jones was the handsomest boy I had ever seen. He had longish dark hair, a lock of which fell forward across his forehead, and blue-grey eyes that smiled, even when his mouth was thoughtful. He had excellent posture, with broad shoulders and well-muscled arms. I realized that he was physically powerful.

"Can I take you out the weekend after that?"

I want to go. "I can't. I'm going to my roommate's house that weekend."

He came right back with, "And how about the weekend after that?" During this conversation, we stood eye-to-eye. Most girls were only interested in boys taller than themselves. I liked having this one right where I could see him.

"School will be out by then. I'll be gone for the summer."

He said, "Okay," and let go of my hand. He walked off toward his car.

That's the end of that. A boy who has been turned down three times in a row isn't going to ask again. I went to my room where Mary Lee was getting ready for bed. I said, "I just met the man I'm going to marry. And I turned him down for a date three times in a row, so I have no idea how it could possibly happen." *I'm being silly again, but it feels like the truth.*

The following Thursday evening, I got a page, saying I had a visitor in the lobby. I went downstairs to find Jeff there. He was neat and clean-shaven. He said, "If you can't go out this weekend, or the weekend after that, or the weekend after that, can you go out right now for ice cream?"

"I'll get my sweater."

While we sat over our ice cream, Jeff explained that he belonged to a fraternity. The night of the dance, he had been at their off-campus house, working on finishing the basement into a place where they could have parties and hold meetings. After doing demo and then hanging paneling for two days, he had been exhausted and just wanted to go back to his dorm room to shower and sleep. To get to his room, he had to walk through the foyer where the dance was being held. He had no intention of dancing, but he saw me and changed his mind. My heart backed up a beat. I desperately wanted to know what it was about me that got his attention, but I suddenly felt too shy to ask. *I wonder if my red hair had something to do with it.*

We told each other a little about our families. Jeff was one of five children. His family lived in Briarcliff Manor, New York, about an hour north of the city by train. He told me that his mother, Mary, had been a nurse, and his father, Robert, worked in Manhattan and was the editor of *Family Circle Magazine*. Since there was no time for a second date, we agreed to write.

Later I looked Jeff's dad up in *Who's Who in America*. Robert Jones was considered a visionary in the publishing world who could spot a trend in the making. He had been responsible for *Better Homes and Gardens* publishing the first handyman book. *I don't care what his father does, but it might impress Daddy.*

Handsome, strong Jeff Jones

58
Get Out

As soon as I got home from school, I wanted to look for a summer job and was excited about the idea of working in a women's clothing store. I told Mother I was going to Goldstein's to talk to Harriet. Daddy came in from the shop right then and said, "No daughter of mine is going to work."

My hands made fists. "But, Daddy. Every college student I know has a summer job."

"Well, you're not everyone, and you're NOT going to work. I won't have it."

We had quite a "discussion," which did nothing to change his mind. After a year of college, during which I had grown used to making my own decisions about most everything, my parents expected me to be just the same as always—and that included going out to dinner with them. There I was, a nineteen-year-old young woman riding in the back seat of the Cadillac to wherever the notion took Daddy. I was so bored in that back seat that I gave myself a manicure with my teeth. Daddy had also sold the Penn Yan, so when I wanted to be on the lake, I took out the Chris, or sometimes drove Daddy's hydroplane, to have something to do. I missed my beautiful car, but I could drive the Vette and go out with Joyce or Leo sometimes.

I met a couple of boys at local dances. One asked me out, and I thought I might like to go until he told me he was in med school and his father was a doctor from a nearby town. *My second chance to date*

(above) Daddy's U2 Commando
Hydroplane; (right) The Chris

a doctor and I could end up
living forty miles from Celina.
Chills spasmed through me.

I met another boy, home
from his second year at Purdue,
and went out with him. When
he was driving me home, he
turned off Harbor Point Drive
just before the boathouse and
pulled into the parking lot of
the state park. He turned off the ignition but left the radio playing softly.
He kissed me a few times, but then his hands started roaming. I tried
stopping him, but he wouldn't back off. *He's getting physical really fast.*
Thanks to Ed and his advice about boys, I knew I had to get away—
right now. I turned up the radio and said, "Dance with me."

"What? Dance? In the parking lot?"

I said, "Oh, yes." I hopped out of the car and, before he could get out, I took off into the shadows. I knew that park in the dark as well as the inside of my own closet.

"Wait. Janice. Come back! Just come back. I'll take you home."

I was over the footbridge and halfway there already. *Doctor Beare's Daughter will never be sent away to a Home.*

Kahoona!

In July, Daddy let me drive the Vette to visit Mary Lee, about an hour north of Detroit. It was a road trip—by myself. I drove with the windows down, my hair blowing all over the place. There were no cigarettes so I could breathe. I had the radio blasting rock and sang along as loud as I could.

Jeff had asked if he could come to Mary Lee's house on Saturday and take me out that night. On Saturday morning, he called to say he had to cancel our date because he had broken both his arms the night before when he fell out of a playground swing. He explained that he was pledge master for his fraternity, and it was Hell Weekend for his pledges. As part of initiation, they played a pledges-against-brothers football game in a park after dark. After the game, Jeff and some of the brothers, all of them drunk, got on the swings and made a contest of seeing who could pump a swing the highest. Jeff was way up there when he yelled, "Kahoona!" and bailed out. He landed on his arms. The brothers took him to the hospital. *I'm not sure I want to date a boy who gets drunk and jumps out of swings, but I still feel like I'm gonna end up with him somehow.*

Mary Lee and I drove to U of D to see Jeff. He was on the front steps of his dorm, watching for us. Both arms were in casts, one of them in a sling. It was obvious he couldn't do much for himself. He was delighted to see me. He was quite stoic and viewed his broken arms as an inconvenience, rather than a tragedy. *If that happened to me, I'd think it a tragedy for sure.* As Mary Lee and I were leaving, two of Jeff's pledges popped up out of nowhere, ready to take him to lunch and feed him. *I'll bet they have to dress him, too.*

A Toupee in a Potted Palm and a Priest in a Lounger

In early August, Daddy needed elective surgery at University Hospital in Columbus for a prostate problem. He was very unhappy about needing the surgery. The night before surgery, he drove the three of us to the hospital so he could be admitted, then I drove Mother to a nearby motel.

Our room was next to the pool. After we went to bed, there was a wild party with a loud band at the pool—right outside our door. I put the chain on the door and closed the drapes. People were yelling and throwing things, and a big fight broke out. *This is not a safe place to be.* I called the office to report the fight, but there was no answer. Then I tried to call the police but couldn't get an outside line without connecting through the office. *We're trapped.*

A man banged on our door, yelling, "Wake up. Let me in!" He rattled the knob so hard the door shook on its hinges. My heart was pummeling my ribs, and my breath was coming in gulps. Mother locked herself in the bathroom, and I grabbed the iron from the closet and stood on a chair behind the door. *If he gets in, I'll bean him with the iron.* Just then another man came along and dragged him away, saying, "That's not your room, Buddy."

The next morning, there were broken bottles and clothing, including bikini tops, strewn everywhere. A man's toupee was lodged in the fronds of a potted palm, and the patio furniture was in the pool. Mother said, "That was some party."

It sure was. I went to the office to check out, but the clerk said, "There's a convention in town, and you won't find another room in all of Columbus. That was our regular Friday night party, and there won't be another one until next week."

We went to the hospital for Daddy's surgery, and there was no time to look for another motel. The surgery went well. When Daddy was out of recovery and back in his room, Mother and I sat with him while he slept, and we talked quietly. She mentioned something she needed to do when she got back to Celina.

Daddy opened his eyes and said, "Well, if you don't want to be here with me, then go on home."

Mother said, "I was just thinking out loud."

Daddy said, "Well, it's a fine thing. Here I am, in the hospital, recovering from surgery, and my own family would rather be somewhere else. You don't give a tinker's damn about me. Janice. Take your mother home."

I felt heat rush through me. *He's irrational again, thinking we don't love him.* "But, Daddy, we can't just leave you here. How will you get home?"

"I'll rent a car and drive myself home."

"The doctor said you can't drive for another three weeks."

"Then I'll call someone. There's plenty of people in Celina who care enough about me to come and get me." His tone was vehement. "Now go home, goddammit." The rush inside me grew into a torrent.

"GET OUT," he yelled. He sat up in bed so fast he almost ripped out his IV.

He means it. But I can't just abandon him. I know what it feels like to be abandoned—to have your family give you away. I said, "Mother and I are going to go get something to eat, then we'll be back." I grabbed Mother's hand and led her from the room. Later, when we came back, Daddy was asleep. When he woke, he said no more about us going home. *I think Daddy might crumble if we ever did leave him alone.*

Back at the party motel, families were relaxing at the pool. There was a priest in a lounger reading a book. *I hope Daddy is ready to go home by next Friday.*

The Three Beares headed back to Harbor Point on Thursday. *Whew.*

59
Sinking Fast

Ann Landers Says

We had just finished dinner at the cottage, and my parents were going to a party at the country club. However, they got into a "discussion" over some "ignorant" remark Mother had made. When it was over, she was crying and exhausted. And it was almost time for the party to start.

"Now what are we going to do?" Daddy said. "You aren't ready to go."

Mother shook her head. "I'm too upset to go."

Another storm was brewing on Daddy's face.

I said, "You go on, Daddy. I'll bring Mother in a little while."

"Everyone will ask me where Lou is."

"Tell them that I decided at the last minute that I wanted to come along, and Mother is waiting for me to get ready."

Daddy left in the Vette. Mother and I sat talking while she calmed down. She said, "Sometimes I want to leave him."

I felt the muscles in my face tense. *This is a big surprise. I never imagined she would even think about leaving him.* "Why haven't you?" *I'm never going to be married to a man who talks to me the way Daddy does to Mother.*

"Ann Landers says in her advice column that if a woman is trying to decide whether or not to leave her husband, she should ask herself, 'Will I be better off or worse off without him?' I'm pretty sure I would be worse off."

She's probably right. Her entire identity is being Daddy's wife, and maybe it's too late to change it. My identity is being Daddy's daughter. "I'm gonna change that someday."

That summer I wrote to boys in Vietnam. In their letters, they described what it was like for them in combat. It was terrible. I felt so sorry for them and what they had to do because of the draft. My letter-writing relationship with each of them was short-lived. Sometimes I would hear from their buddies that my pen pal had been killed. *Please let this awful war be over soon.*

So Damn Careless

A week before school would start, I couldn't wait to get there. I got out my trunk and laid my clothes out on the bed to decide what I would take with me. Mother came into my room and said, "Why are you packing now? You're aren't leaving for another week."

"I'm planning what to take and how it will fit into the trunk."

She said, "You're happy about going back to school."

Uh-oh. I had let my "I'm-so-sad-to-leave-my-mother mask" slip right off my face. I pasted my somber face back on. It was too late. She was deeply hurt. *My God, Janice. You're nineteen years old, and you still manage to cut her to the quick. You're so careless sometimes.*

The night before I left for school, Daddy started an argument with Mother over nothing. *He does this every time, right before I leave home. It's like he's mad that I'm leaving him with just Mother.*

Pinned

While I was moving in the dorm, Jeff showed up to meet my parents. He wore a white shirt, sport coat, and a tie. The top half of him looked nice. However, his jeans had seen better days. When Mother was getting in the car to start back home, she said, "He seems nice, but someone should teach him how to dress."

Daddy said nothing. *At least he didn't tell me to get rid of Jeff.*

Every Friday night, Jeff took me to a fraternity party. We sang raucous songs, played records, and danced. There was lots of beer and liquor. I had tried alcohol many times at my parents' parties and didn't like it. After one drink, it gave me a headache and made me sleepy. However, it made Jeff and the brothers do silly things. One brother recited the Greek alphabet while doing handsprings off the back porch of the frat house—in the snow. Most all the boys smoked. The first time I saw Jeff smoking a cigarette, I said, "I don't date boys who smoke."

He threw his cigarette down, stepped on it, ground it out, and said, "I just quit."

I came right back at him, saying, "I know about quitting. If I ever see you with a cigarette or smell it on your breath, then I'm done." *Wow. I sound like Daddy giving an ultimatum. What right do I have to tell Jeff what to do? We've only just started dating.*

Jeff was taken aback. He said, "I think you mean that."

I do mean it. "You have no idea how much I hate cigarettes." Then I added, "You should also know that I don't clean fish, cook fish, or eat fish—never, ever." He stared at me a few seconds, then we both laughed.

When Jeff wasn't with his frat brothers, he had a quiet personality. Once in a while his quirky sense of humor would pierce his calm veneer, which made it even funnier. I learned that Jeff felt things deeply and cared about others. He watched me most all the time, with those eyes that were sky blue when he wore a blue shirt and steel gray when he wore gray or white. Whenever another boy talked to me, he draped his arm around my shoulder and pulled me against him. I felt a kind of connection to him that I couldn't explain. It was like we somehow knew, deep down, that we needed each other, even though the reasons weren't clear.

Formal dance at Marygrove

In October, Jeff asked me to wear his fraternity pin. He said being pinned meant we were engaged to be engaged. I was thrilled to wear it. *I hope Daddy likes him, because no matter what, I'm keeping this one.*

Just in Time

When I went home for Christmas break, wearing Jeff's pin, Daddy said nothing about it. Perhaps he didn't even notice because Mother was very sick. She had jaundice and a fever. She couldn't eat and was in pain. "She has a mass in her pancreas," Daddy told me. "I can feel it."

Pinned!

Poor Mother. I don't want to lose her.

Normally, Roberta and I would put up the spectacular spectacle as soon as I got home on break, but instead The Three Beares got in the Caddy and drove to Columbus, where Mother was admitted to University Hospital. Daddy checked us into the party motel. I told him it wasn't a good place to stay, but all the other motels were full up for the holiday. *I hope we'll be checked out of here before New Year's Eve.*

Mother was diagnosed with acute pancreatitis and was being treated with antibiotics and painkillers, but they weren't doing her any good. She was getting worse, day by day. On Christmas Eve, Daddy said, "If I can't figure out what's causing this, she's going to die."

Christmas Day, I felt as if I'd thrown a heavy anchor overboard, the rope caught round my ankle, and I was being dragged down, down. *My family is sinking fast.* The morning after Christmas, Daddy woke me up while it was still dark outside. He said, "I know what it is! I have to get to the hospital before Lou's doctor makes his morning rounds." He slapped some money on the dresser. "Get some breakfast at the restaurant. I'll come back for you later." With that, he was gone.

I smiled because I knew Mother was going to get better. The hard diagnoses had always come to Daddy in his sleep. He would go to bed pondering a case, and the answer would jump into his mind when he woke up. He had figured out that Mother's pancreatitis was caused by one of her diabetes medicines. As soon as she was taken off it, she began to get better. On the morning of New Year's Eve, she was released from the hospital, and Daddy and I checked out of the party hotel. *Just in time.*

Juicy Fruit

When we got back to the house-in-town, there was no Christmas tree. No presents lying about. No preparations for a gay New Year's

Eve party. However, there was ham and the makings for sandwiches in the fridge and a plate of homemade chocolate chip cookies on the counter. *Happy New Year. And God bless Roberta. I'm going to pass on the cookies, though. They give me pains in the right side. Pains that are all in my head.*

That evening, Daddy handed me a present wrapped in Christmas paper. I peeled off the paper and opened a small jeweler's box. Inside, nestled in cotton wool, was a single stick of Juicy Fruit gum and a note. The note said: "I may look like a stiff, but when chewed, I'm a softie. When pulled through the teeth and air is forced through me, I make exciting, popping sounds, sometimes weird and often scary."

It was signed: "Young Juicy." It was the only Christmas present that any of The Three Beares got that year. And it was the best gift Daddy ever gave me because he made it himself.

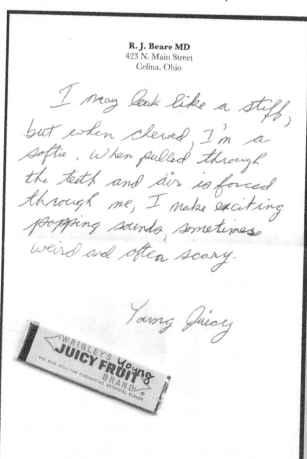

60
Even if He Were a Heathen

My Fancy Singer

I finished my sophomore year at Marygrove and was home at the cottage for the summer of 1967. A few days before my twentieth birthday, Daddy said, "I can't think of anything to get you for your birthday. So you name it, Kiddo. Anything you want."

I didn't hesitate. "I want a sewing machine."

"WELL, HELL."

The next day, Daddy took me to the Singer store and bought me the fanciest machine they had. He arranged sewing lessons with a former patient who was a retired home-economics teacher. I bought a simple pattern and some cotton fabric, and she guided me through sewing a sundress for myself. I sewed the summer away, making a tweed, lined-wool skirt and matching vest and a plaid skirt and a gray vest. I designed my monogram and used my fancy Singer to embroider it on the vests.

I was sewing one day when I got a sharp pain in my lower right gut. I ignored it and kept sewing. The pain grew until I couldn't sit up straight. *What if this is appendicitis and it gets so bad it ruptures?* My thought shot a bullet of fear through me. I found Daddy and told him. He had me lie down on the bed and examined my abdomen. He said, "It's a bit tender, but you don't have a fever. It's probably just gas."

He doesn't sound a bit concerned. I'll have to stick it out alone like all the other times and hope for the best. Daddy pays attention and takes good care of me when I'm sick. But if I have a symptom that could mean I'm REALLY sick, he wants to ignore it. I think he's more frightened of his daughter being REALLY sick than he is of dogs. Either that or I'm a hypochondriac. Maybe I am.

In July, I saw on the news that a riot had started in Detroit in an inner-city neighborhood between the police and residents. It expanded to other parts of the city, with fires, looting, and sniper fire. People were being killed. *You don't have to go to Vietnam to go to war. You can just go to Detroit.* Jeff was living in a rented flat a few miles from the inner city, but the rioting had spread. I tried calling him, but all the phone lines to Detroit were busy. I could only watch the news and hope he was okay. Forty-three people were killed. More than a thousand were injured, and thousands were arrested. It was the worst riot in our country since the Civil War. President Johnson had to send in the army and the national guard to get things under control.

On day three, I finally got through to Jeff. The garage behind his house had been set on fire, but he and the brothers put it out. I realized I would be completely lost without him. *I think I've been lost for my entire life until he found me at that dance. He told me that he feels lost, sometimes, too. I think that our real home is with each other.*

My junior year at Marygrove was wonderful—Jeff and I were smack in the middle of a big, happy college family made up of his frat brothers and my Marygrove friends. *I feel like I belong, and it's amazing.*

It Was Aunt LaVaun

The summer of 1968, Jeff came to the cottage for the weekend. We had dinner that evening with my parents, and then they left to visit Uncle Paul and Aunt LaVaun in town. Jeff and I were still sitting at the table. I stood to clear away the dishes when he took the plate from my hand and tugged me to sit in the chair next to his. He said,

with a blank face, "There's something in my shirt pocket. . . ." His eyes
went to the pocket, as did mine. He dug his fingers into the pocket and
fumbled around. "Well, I think I had it here. . . . Maybe not. . . . Oh
. . . here it is." He drew out an engagement ring, gently placed it in my
hand, and said, "Well?"

I let out a jubilant laugh. Then I examined the ring in my hand.
It was white-gold with a solitaire diamond that made the light dance.
It was exactly as I had described the perfect ring to him some time
before. I jumped out of my chair, onto his lap, and hugged him hard.

"I guess that's a 'Yes,'" he said, laughing and hugging me back.

"It's an 'Of course.'" We had been unofficially engaged for a long
time; however, I had no idea when the ring was coming. I handed it
to him and said, "Put it on me, please." I held out my left hand, and
he slid the ring on my finger.

He said, "Now can I have my fraternity pin back? I haven't had
a chance to wear it for two years." He unpinned it from my shirt and
pinned it on his. Then he sighed and said, "It's going to be a long year
until next summer." Jeff had already graduated and was working part-
time as an engineer at Ford Motor Company, while also working on
a master's degree. He had wanted to get married after my junior year,
but Daddy would not hear of it.

I hopped off Jeff's lap and grabbed a calendar that showed 1969. I
said, "My parents' wedding anniversary is on July 12, and that will be
a Saturday. So how about July 12, next summer?" *I'm throwing them
the only bone I can dig up.* I wanted to show my ring to my parents—
especially Daddy. He already knew I was going to marry Jeff, but the
ring made it real, and I wanted him to see it in front of other people
—in case he decided to have a rant. We left the dirty dishes on the
table, drove into town to the Nickels' house, and found them and my
parents on the back porch.

Casually joining the conversation, I suddenly felt shy and hid my hand in my lap. *Why don't I want him to see it? Because even though he knew it was coming, it's going to be a blow.* Jeff was watching me, a question on his face. I moved my left hand to my knee. The ring caught the early evening rays of the sun.

Aunt LaVaun said, "Janice. I see an engagement ring on your finger. Congratulations to both of you."

Daddy made a gurgling choke then got control of himself. Mother oohed over the ring with Aunt LaVaun, while Uncle Paul went to find a bottle of champagne. Daddy's face looked like it belonged on a totem pole. *It's amazing that Daddy has never tried to force me to get rid of Jeff, who is neither a doctor nor a lawyer. I think he's relieved that I picked a Catholic boy with an education. What Daddy doesn't know is that I would marry Jeff if he was a farmer and a heathen and I had to run away from home to do it.*

Don't You Touch That Car

For my senior year, I went back to Marygrove, driving the Corvette. Daddy had given it to me because I needed a car for my internship at Catholic Social Services in Detroit. Part of my job was to make home visits to clients in the inner city. Driving a Corvette into the neighborhood where the riots had been was a terrible idea, but it was the only car I had.

One time, when I parked outside a client's house, three men on the neighboring porch grabbed baseball bats and walked toward me. I felt a jolt of danger, and was about to scramble back in the car and get out of there, when my client came out on her porch and yelled, "Leave her alone. She's the social worker, and I need her help."

They backed off. As I followed the woman inside, she leaned out the door and yelled, "Don't you touch that car or let anybody else touch it neither."

When I came out to the car after my visit, I found a man with a club sitting on the curb, guarding it.

One afternoon in social services class, I had a dull pain in my lower right side. I ignored it. I stayed up late that night studying, and the pain stayed with me. The next day, it intensified until late that night it got so bad that I couldn't stand up straight. It was the same pain that Daddy always said was gas. *I know what a gas pain feels like, and it's not this. THIS is not normal. THIS could be bad. THIS is the second day with this pain, and it's not going away. I HAVE to do something to take care of myself.* I decided to drive myself to an emergency room, but I couldn't get out of the dorm in the middle of the night without permission from the school nurse. She said I should go to the hospital, and she would call my parents.

"Don't do that," I said. "I'll call them myself if I have to have surgery."

She said, "I have to call them. It's part of my job."

"Then I'm not going."

"But this is a true emergency," she argued.

"If you're going to call them, then I'm not going."

She thought it was imperative that I go, so she gave in.

At the hospital, a doctor examined me. While he was in the room with me, a nurse came in and said, "Doctor, that girl's father is on the phone, and he wants to talk to you."

Damn the school nurse. She lied to me. The doctor was gone for some time. When he came back, he said, "Your white count is slightly elevated, but you don't have a fever. We're going to keep you until morning to see where this is going. I explained everything to your father, who told me he is a doctor. I promised to keep him updated. Now you get some rest."

Thank God that Daddy would never yell at another doctor. My pain subsided overnight, and I went back to Marygrove where the school nurse found me and apologized for calling my parents. "I had to do it, but I'm sorry I did. Your father was furious at me for sending you to the hospital. I've never heard such language. I feel sorry for you, having to live with that."

I feel sorry for me, too, because now Daddy is insisting that I come home this weekend, and all hell is going to break loose.

When I got home, the first thing he did was look me over and feel my belly. Then he gave me a lecture about how going to a hospital and complaining about pain in my gut could have got me into all kinds of trouble. They could have run all kinds of tests on me. Those tests had risks or—God forbid!—they might have operated on me to see what the problem was. "People DIE from exploratory surgery," he hollered. *He sounds more scared than mad—like he's afraid of what might happen to me in a hospital when he's not there to make all the decisions and to be in control.*

～～～

Jeff graduated in December with a master's degree in mechanical engineering and went to work full-time for Ford Motor Company. We picked out an apartment together where he would live until I moved in after we got married. It was a one-bedroom apartment with a small kitchen and a large living room with a slider that opened onto a balcony. It had just been built—brand-new—like us. There were two weekday afternoons when I had no classes, so I brought my sewing machine to the apartment and went to work on all those bare windows. I sewed drapes and daydreamed about living there with Jeff, in *my own home.*

It's Already Paid For

I graduated from Marygrove with a degree in social work in June 1969. For a graduation/wedding present, Daddy was going to buy Jeff and me a new car. It would be a Ford, since Jeff was an employee. The three of us went to the dealer in Celina and I chose an LTD. Daddy and Jeff agreed it was a good choice, except Daddy thought it should have a big, 429 hp engine, and Jeff wanted a 325 hp engine—enough power, but still economical. I liked driving a powerful car, but was happy to go with what Jeff wanted.

Jeff was at the cottage when the car was delivered. A small plate on the front fender said: "429." *Daddy did that.* I thought about how much fun it was going to be to drive, but Jeff thought about all the gas that monster was going to eat. He said, "That engine isn't what we ordered. It's a mistake."

Daddy said, "I changed the order. I can't have my daughter driving a car that doesn't have enough oomph to get her out of trouble on the freeway."

"Let's take it back," Jeff said. "I want the smaller engine."

They both looked, expectantly, at me. My heart hit the gravel of the driveway. *I have to choose between my father and my future husband.* I wanted to run and hide my face in my mommy's skirts. Instead, I took a deep breath and said, "It's too late to take it back. It's already paid for." My heart was groveling in the gravel now.

Jeff gave me a scowl, and Daddy, a big smile. My heart groveled some more. *Jeff really wanted the smaller engine, but he'll be okay with my decision. On the other hand, if I tell Daddy to take his gift back, he's going to make a huge scene just days before my wedding. Wow. Am I just trying to avoid trouble like Mother? Yes, I am. She's the one who showed me how to grovel.*

61
At the End of the Rainbow

Mrs. Jones

In July, The Three Beares moved back into the house-in-town, leaving the cottage to serve as headquarters for Jeff and his groomsmen—five of whom were his fraternity brothers, and the remaining one, my cousin, John.

On July 12, my bridesmaids and I dressed for the wedding, then set out to walk down the alley to church. Why drive when we lived next to the parking lot? Daddy walked beside me, and I carried my gathered-up train in my arms. I wore a white satin dress trimmed in beads and lace, but instead of a veil, I chose a lace mantilla that floated out yards behind me in the breeze. Trailing after me were Mother and my six bridesmaids—my roomie, Mary Lee, three other Marygrove friends, and my two girl cousins, in their identically styled, long, chiffon dresses, each one a different color of the rainbow. Their headpieces, in the colors of the dresses, were made of horsehair loops that had two floor-length veils attached in the back, and two short bouffant veils in the front. The veils—hovering over their faces and buoyant behind them as they walked—gave them an ethereal air.

As I walked past the back of the high school, I remembered the times I'd skipped morning Mass, then sneaked into the back door of the school to mix with the crowd coming in the front door. As I looked at the church parking lot, I pictured two ghostly houses there—the furniture store and Nora's.

When we arrived in the church vestibule, I peered through the crack in the double doors to see that the church was packed. While 200 family and friends were invited to the reception, anyone who wanted to see the wedding could come to the church. *There's Jerry who let me ride his Arab mare. And the woman who taught me how to sew. And over there . . . the patient who baked my cousins' and my birthday cakes every year, even though no one asked her to do it. Is that a gaggle of nuns crammed in the corner? Along with a stray priest?*

"Come away from the doors." It was Harriet from Goldstein's who had appeared in the vestibule to arrange my train and mantilla. No one had asked her to do it. I loved the Goldsteins.

The organ struck up. Harriet opened the doors. My bridesmaids promenaded up the aisle, one floating color after another. Daddy tucked my hand in his arm and said, "Here we go, Kiddo."

Once through the doors, I looked past the progressing rainbow and saw Jeff at the end. His eyebrows raised and his mouth formed the word, "WOW." I suddenly remembered that night when I was sixteen and falling asleep after my first date. I had imagined that my future husband would have the last name of Jones. I also remembered all the times I wished that someone would come to take me away from my parents. *Someone named Jones has come at last, and he is taking me away.* I looked up at Daddy. Tears were flowing down his face. My heart stopped. Then I felt the blood in my veins slow down and stop, too. *I've never seen Daddy cry.* Then my heart gave a tremendous beat and my blood flowed again. I wanted to stop walking and hug Daddy, but of course, I didn't. His tears were still falling when he gave my hand to Jeff.

I'm a Jones!

~~~

After the reception at the country club, Jeff and I left for Gatlinburg on our honeymoon. He was at the wheel of our new car, while I was watching out the rear window as the house-in-town grew smaller, and smaller, then disappeared. When we passed the Celina city-limits sign, I heard Daddy's voice say, "We're away," just like he did every time we left town for Florida. Now it was me who was "away." I started crying.

"What's wrong, darling?" Jeff asked.

"Nothing." My crying grew into sobs.

"Should I pull over?"

"Keep going. I'm not unhappy."

"You're not?"

"No." *I'm terrified.*

He was really concerned now. "I'm pulling over."

"Don't do it!" I leaned forward in my seat and pointed down the road. "DRIVE!"

Jeff drove. I sobbed all the way to Cincinnati. I wasn't crying for myself. I was crying for the Two Beares I'd left behind. The special child they had chosen for themselves had just walked out on the job.

My Roberta

62
Still Doctor Beare's Daughter

We honeymooned in one of my favorite places—Gatlinburg. As we were driving in the foothills of the Smokies, I realized that this was my first drive through mountains without The Pot. It was as though marriage had cured me of car sickness. And let's not forget the absence of cigarette smoke.

I took my new husband to the riding stable and introduced him to Mr. McCarter. We rode together to the apple orchard where I had once been stung by wasps. Sweet freedom was tempered with anxiety. *How are the Two Beares doing back in Celina?*

Riding at McCarter's stable on our honeymoon

On July 20, in our motel room, Jeff and I watched Neil Armstrong become the first man to walk on the moon. I immediately called Daddy to ask him if he'd seen it. We had a short conversation about the space program, then Mother got on the phone, said a feeble *hello*, and we hung up.

Jeff said, "Why did you call your parents?"

"To talk about the moon landing." *I did it because I miss them and because I want to make sure they're doing all right without me.*

Dump the Ice Cubes

The first time my parents came to Michigan to visit Jeff and me in our apartment, Daddy walked in with a grocery bag and plunked it on the kitchen counter. "I brought a few things from Jerry's for your freezer." He started pulling out packages, wrapped in butcher paper. Each one had a handwritten label: hamburger patties, ground round, chicken breasts, pork chops, and so on. *I might just manage to fit it all in the freezer if I remove the ice cube trays.*

Drive Around the Block

The first time Jeff and I went to Celina to visit for a weekend, I told Mother I wanted to go to lunch with Joyce, my old roller-rink pal. "You're only here for two days and you want to spend time with her instead of me?" That old familiar hurt look had crept over her face.

I understand that she misses me. I understand that it's harder for her with Daddy now that I've moved away. What I didn't understand —until now—is that my job isn't over just because I got married. Thank God I don't live right down the block.

And so I never did get to see Joyce or any of my other friends when Jeff and I visited my parents. However, there was that one time when Mother sent me out to the front porch to bring in the newspaper. I saw Mr. Becker sitting at a red light in front of the house. I ran out to the car, jumped in the passenger seat, and said, "Drive around the block . . . slowly."

Mr. Becker like to have leapt out the driver's side window. When he realized it was me, he reached over and tousled my hair. During our short ride, I asked about Joyce and Mrs. Becker. When we got back to the light at Main, I hopped out of the car, picked up the newspaper, and went inside to Mother with a big smile on my face. *I feel like I did the time I told her that a stranger cat was my Tinker.*

In late February, Jeff and I flew to Florida to see my parents for a few days. Jeff had never been to Florida, and my parents were staying right on the beach. They were spending every winter there now. We had a nice time. Daddy always behaved himself in front of Jeff, and I got to see Mary and Owen Pogue, who were wintering just a block from my parents. We went to a cocktail party, and Mother introduced me to her new Florida friends. One woman smiled and said to me, "You look a lot like your mother."

She's being polite—I don't look a thing like her. I opened my mouth to say that I was adopted, when I felt Mother's nails digging into my arm. I got the message and said nothing.

Later Mother said, "At the party . . . the people here don't know you are adopted, so I don't have to tell them." She gave a little giggle.

It was back in Michigan, in April, when Jeff and I had been married seven months, that I realized I might be pregnant. I felt my heart open as wide and deep as the Grand Canyon. *I might have a relative growing inside me.* A neighbor referred me to her obstetrician, who confirmed it. My due date was early December, so I must have gotten pregnant in late February. When I told Jeff, he shouted "KAHOONA," picked me up, and kissed me while he danced on the carpet. We decided to call and tell our parents. Jeff's were surprised and delighted. Mine were delighted but not surprised. Our phone conversation went like this:

Me: "Hello, Daddy. Can you get Mother to pick up the extension."

Daddy: "Lou. Get on the phone. Janice is finally calling to tell us she's pregnant."

I hadn't seen them since Florida in February. *I should have known. Daddy always could spot a pregnant woman in the P & B long before she knew about it herself.*

Yet Another Mother's Day

It was May, and Mother's Day was coming. My parents were at the cottage for the summer. I thought about going home to see Mother, but she hadn't asked me to come, and I was relieved. I mailed her a card and a gift. Then I called her that Sunday morning to wish her a happy day. In a teary voice, she said, "This is the first Mother's Day without you. I thought you were coming home."

"I didn't know you wanted me to come. You never said anything."

"How could you forget me on Mother's Day?"

"I didn't forget you, Mom. Didn't you get the package I sent?"

"Oh, that. I got it, I guess."

"If you got my gift in the mail, why did you think I was coming home?"

"I assumed you were going to show up to surprise me. You surely couldn't stand to be away from me on Mother's Day."

I never imagined it would be worse for her if I wasn't there. *I should have known.* "I'm sorry I didn't come, Mom. I hope the rest of the day will be better for you." She hung up in tears. *I have a feeling the rest of her day isn't going to get any better.*

At two a.m. the following morning, the phone rang and jerked Jeff and me awake. When I answered, Daddy said, "Your mother had a massive heart attack last night. I've got her in the hospital in Dayton. The cardiologist says if she lives another two days, she might survive."

My heart felt like it had been attacked, too. *Please, God. No. I don't want to lose her.* "I'll be there soon as I can," I said.

Mother had suffered the heart attack in the car the previous evening, while they were driving home from dinner. When she slumped in her seat, Daddy reached over and found she had no pulse. He pulled over, managed to restart her heart, and took her to Dayton.

Jeff and I arrived at the hospital in the afternoon. When Mother saw me, she started sobbing. I went to her and took her hand. She said, "I don't want to die. I'll do anything! I'll never smoke another cigarette. I'll eat healthy. Anything—if I can just get well."

I've heard this before. Instead of feeling sorry for her, I felt mad. Mad because she loved her goddamn, shitty cigarettes more than she did me. Then I felt guilty for feeling mad, and felt horrified that she might die. Then I realized she had her heart attack on Mother's Day. *Of course she did.* Jeff and I stayed at the hospital until Mother's doctor decided the worst was over.

When Mother got out of the hospital, she went back on her diet and gave up cigarettes—again. She had no choice. There was no way she could get any because she couldn't drive and because Daddy had given orders to Roberta, who had been known to buy them for her in the past. *I hope he spoke to Aunt Mildred, too.*

A Simple Box of Cottage Cheese

In June, Jeff had to go to Arizona for two weeks for his job. When Daddy learned I was going to be home alone, he insisted I come to the cottage for those two weeks and help him take care of Mother. I wished I hadn't mentioned that Jeff was going to be away. I didn't want to go home, but it was something Doctor Beare's Daughter was expected to do, and I was still her. "I'm waiting."

At the cottage, I fixed Mother's meals and took short walks with her while Daddy played golf. We had lots of time to talk. I had heard of people who had died and were brought back to life, remembering going toward a white light. I asked her, "Do you remember anything from when your heart was stopped?"

"The only thing I remember is that while Ralph was working on me, I heard a voice screaming, 'DON'T LEAVE ME.'"

Then she reminisced about the day she and Daddy brought me home from the adoption agency. "When we went to Dayton to get you, you were sick with a bad chest cold. Normally the agency wouldn't let a baby go to a new home until the baby was healthy, but because Ralph was a doctor, they let you go. I was so excited to get you that I got a new outfit and wore my fur. On the way home in the car you threw up all over me. My fur was a mess." She screwed her face up at the memory. Then she went on. "We got you in October and you were still sick at Thanksgiving. My whole family gathered at my sister, Nell's house in Indiana. Ralph said we shouldn't take you there, because you were sick, but I just had to show you off to my family. I dressed you all up and there I was, showing off my new daughter, and you wouldn't smile or look cute for my family. You were just so darn sick."

I felt like apologizing for my behavior, then realized how ridiculous that was.

~~~

When Jeff got back from his business trip, he came to the cottage in the late morning, planning to drive us home the next day. I was getting lunch ready for everyone and realized we were out of cottage cheese. Daddy liked cottage cheese every day for lunch with fresh fruit. I was headed out the door to the store when Daddy came in the kitchen and said, "Where are you going?"

"To the store. We're out of cottage cheese."

"Never mind," he said. "I'll have a sandwich."

"It's no trouble. I'll be right back." I grabbed the keys to the Cadillac off the hook near the door.

"It's okay. I don't need cottage cheese."

This conversation is beginning to sound like the old "Do-you-want-to-come-along-out-to-dinner-it's-really-fine-if-you-don't" discussion. I dug in my heels. "I'm going to the P & B. I'll be right back."

Now Daddy was walking toward the door, saying, "Don't be silly. Fix me a sandwich. I don't want to wait. I'm hungry."

Daddy has always caused trouble the day before I leave home. He did it when I left for camp, and when I left for Austria, and every time I left for Marygrove. I became even more determined to get the cottage cheese. "I'm going. Won't take long."

Now he was standing in the doorway, blocking the door. My gut felt VERY uneasy. I tried to push past him, but he was as solid as the door behind him. I tried to duck under his arm, but he lowered it and said, "Just make me a sandwich, Kiddo."

The old familiar fear-pain was gripping my chest. My hands were shaking. I dropped the knife on the floor three times before I got the peanut butter on the bread.

Mother, Daddy, Jeff, and I sat down to eat at the table. Daddy took one bite of his sandwich, put it down, and said, "I really wanted cottage cheese." His words struck all the most tender places in me and flayed them to fragments. *I should have gone out the other door and walked around the house to the car to get to the store.*

"All I wanted was a SIMPLE BOX OF COTTAGE CHEESE. You don't care about your Daddy anymore."

The flayed fragments of my tender self blew around inside me like dust shook out of a cleaning rag. Mother jumped in. "For God's sake, Ralph. You're getting irrational."

He turned his venom on Mother. "SOME PEOPLE should keep their mouth shut and their ignorant ideas to themselves."

Mother was still very weak from her heart attack. Her face turned white, and she looked like she might have another one on the spot.

Daddy turned back on me and said, "You don't give a tinker's damn about your poor father who just wanted a simple box of cottage cheese. You should be ashamed of yourself for being so son-of-a-bitching, goddamn disrespectful."

I feel like throwing up. I glanced at Jeff. He was sitting there, shocked and mute as if he couldn't comprehend what was happening and had no idea how to react. *This is the first time Daddy has let go in front of him.*

Daddy opened his mouth to rage on, when Mother, who looked as if she was struggling to keep from falling out of her chair, choked out, "Ralph. She's three months pregnant. Do you want her to lose the baby?"

Daddy shut his mouth.

I realized that I was so worried about Mother having a heart attack that it never occurred to me that my being smashed to bits by Daddy's tongue might cause a miscarriage. *I can't take anymore.* I got out of my chair, ran to the bedroom, slammed the door, threw myself and my baby on the bed, and bawled. Jeff was right behind me. He lay down next to me and pulled me close. I snuggled into him. Now Daddy stuck his head in the door and said, "I'm sorry, Jeff. I shouldn't have said those things."

My God. He apologized! But not to me. No. He apologized to Jeff, for crying out loud.

Then Daddy said, "I know you were planning on going back to Detroit in the morning, but maybe it's best you go now."

I didn't want to leave Mother while she was still so upset and looking so awful, but then she appeared in the doorway and told me to go. As I was getting in the car, I felt cleaved into two pieces—a small rock and a boulder. *Jeff has the rock, and my parents have the boulder. Somewhere, cast off to one side, is a leftover pebble for me.* Mother reached in the car window, got hold of my arm, and whispered in my ear, "Be happy." A squirrel, popping out of the glove box, graciously offering me a nut, would have been far less surprising than those words that had popped out of her mouth.

Happy is something Mother has never been, but I think she really does wish it for me. It seems selfish for me to be happy when she is so miserable, but maybe I should be a little selfish sometimes. Mother has showed me how.

63
Thank You, Uncle Doc

Meeting a Relative for the First Time

After my pregnancy was showing, and my little relative was turning and kicking, whenever I saw Daddy, he put his hand on my belly and said, "How's little Ralph in there?"

Daddy assumes I'm having a boy, and he wants me to name the baby after him. I wanted to name a boy baby Jeff. However, Jeff did not want his son to be a junior. If not Jeff, then I did like Ralph. It was an uncommon name that would stand out from the other Jones boys of the world. *And it will certainly please Daddy.* Even though Jeff was not fond of Daddy, he also liked the name "Ralph." Jeff's father was "Robert," so we decided on "Ralph Robert" for a boy.

I had a boy. When the nurse gave him to me to hold for the first time, I felt I already *knew* him. It seemed as if he *knew* me too, I said, "Hello, Ralph Robert. I'm your mother. You have a wonderful Daddy that you haven't met yet. We are going to love you and protect you and prepare you to one day be able to love and protect yourself. Oh, look at that. You have my nose. And my chin. And my brown eyes." In fact, except for his light brown hair, Ralph Robert didn't look anything like the Joneses. *He looks like me in some ways, and the rest must have come from my ancestors. I wonder which side he looks like the most— my birth mother's people or my birth father's people? I wonder which side I favor? My records and birth certificate are sealed by law. Why aren't adopted children allowed to know where they come from? Why do people who do know where they come from think those of us who don't shouldn't be allowed to have the same information that they take for granted? The more I stared at my beautiful son, the angrier I felt. At least Ralph will know his story.*

~~~~

When Ralph was eight months old, I had a sharp pain in my lower right side. *There it is again. And it's building. I think it's my appendix, but when this has happened before, Daddy told me it was all in my head.* The pain was getting worse. It soon had me doubled over. I was terrified. I wanted to go to an emergency room, but I remembered the time I did that and the blistering rant Daddy had at the school nurse and later at me. While I had an obstetrician for Ralph's birth, I had never had a primary care doctor for me. I couldn't have one because Daddy wouldn't like it. He didn't want me in the hands of some quack, and anyone who wasn't him or Uncle Doc was likely to be a quack. *I don't think he could handle it if I went to another doctor or had to have surgery. It's a hell of a thing, isn't it? If my appendix ruptures, I could die and leave Ralph without a mother and Jeff without a wife. Daddy is wrong about me—I DO have the sense God gave a horse. What's crazy is ignoring it just so Daddy doesn't have to cope with the threat of his daughter being REALLY sick.* I found Jeff and said, "Take me to Celina. Right now."

"Right now? What for?"

"Something is really wrong with me, and it's time I found out what it is."

While we drove to Celina, Jeff kept asking me how my pain was. And if he should look for a hospital. The pain was bad, but I was mad. I was loaded for Beare. "Keep driving."

When we got to the cottage, I walked inside, hunched over from the pain, hobbled over to Daddy and said: "I'm sick. I think I have appendicitis. I also think there's something wrong with my liver or my gallbladder. Every time I eat Roberta's chocolate chip cookies or her pecan tarts, it makes me sick. Then there's my stomach. It hurts a lot of the time. I came home to ask you to help me figure it all out. If you won't do it, then I'm getting back in the car and going home where I'm going to get out the yellow pages and go see the first doctor my finger lands on." *If there's anything that Daddy might fear more than his precious daughter being REALLY sick, it's probably his precious daughter under the care of a quack.*

Daddy said, "Go in the back room and lie down. I want to feel your belly. He came in and palpated my abdomen. Then he said, "Stay here and rest. I'll be back."

About ten minutes later, Uncle Doc showed up to examine me. Then he walked out into the hall, shut the door behind him, and started yelling at Daddy. "What the hell, Ralph! I think she has chronic appendicitis. It comes and goes, but one of these times when it comes, it will rupture. She could die. And it will be your fault."

Thrill and fear were arm-wrestling in my gut. Hearing Uncle Doc stand up to Daddy for me was exhilarating. I was afraid of what Daddy might have to say to Uncle Doc. Instead he came back into the room and said, "I'll set up some tests for you at the hospital."

Thank you, Uncle Doc. I'm going to get the help I need, and Daddy is going to deal with it.

The tests showed that I didn't have an ulcer—my stomach pain was likely caused from stress. *The stress of being Doctor Beare's Daughter?* But I did have large gallstones, and my appendix was inflamed. I needed them both taken out. It was going to be a big, open abdominal surgery. Uncle Doc, who was still in practice, found a surgeon for me near my home in Michigan and made the arrangements.

I had the surgery. There were complications. I was in the hospital for ten days. Jeff brought Ralph to the hospital every day so he could see me. Daddy haunted the halls, drove the doctors crazy with his questions, and bullied the nurses into letting him read my chart. I was grateful to have him there. The day before I was to be released, Daddy said, "Your mother and I are going home this afternoon, and I think we should take Ralph with us. You won't be able to pick him up or carry anything for six weeks, and your husband has to go back to work."

I had been so sick that Jeff and I had not even made a plan for when I came home. At nine months, Ralph was already walking—running, actually. Mother didn't have the stamina to take care of a baby, but I knew I could trust Daddy with the job. *I have no idea how Jeff and I can cope right now without Daddy.* "Please take him." *Jeff will be relieved. He's been so worried that he would get into trouble at work if he takes any more time off.*

Lucky

In the winter of 1972, when Ralph was two, Jeff and I bought our first house. Two days after we moved in, I kept hearing Daddy's voice in my head the day I won the puppy in Mr. Kohnen's class: "When you grow up, get your husband to buy you a dog." Jeff bought me a golden retriever named Lucky. He was a one-person dog, and he decided that I was his person. He was always near me. If he was sleeping and I moved from one room to the next, he woke himself up and followed me. If I felt fear, he put himself in front of me, looking for the danger, ready to take it on. My stomach always felt better when he was watching over me. I felt privileged to have such a special connection with an animal. *Daddy is not going to be happy that I followed his advice.* I told him on the phone that I had a dog.

I have a dog!

"The hell you say. You wouldn't do a goddamn thing like that."

"I really did get a dog, Daddy." I suddenly felt like a naughty child.

"Well, if some people choose to have a goddamn dog that's their business, but if I choose not to visit a house where there's a goddamn dog, then that's my business."

I'm not going to give up my wonderful Lucky. I said, "I hope you'll come. When you're here, I'll put the dog away."

I wasn't sure if Daddy would come to visit again, but he did. While he was there, I kept Lucky in the basement or out in the fenced back-yard. One day, Daddy was sitting at the kitchen table about to take a bite out of a sandwich. I could see in the light from the kitchen window, a golden dog hair on top of the bread. I was about to say something, then realized that it might disturb the uneasy peace, so I held my breath, and watched my father eat dog hair. It was hard not to smile.

Later, when I went to bring Lucky in from the yard, he was gone, and the gate was standing open. I lost balance and rocked on my feet. *My wonderful dog is lost. I never should have left him outside so long without checking on him.* Jeff and I left my parents to watch Ralph while we went looking for Lucky. Jeff took the car and drove the neighborhood. I searched on foot.

After an hour with no luck, I felt devastated and slogged toward home. When I turned the corner, there was Daddy, standing in the middle of the street, looking. It was a cold winter day, and he had on one of Jeff's knit hats and a pair of garden gloves. He was looking for my "goddamn dog." *What was he going to do if he spotted Lucky? Grab him by the collar and put him in the house?* I felt a rush of love for Daddy. I went inside to get warm, but Daddy stayed out in the cold to look. *He's still taking care of me, trying to make me happy, even if it means he has to grab a goddamn dog that he's afraid of.* Fortunately, Jeff came home with Lucky in the car, who was beside himself to see me, and I was thrilled to have him back.

64
Ralphnrachel

Daddy's Voice

One spring day in 1972, while Jeff was at work and Ralph was still two, he was sitting on the floor and getting bored, so I turned on the TV to *Sesame Street* to keep him amused. I sat on the couch and watched Muppet Bert in the bathtub singing to his rubber ducky and I found myself singing along until I realized that Ralph was gone. He was a quarter horse on two legs who—in the time it took to sneeze—could wheel and run and disappear. *How long has he been gone?* I dashed upstairs and into his room. Not there. I checked out the entire second floor. Back downstairs and into the kitchen, I noticed that the door to the basement stairs was ajar. When I spied Ralph standing halfway down the stairs and drawing on the wall with crayons, I let out a long breath. I sat just below him, so he couldn't fall down the stairs. The entire length of the stairs, lime and lemon and lavender lines and squiggles embellished the white, sprayed-on cement. I squeezed my eyes tight, gritted my teeth hard, and mentally cussed.

I got a spray bottle of cleaner and a brush and went to work on Ralph's art. It did not scrub off easily. My arm ached. It seemed like my entire life was nothing more than watching this little tornado so he didn't accidentally cause his own death. I grabbed Ralph, stood him on the stairs, and gave him the brush. "Scrub," I commanded.

He scrubbed.

I started lecturing. "See how hard that is to clean up? Do you? What were you thinking? Why do you do these things to me?"

Ralph scrubbed faster and harder. He began to cry.

"WHY ARE YOU CRYING?" *Oh my God. That's Daddy's voice—coming out of me.* I grabbed Ralph and hugged him. Then I heard Grandpa's voice, "Tut, tut, tut, Kiddo. That's not the way." I took the brush from Ralph and wiped his tears on my shirt. "Let's go outside in the yard and take a walk around the garden. Then we can play in the sandbox for a while." *I'm never going to let Daddy's voice come out of my mouth again. And I'm going to watch out for Mother's voice, too.*

Another Relative

In 1974, Jeff and I had a baby girl. *Now I have two relatives.* We named her Rachel Anne, after my favorite soap opera character and because we thought it was a beautiful name. And because the name

Ralphnrachel

went so well with "Ralph" when we called them at the same time, as in "Ralphnrachel!"

Rachel had the Jones head and cowlicks. She had Jeff's dimples and his smile. She had light blonde hair, like Jeff had had when he was born. She had Jeff's sister's eyes. I didn't see anything of me in her, but it didn't matter, because I *knew* she was mine. And she *knew* it, too. Both my children seemed to know me as their mother from the minute they were born. They fussed or cried if anyone else picked them up—even their daddy—at first. Then they quickly *got to know* Jeff, and other people who fed and held them. But they never had to *get to know* me. They already knew me by the sound of my heartbeat and voice. *I must have known my birth mother that way, too. And where was I for the first four-and-a-half months of my life before I was adopted? Did my birth mother feed me and take care of me all that time? Or was I passed around before I landed with the Beares?* For the first time, I realized that being taken from my birth mother must have been a monstrous death, and I must have felt the pain of that death.

～～～

Daddy sold the cottage in 1976. In 1979, Uncle Doc retired, and Daddy sold the house-in-town to the church. He and Mother moved to Florida, permanently. My parents got an apartment just a block from Mary and Owen Pogue.

In 1980, Daddy was diagnosed with lung cancer, even though he hadn't smoked a cigarette in twenty years. He had radiation and some chemo, but it didn't do any good. It was near the end. I flew to Florida to be with my parents.

65
May 3, 1981

Daddy was dying in the hospital's hospice wing. He was drifting in and out of a coma, each breath a strangled gurgle. Mother and I were sitting with him. It was late afternoon, and we'd been there since early morning. With her heart condition and diabetes, Mother looked so old and used up that I was afraid she might faint.

I took Daddy's hand and told him I was going to take Mother back to the apartment.

He stirred, opened his eyes, and fixed them on me. "Go take care of her . . . . Kiddo." His voice was a raspy whisper. He took a labored breath, then muttered, "Make sure . . . she eats . . . takes her insulin . . . put her to bed . . . then . . ." His voice ran out.

I said, "We'll be back in the morning to sit with you."

He opened his mouth, closed it, opened it again. "I won't be . . . here . . . in the morning. . . ."

I turned to Mother and said, "I'll be right back." I went to the nurse's station and asked Daddy's nurse, "Can you tell me if my father will last the night?"

She looked at me kindly, shook her head, and said, "I'll be very surprised if he does."

I felt a boa constrictor wrap itself around my heart. I walked back into Daddy's room. Mother saw me, got up, and walked wearily into the hall, expecting me to follow.

I went to Daddy. I kissed him gently on the forehead. His eyes fluttered open. He said, "I'm going to die, and not . . . one . . . of my family will be here . . . with me." The boa constrictor tightened its coils and squeezed.

Searching my face, Daddy whispered, "Take your Mother home. Then come back, Kiddo. I'll wait . . . for . . . you." His eyes closed and forced a tear down one sallow cheek.

That vicious snake clamped down on my heart and tried to force the life out of it. I grabbed the IV pole to keep myself from falling.

I can't do this alone—watch him leave.

Daddy didn't stir. He had slipped back into a coma. I quietly opened the patient closet and grabbed the plastic bag hanging there. I took Daddy's pants and belt, his shirt and socks, and put them in the bag.

Then I picked up one of his size thirteen wingtips. I imagined its heel kicking our living room carpet in time to music from the Scott. I picked up the other shoe. I could see it on the gas pedal of the Corvette. I dropped the shoes in the bag and looped it over my arm. I looked around—nothing else I would have to come back to collect.

On my way out the door, I snatched up the potted plant someone had sent him. I glanced back at the bed and whispered, "Goodbye, Daddy."

I said no to him for the first time in my life.

Daddy died that night. And like a mirror in a frame, dropped on concrete, I shattered into shards, leaving a single, jagged chunk, desperately clinging to the edge of an otherwise empty frame. *How can I live without Daddy? How could I have left him to die alone?* I sat on the floor in a corner, unable to get up, to get dressed, to eat. The weight of grief and guilt held me down.

I went into therapy. It was having to crawl out of my corner to get there that kept me functioning—barely. The therapist's first question was, "Why are you here?"

I said, "My father died." Then I surprised myself and said, "I'm adopted." It was the little voice, speaking up, loud and clear. I had a lot of work to do—picking up the broken pieces of myself and fitting them back together.

Mother was in very poor health. I wanted her to come to Michigan where I could take care of her. Roberta wanted Mother to move in with her in Celina. But Mother was determined to stay in her apartment.

I was still in therapy fifteen months later, when Mother died, alone, of a heart attack—an ashtray of cigarette butts on the table next to her. She was found by Owen Pogue, God bless him.

The vow I had once made to outlive my parents was fulfilled. I felt as guilty, as if I had committed murder and gotten away with it. Keeping them safe and happy was my job—the reason they adopted me. I had failed them.

In therapy, I discovered that the broken pieces of Doctor Beare's Daughter would not fit back into my frame. She had died with them. Now I needed the real pieces of me—the pieces that the world didn't want me to find. And so . . . I set out to search for them.

After my parent's death, I received many cards and letters of condolence. One very good Catholic woman sought to comfort me when she wrote, "You will see them again in heaven." The thought of seeing them again was terrifying. I would have to go back to being Dr. Beare's Daughter. But after I completed my search—became whole and real —I knew that I if I could see my parents again. I would greet them with compassion, and without fear. I couldn't go back to being Dr. Beare's Daughter, even if I wanted to.

The story of my search, and the stories of my birth families are told in the sequel to Dr. Beare's Daughter: *Conceived in a Canoe: An Adoptee's Search for Her Roots,* to be published in late 2025. Read Ralph and Lou's story, and other stories about The Three Beares that were not included in this book at LouJanPress.com.

Thank you for reading
Dr. Beare's Daughter.

Book reviews are so important.
I'd be grateful if you'd post one on Amazon.

About the Author

As told in this true story, Janice Jones grew up in Celina, Ohio, as the adopted daughter of Ralph and Lucinda Beare. Jones has worked as a freelance editor and writer, and she invented a way to use jigsaw puzzles to teach reading skills to children.

The two things Janice values most in life are truth and connection —to family, friends, and the world at large.

Those who know Janice enjoy her eccentric personality. Her hobbies are gardening, sewing, riding her e-bike, singing, and playing music on piano, guitar, harmonica, and Cajun accordion with other amateur musicians.

Her young adult novel, *Secrets of a Summer Spy,* reminiscent of her summer days growing up on Grand Lake St. Marys, was previously published by Macmillan in 1990, and the updated version ©2024 is available on *amazon.com* and *barnesandnoble.com*.

Acknowledgements

Special thanks:

My family

Pauletta Bednas, Head Cheerleader

Teresa Crumpton, Editor

Adrienne Ross Scanlan, Editor

Rebecca Finkel, Book Design

Nick Zelinger, Cover and Graphics

ForeverStudios.com, Photo Restoration

Elizabeth Sain, Proofreader

Marty Lentz, Proofreader

Melissa Carmean, Amy Santeel, Sarah Simpson, and Donna Grove, Beta Readers

Seth Schurman MD, Serendipitous Inspiration.

Thanks to everyone who helped with research, provided reviews, photos, or permissions to use their names/photos/newsclips/quotes:

Mary Lee Woodhams, Joan Schweickert, and Mary Beth Kaak, college roomies

Susan Gilkey-Priest and Karen Hiles, Harbor Point girls

John Beare MD, my cousin

Joe Tom Sayers, Hereditary Keeper; Member of the Batchewana First Nation

Betsie Norris, Founder and Executive Director of Adoption Network Cleveland

Steve Cron, grandson of "Aunt" Mildred and "Uncle" Charlie

Pat Neveau and Connie Gray, researchers at the Mercer County District Library

Matt Hess and Heidi Pierron, The Shrine at Maria Stein

Anne Heffron, author of *To Be Real*

Leitzell Studios, Celina, Ohio

Aaron Snyder, General Manager, *The Daily Standard*

Bryant Billing, Editor-in-chief, *Sidney Daily News*

David Trinko, Editor, *Lima News*

Rich Gillette, Managing Editor, *Dayton Daily News*

Alec Demsey, Survivor Classic Car Services

360

Notes

1. Valentina P. Wasson. *The Chosen Baby*. New York and London; J. B. Lippincott, 1939.

2. Bobby Burke and Horace Gerlach. "Daddy's Little Girl." Ocheri Publishing, 1949.

3. Andrew B. Sterling and Kerry Mills. "Meet Me in St. Louis, Louis." New York; F. A. Mills, 1904.

4. Ed Haley. "The Fountain in the Park." New York; Willis Woodward & Co., 1884.

5. Hank Williams. "I'm so Lonesome I Could Cry." Cincinnati, Ohio; Herzog Studio, 1949.

6. Theodore F. Morse and Howard Johnson. "M-O-T-H-E-R A Word that Means the World to Me." New York; Leo Feist, 1915.

7. Buck Ram. "The Great Pretender." Panther Music Corp., 1955.

8. Ray Henderson and Sam M. Lewis and Joseph Widow Young. "Five Foot Two, Eyes of Blue" (Has Anybody Seen My Girl?). New York; Leo Feist, 1925.

Made in the USA
Las Vegas, NV
28 February 2025

18809084R00207